Christian Much

Goin' Home
and Far Away

Christian Much

Goin' Home and Far Away

How Dvořák and Other Curious Minds Shaped American Music

English translation
by Kate Mueser

CHRISTIAN MUCH spent his career as a diplomat and writes about the topics close to his heart: politics, international criminal law, bridging cultures, and his life-long hobby: music.

Born in Luxembourg, he currently divides his time between southern Germany and South Tyrol in northern Italy. *Goin' Home and Far Away* is his third novel.

Original Edition: Wolke Verlag, Germany 2023
© Christian Much
The cover design uses details of a photo taken by the author of the facade of the Ottendorf Library.

ISBN 979-8-218-49689-0

Foreword

This book tells a story that could not have happened in real life.

The main characters have long, deep conversations with each other, even though they did not live at the same time. The South Tyrolean music student Petra and her Nigerian boyfriend Bukar were born in the early 1990s. Amy Beach lived from 1967 to 1944, Antonín Dvořák from 1841 to 1904, and Bud Powell from 1924 to 1966. Calliope, alias López, the elderly librarian, is timeless, which can either mean that she has always been alive— or perhaps never actually was. All this makes the book a work of speculative fiction.

But it's a novel that is infused with elements of non-fiction, revolving around a fascinating but largely unknown chapter in music history: the interplay of white, Black, and Indigenous music after 1890. The musical and historical introduction at the beginning of the book attempts to provide enough background to understand the story. The subsequent chapters lack the scope and methodology to be considered pure non-fiction. Historical details are included to the extent that they are relevant to the plot.

Those interested in learning more about the musicians and the American musical eras referenced in the story can take advantage of the music tips scattered throughout the book. Farwell, Chadwick, Dawson, Price, Still, Griffes, Ballard, Cacioppo and the others are hidden treasures worth discovering! The QR codes lead to recordings on Idagio and YouTube ♦. I have personally selected the listening examples which are admittedly somewhat arbitrary. There are other recordings out there which may be just as good, or even better.

In addition to music history, the book deals with the militant Islamist organization Boko Haram in Nigeria, the International Criminal Court in The Hague, the notion of transitional justice (judicial issues that typically arise in the transitional phase following a conflict), and to some extent with the mythology of the Ancient Greeks and the Diné (also known as the Navajo).

Given the novel's themes, it is inevitable, but not unintentional, that arguments from present-day debates on identity and cultural appropriation can be found in the protagonists' conversations. The novel can and should be read as a ballad about identity politics, keeping in mind that a ballad can only tell one story. This book is not a treatise on identity politics in the guise of a novel; such a text would have required a more nuanced presentation of each of the various positions and counter-positions.

All of this may sound rather weighty, which indeed it is. Nevertheless, I hope this book will find an inquisitive readership that is not overwhelmed by the amount of material addressed, but, on the contrary, sees it as confirmation that the world is colorful, diverse and full of unknown treasures; that identities are composed of an infinite set of variables that extend well beyond our own collection of experiences and are constantly shifting and recombining; that identities are rarely an end, but rather the beginning of something new. Only this kind of openness will lead us away from narrow, static and, in extreme cases, racially based definitions. Linking identity to a single quality, especially a gene or gender, and cramming that identity into a corset that ignores an individual's many other qualities and potentials, is an attitude that should be viewed with suspicion by anyone who values emancipation.

Music is, and has always been, a realm of acceptance and openness where identities can unfold boundlessly. Interculturality was cultivated in music long before the terms *world music*, *crossover* and *fusion* were introduced. The real question is not *whether* cultural discourse with the other should take place, but *how*.

In this book (see page 147), Amy Beach's Four Commandments are, unfortunately, fictional. One of their central elements is respect, which brings me to an important point: If there is any terminology that might be considered offensive in today's language, I hope that the context will either clarify why the use of a particular term is justified in a particular rhetorical situation, or explain the problematic nature of the term, or demonstrate that I disassociate myself from the term. It is certainly not my intention to be dis-respectful to anyone.

Biographical and musicological details are the result of my detailed research. The cook's name in the historical Minton's Playhouse in Harlem really was Adelle; Dvořák really did read

Národní listy in Café Boulevard. Now long forgotten, Charlotte Hubach was the librarian who organized the exile art events in the Ottendorfer Library mentioned in the book. Furthermore, the massacre perpetrated by Boko Haram in the Baga region in early January 2015 took place as Bukar describes it.

I have not cited sources for every detail, lest the book become more of an academic paper and less of a novel. On the contrary, while the scenes and dialogues in the book are based on everything I learned about the characters' ways of thinking, they are purely fictional.

One example is the interaction between Amy Beach and Béla Bartók. Bartók deserves to be highlighted because of the parallels, but even more so because of the differences, between his and Arthur Farwell's biographies. In reality, Amy Beach and Béla Bartók only met once, in February 1928 in the New York salon hosted by composer Ethel Hier. Although Beach was an assiduous letter writer, there is no evidence of any correspondence between her and Bartók. The Bartók letters I quote in the book were actually written to other people.

Beach did meet Farwell in person and, since they both liked to write, it is quite possible that they corresponded, although this is not documented. The Arthur Farwell Collection at the Eastman School of Music does not include any letters from Amy Beach.

It is also fiction that Bud Powell's grandfather visited the Chicago World's Fair in 1893 and that he was so shocked by what he saw there that he believed he'd experienced it himself. The incident is not far-fetched, however. Members of the Fon people, an ethnic group from what was then known as the Kingdom of Dahomey, now southern Benin, were indeed on display at the fair. The grandfather's indignation at the dehumanizing show is representative of the reaction of Black visitors at the time.

In the interest of transparency, I would like to thank those who were kind enough to share their knowledge and inspiration with me during the process of researching and writing this book: Joseph Horowitz, the author of three extremely insightful, intelligent and tasteful books about classical music in the United States, about Dvořák's ›prophecy‹ and the ›moral fire‹ of some of Dvořák's American contemporaries; the leading Dvořák expert Professor Michael Beckerman who, among many other interesting tidbits, provided me with a short letter from Amy Beach that plays a small but important role in the book; pianist Virginia Eskin, a specialist on Amy Beach and other American women composers, who remains vibrant despite her advanced age and who wrote a very inspiring children's book about Amy Beach which unfortunately was never published; Curt Cacioppo, a culturally aware American composer who has critically examined the Indianist movement and demonstrated how the historically ambivalent interaction between white and Indigenous musicians can be approached in a respectful, musically captivating way in the present age.

I greatly benefitted from the following background literature: Adrienne Fried Block's biography of Amy Beach; Guthrie P. Ramsey's biography of Bud Powell; Klaus Döge's biography of Dvořák; and the rather uninspired but precise chronicles of daily life kept by Dvořák's assistant Josef Kovařík and by Walter S. Jenkins, an acquaintance of Amy Beach. Professor Beth Levy's insightful and assertive synopsis of the history of music and society in the American West, entitled *Frontier Figures*, was also impressive and served as a contrast to Evelyn David Culbertson's extremely well-meaning biography of Farwell. Heidi J. Todacheene's article in the Tribal Law Journal on the Navajo Creation Story (2014) was my major reference for Diné mythology. Tibor Tallián's biography gave me a better understanding of Béla Bartók. Wolfgang Rathert and Berndt Ostendorf's monumental work, *Musik der USA*, published by Wolke Verlag (my German publisher), delves much deeper than this book into the phase of self-discovery in American music, the Indianist movement, the musical expansion of the pioneering spirit in the American West, and the origins, significance and identity of blues and jazz.

I would like to thank all of my early readers for their stylistic criticism, especially my daughter Valerie and Richard Lomax. Kate Mueser, with her dual qualifications as a writer and pianist, did a marvelous job of providing an English translation that is savvy, spirited and idiomatically unerring.

Finally, a very special thank you goes to my partner Hanni. Without her, our research trip to New York City in April 2022 would not have been so fruitful and enjoyable. For a whole year, she forgave me for having my head in a different place and time. But why should my head be better off than Amelie's, Tony's or López's?

»How should I begin?«

Sipping her espresso, Petra stares at her computer screen, half expecting the answer to jump out at her.

Bukar stands behind her. He puts his hands on her shoulders and leans down to give her a quick kiss on the forehead.

»It's not like you're writing for the very first time,« *he says.* »Okay, okay, I know it's your first novel and not a term paper. But the rules are the same, right? Just keep it simple. And forget the hype about the first sentence. It's not that important. I never decide whether or not I'm going to keep reading after just one sentence.«

»Really? And that's coming from you?« *asks Petra.* »Didn't they hammer it into you, back at the *Lagos Herald, that the first sentence is the most important?*«

»Yeah, they did. But there's only one rule for writing a good first sentence: It shouldn't be terrible. You only tell people to focus on their first sentence if you know they can't write anything good after that. You're not one of them.«

»Enough compliments, Bukar. Come on, help me!« *begs Petra.* »How should I begin?«

Bukar goes into the kitchen and puts on an apron, planning to stay there for a while. Silence is his reply to Petra. She'll figure it out on her own.

Petra understands. She looks out the window. It's raining and damp air seeps through the edges of the warped wooden window frames. It takes muscle and finesse to shut them all the way. The weather app shows precipitation for the foreseeable future. Rain, rain and more rain, from the North Sea all the way to Brussels, where it has no intention of leaving. It's here to stay, like the Belgians who cling to a beer and a bowl of mussels in their favorite restaurant, or to the foosball table in the local pub, lest they be washed away by the autumn blues.

»Should I begin with Tony and Amelie, explaining who they are and what they have to say? Or with López? No. Not with López. I still don't get her.

Maybe with Bob? Should I go chronologically and explain why we went to New York—because of my writer's block with my dissertation and your frustration with the Boko Haram trial? Or should I tell the story from the end and explain our hope that a homecoming can also be a new departure?«

Bukar, still wearing his apron, comes back to the living room with two glasses. He pauses and looks at Petra quizzically. »Say that again.«

»Say what? I've been talking this whole time.« Petra looks confused. »What should I say again?«

»Your last sentence,« insists Bukar.

»Why?«

»It was a good sentence.«

Petra thinks for a moment, trying to remember what she had just said. »Every homecoming is a new departure. That one?«

»Yes, that one. But you didn't say it like that. Homecoming is departure. A equals B. That's too categorical. You said it more conditionally, and you mentioned hope. Returning home means first of all that once you are at home you want to stay there and not pick up and leave right away. You sleep in your own bed, you get back to your routines, you're happy because everything is back to normal. You feel like you're in a beautiful garden. The herbs smell nice, and they heal and strengthen you. But then…«

Bukar's eyes flash with inspiration as Petra's widen. »…then comes the day when you listen to your inner self.«

Bukar paces like a cat ready to jump. »There's a little restless spirit inside of you that's whispering: 'Don't be so complacent, there may be ways to find an even better balance in life. Your inner self could be happier. You could feel more complete.' And you look into the distance and say, 'I'm going away. Where to? To the next homecoming.'«

Ever since they met over two years ago, Petra has admired Bukar's eloquence. He can hold a moving speech, win a crowd at the drop of a hat with both his astute arguments and convincing gestures. He is a journalist through and through.

»You mean I should say that every homecoming holds the chance of a new departure?«

»Yeah, just like that. Isn't that what you would say about our trip to New York?«

»I guess so. Definitely about Tony, the musical nomad. And Amelie and Bob…«

Bukar takes off his apron, sits down next to Petra on the couch, and hands her one of the glasses he's been holding. He sets his on the coffee table and puts his arm around her, pulling her close.

Suddenly, Bukar jumps up, releases Petra from his embrace, and dashes to the bookshelf. »You know what I'm going to turn on.«

Bukar taps his index finger against his mouth, closes his eyes and waits for the music to start. As the first notes shyly emerge from the piano on the recording, he begins to imitate Bob's raw, jagged voice, teetering back and forth with short squarish movements, just as Bob always did: »Listen, folks. 'Goin' Home' from Dvořák's New World Symphony, an American work full of Bohemian homesickness. Second movement. Gorgeous melody! Sounds like a spiritual, but it's not. Until William Arms Fisher came along—Dvořák's pupil. His lyrics and choral writing make it sound like a gospel song. And then Art Tatum! ♦ Fisher's Bohemian gospel song now becomes a real American jazz number. Right hand. Romantic yearning. And then it suddenly races up and down the keyboard. Left hand. Jumps like a good stride piano piece but with the strangest harmonies. Crazy! Dvořák, Scott Joplin, Liszt, Tatum! All in one piece! Hey, guys, are you with me? How often has this piece been put in a box, settled there, then been pulled out again? Yeah, that's true art. Give and take. In art, there's no virgin conception. Remember that before you judge others.«

Bukar stops and looks at Petra, his eyes sparkling. She shakes her head in disbelief, recalls her farewell from López, and wipes away a tear. »You remembered all that, word for word?« she asks.

»Oh yeah. How could I ever forget? I only caught half of your insider talk with Tony and Amelie. But what Bob said stuck with me. I think of it when I'm feeling hungry and curious,« he says.

»Don't be so modest, Bukar,« says Petra. »You understood a lot. You – you hungry, curious journalist. I'm always amazed at how easily you pick up new things!«

»You think so?«

»Before our trip, you didn't know what stride piano was.«

»True,« admits Bukar. He sits down and taps a hopping bass line on his thigh with his left hand—a pattern typical of stride compositions which relied *on ragtime bass techniques brought to virtuosic perfection by musicians like Duke Ellington and Art Tatum.* »Um-ta, um-ta.«

Petra waves Bukar back to the couch. »Hungry and curious would also make nice opening words, wouldn't they?«

»Definitely! Later, baby, when we turn off the light. But for the book, I think that the homecoming and departure stuff is better.«

Quite a flirt, thinks Petra. Even after two years together, he still gives her goosebumps.

»And what are you going to call it?« *asks Petra.*

»Wait a sec...I've got it!«

And so, Petra puts her fingers on the keyboard of her laptop and types:

GOIN' HOME

Every homecoming holds the chance of a new departure. Since we returned from New York exactly one week ago, this has become increasingly clear, even though both of us can only guess where our departure will take us.

The day before yesterday, I sent a long email to my thesis advisor in Innsbruck. I'm sorry, I wrote, but I won't be able to write anything good about our agreed topic in time. Antonín Dvořák and Amy Beach as opposites in the debate about a national style of music in the United States—a harbinger of today's identity politics? I find the topic problematic for several reasons.

Petra stops typing. Instead of delineating, in typical academic language, everything she finds problematic about the topic, she asks herself who she is writing for in the first place. A small circle of musicologists? Or a new, broader audience? For people who want to discover a fascinating chapter in music history? For those who are also interested in learning about the historical context? Yes, for them. She'll have to give a little background. Petra starts again:

Musical and Historical Introduction

In June 1891, Jeannette Thurber, President of the New York Conservatory of Music, asked Czech composer Antonín Dvořák to become director of the young but ambitious institution. For music circles in the US, Dvořák seemed predestined for the job, given his role in heralding a Czech national school of music that drew on Moravian and Bohemian folk styles.

Jean Sibelius, a pioneer of the Finnish national school of music, was also considered for the job, but he had a reputation for drinking too much.

Dvořák was offered an annual salary of $15,000—ten times what he was earning in Prague. After some hesitation, he accepted the position, although it wasn't an easy decision for him. Through the influence of Johannes Brahms, he had received an equally lucrative job offer at the same time as director of the Vienna Conservatory. But what would people say in his homeland, anti-Habsburg Bohemia, if he accepted?

The United States was in the midst of an era of optimism, and recruiting Dvořák was considered a major coup. The country was celebrating the 400th anniversary of Christopher Columbus's discovery, trade was booming, and industrialization was on the rise, all of which fed the country's subcutaneous conviction that it was exceptional. Dvořák was there to ›help add the new world of music to the continent which Columbus found‹, as patron and millionaire Thomas Wentworth Higginson said in his opening remarks at Dvořák's welcome concert on October 21, 1892.

In addition to Thurber, other influential figures in the American music scene, including the vocal music critic Henry Krehbiel[1], expressed the view that it was time for America to free itself from dependence on other cultures. Musically, this meant liberating itself from the monopolistic influence of the German conservatories, removing the role model function of the German and Austrian musicians and conductors who kept pouring into the US, and enticing audiences to accept concert programs with an unmistakable American flair rather than their beloved standard fare of Beethoven and Wagner.

Only six months after his arrival in New York, encouraged by his interactions with the conservatory students and with his Black assistant Harry Thacker Burleigh[2], Dvořák made an important announcement in the *New York Herald* on May 21, 1893:

> "I am now satisfied that the future music of this country must be founded on what are called negro melodies. That must be the real foundation of every serious and original school of composition to be developed in the United States. (...) These beautiful and varied themes are the product of the soil. They are American. (...) In the negro melodies I discover all that is needed for a great and noble school of music. They are pathetic, tender, passionate, melancholy, solemn, religious, bold, merry, gay, or what you will."

---

1   Henry Krehbiel (1854-1923) was a German-born music critic for the *New York Tribune* (1880-1923) and an influential *primus inter pares*. He promoted Dvořák's *New World* Symphony and supported his views on the value of African-American music, both in his published texts and through his own studies (*Afro-American Folksongs*, 1914).

2   Henry "Harry" Thacker Burleigh (1866-1949) was an American baritone, composer and arranger of hundreds of spirituals (e.g. *Deep River*). Dvořák's assistant at the National Conservatory, he was one of the reasons for his interest in African-American music.

In the summer of 1893, Dvořák spent his vacation in Spillville, Iowa, a small rural town that had been settled by Czech immigrants. One of its residents was Josef Kovařík, a young man who would become Dvořák's assistant throughout his stay in the United States. In Spillville, Dvořák met many Indigenous Americans and became familiar with their music. In December 1893, he expanded on his declaration of love for American music in an article in the *New York Herald*:

"Since I have been in this country, I have been deeply interested in the music of the negroes *and the Indians* (...) and I intend to do all in my power to call attention to their brilliant treasure of melodies."

It was this mindset that guided Dvořák's work on his *New World Symphony* ♦ which was premiered to great acclaim in New York on December 16, 1893.

His comments about making Black and Indigenous music a foundation of American music were met with both approval and criticism. Composer Edward MacDowell[3] argued that a national American music was just as superfluous as any other national music. The language of music was universal, not national, he said. Detractors, such as music critic Philip Hale from the *Boston Herald*, claimed that ›the Negroes‹ lacked musicality and called their music a cacophonous product of an inferior culture—unfit to serve as a basis for American music.

Wunderkind pianist and composer Amy Marcy Cheney raised her finger and pointed out that Black Americans had migrated to the country just like everyone else (with the exception of ›Indians and Esquimaux‹) and, for that very reason, could not form the basis of an autochthonous American music. After the success of her youth, she was about to establish herself as an adult artist in Boston. Her marriage to the surgeon Henry Harris Aubrey Beach gave her access—as Mrs. H.H.A. Beach—to the upper echelons of Boston society.

Amy Beach formulated her stance as part of a collection of reactions to Dvořák's recommendations in the Boston Herald in May 1893:

---

3   Edward Alexander MacDowell (1860-1908) was an American composer and pianist.

"In order to make the best use of folk-songs of any nation as material for musical composition, the writer should be one of the people whose music he chooses, or at least brought up among them."

Beach then wrote—in part to back up her stance—one of her most popular early works, the Gaelic Symphony ♦ in E Minor, Op. 32 (1896), which bore similarities to Dvořák's *New World* Symphony No. 9 in E Minor, Op. 95 (1893), but made use of the Scottish and Irish folk music of her ancestors rather than the African-American and Indigenous American melodies that inspired Dvořák. In later years, Amy Beach seemed to have a change of heart. Some of her best compositions, including her Quartet for Strings in One Movement, Op. 89 (1922), her Theme and Variations for Flute and String Quartet, Op. 80 (1916) and *Eskimos— Four Characteristic Pieces for the Pianoforte*, Op. 64 (1906), were based on Inuit melodies. She also looked to Southeastern Europe in her *Variations on Balkan Themes*, Op. 60 (1906), and to Northern Italy in her *Tyrolean Valse-Fantaisie*, Op. 116 (1914).

What exactly was the controversy between Dvořák and Beach over the foundations of American music all about? Nothing more than one of many heckling points between puritan Boston and cosmopolitan New York City—between two metropolises whose residents proudly traced their arrival to either the Mayflower or Ellis Island?

Or were Dvořák and Beach merely trying to achieve something for themselves, regardless of the principles they invoked? Did Dvořák simply check off expectations attached to his well-paid position at the New York Conservatory by coming up with a recommendation that was a natural choice for him—folk music? And was Beach, the daughter of wealthy Bostonians, simply trying to defend her artistically dominant place in a society that was being challenged by a huge wave of non-Anglo-Saxon immigrants and other parvenus?

These explanations would fall short.

Dvořák and Beach's controversy extended well beyond the two of them. Beginning in the United States prior to Dvořák's arrival, it continued to generate discourse well into the next century. During the 20th century, musical trends unfolded that Dvořák had initiated, but whose paths and dimensions could hardly have been predicted during his stay in the United States.

One of them was the rise of African-American music. This was not only the most important trend for the long-term development of American music, but also the one most clearly attributable to Dvořák. One of the first Black musicians to achieve success was Dvořák's aforementioned assistant, Harry Burleigh. Others followed: composers who were spliced as equals into the panopticon of the Western-oriented Late Romantic canon, often as explicit successors of Dvořák but with their own styles. Unfortunately, their names have fallen into oblivion: William Dawson, Florence Price, William Grant Still, Nathaniel Dett.

Another, even more significant African-American contribution to the musical identity of the United States was the rapid development of jazz. Its origins can be traced not only to New Orleans and gospel, but also to the minstrel shows of the mid-19th century. These deplorable spectacles reflected the rampant racism of the time. Popular pieces of music by white and Black composers were presented by both white and Black performers in blackface. The shows were a racial mockery. Nevertheless, they allowed Blacks to share their own African-American music with a mainstream audience in exchange for renouncing their dignity. Among the Black composers and soloists who initially made a name for themselves in the minstrel shows were the legendary jazz pianist Jelly Roll Morton (1890-1941), ›Empress of the Blues‹ Bessie Smith (1894-1937) and the swing and bebop saxophonist Lester Young (1909-1959).

Looking back at the 20th century, jazz is America's signature music. Around the turn of the 20th century, jazz (that is, ragtime, one of the original incarnations of jazz) had already found its way into Western art music in works by composers such as Stravinsky, Ravel and Debussy. Jazz became one of the most important forms of popular music, not only for the Black community: One form, swing, was largely played by white big bands. American composers such as Gershwin and Copland were also influenced by jazz.

Dvořák had opened the doors for the inroads African-American music was to make in both the classical and jazz scenes. He adored Black music despite the dismissive zeitgeist.

The controversy over the development of a national American musical style was embedded in a much larger socio-political debate at the time about the country's greater purpose, its ›manifest destiny‹. This concept fused American exceptionalism, nationalism and expansionism into an overarching sense of mission and included the notion that the United States had a duty to spread its culture not only among the Indigenous people within the country but also to all those beyond its borders.

By 1890, the Wild West was considered to have been conquered. The next step, so people were told, was to go beyond the domestic reforms called for by the Progressives[4] to address social and political grievances such as poverty among the rapidly growing proletariat, corruption, and deficiencies in the democratic system. Beyond that, it was said, there was a need for a new societal challenge to maintain the strength and vitality that had been acquired during the winning of the West. The exact content of this societal challenge was open to interpretation.

Theodore Roosevelt, who would later become the ›big stick‹-bearing President of the United States from 1901 to 1909, suggested in his 1884 bestseller *The Winning of the West* that the United States should continue to cultivate its pioneering spirit and go-get-'em cowboy mentality.

Historian Frederick Jackson had a different answer. His 1893 speech at the Chicago World's Fair was probably heard by two illustrious visitors to the fair: Antonín Dvořák and Amy Beach. The solution, according to Jackson, was not to be found in Roosevelt's cowboy machismo. Instead, he said, a coordinated effort, not unlike a crusade, was needed to civilize the ›underdeveloped‹ cultures, that is, the African-Americans and Indigenous people—including their music.

His proselytizing approach was rooted in the popular doctrine of Social Darwinism which transferred biological rules, including evolutionary selection, to human societies. Darwin himself had never intended his theories to be applied to social or cultural settings. According to Social Darwinism, Western civilization had prevailed over other civilizations which were therefore doomed to remain at a lower level of development. The pseudo-scientific theory provided a cheap basis for racism and paternalism.

Musicians interested in the music of other cultures had to navigate through these inchoate ideologies, much more vaguely defined at the time than they are now in retrospect. Culturally open-minded individuals sought

---

4   The period between 1890, the end of the Gilded Age, and World War I is known as the Progressive Era, which was characterized by social and political reform.

understanding rather than exclusion—but how? Respectfully distanced acquaintanceships, a quest for commonalities, joyful embraces, syncretism? These conceptual uncertainties manifested themselves in the way white composers treated Indigenous music. While the various strands of African-American music managed to gain recognition in the mainstream music business on their own (though not without difficulty), Indigenous music received attention only through the bias of white composers who became known as *Indianists*.

The term is controversial. For one thing, it's ambiguous. For example, should Indigenous American composers who write music according to the conventions of classical music but draw on elements of their own musical tradition[5] also be called Indianists?

More importantly, the term is tainted by its association with the colonial word ›Indians‹, a blanket moniker that lumps the culturally diverse Indigenous people of North America together into a single category of perceived underdevelopment which then provided a Darwinian justification for the white colonists' systematic campaigns of displacement and extermination.

Today, at least, the term ›Indianist‹ is rejected by many composers who deal with Indigenous American music[6]. For composers in the decades just before and after 1900, it was still in use, despite some people's reservations and regardless of the fact that the Indianists themselves were hardly a homogenous group.

What exactly were the Indianists after? For some, ethnomusicology was their primary interest. They approached Indigenous American music with curiosity and respect, though not always without prejudice, and generally

---

5   Examples include Fred Cardin (1895-1960) and Louis Wayne Ballard (1931-2007) ♦, both of the Quapaw Nation of Oklahoma. Cardin received a degree in composition from the Curtis Institute of Music in Philadelphia in 1927 and composed numerous works according to the traditions of Western music. He performed them himself as principal violinist in the Indian String Quartet and the Indian Art and Musical Company. Ballard studied composition with Rózsa, Milhaud and Castelnuovo-Tedesco, among others, but resisted assimilation more than Cardin and developed his own personal, contemporary style. Nevertheless, he said that Dvořák's recognition of Indigenous American music was an inspiration to him.

6   Such as Curt Cacioppo (1951-) who composed the string quartet *Kinaalda (The Rite of Changing Woman)* ♦ as a part of the cycle *Womb of the Sacred Mountain* about the Diné Bahane', the creation myth of the Diné (Navajo).

had a penchant for the exotic. Their goal was to accurately document the music, not only its melodies and rhythms but also its ceremonial significance. Among these Indianists were the ethnologist Franz Boas (whose 1888 field report *The Central Eskimo* served as a source for Amy Beach in writing her *Eskimo* piano pieces) and the ethnomusicologist Alice Fletcher, whose *Study of Omaha Indian Music* (1893) was read and interpreted by numerous composers, including Dvořák and Beach.

Others were simply motivated by artistic curiosity about a foreign tonal language and the compositional ›high‹ achieved by integrating these new experiences. Today we might refer to it as fusion, although fusion could result in just about anything: dressing up an ›exotic‹ voice in a Western costume; uninhibitedly turning the ‹exotic‹ into something kitschy; selectively picking and choosing borrowed elements to assemble a cliché of primitive music.

The Indianists represented a wide spectrum of viewpoints, and even the more respectful ones slipped up now and then.

Amy Beach's attitude toward Indigenous music underwent a surprising evolution. Originally, at the time of her controversy with Dvořák, she insisted that composers should only write music according to the culture to which they belonged. A short time later, she became interested in Inuit melodies, and then in other Indigenous American melodies. At first, she harmonized the Indigenous melodies in a Late Romantic style, but later developed her own approach. Preserving the distinct otherness of the Indigenous melody, she added a stylistically different, mildly modernist accompaniment. The result was a cultural hybrid in which neither side lost and both sides gained.

Edward MacDowell, a Late Romantic composer influenced by German music throughout his life, composed his orchestral *Indian* Suite No. 2, Op. 48 (1897) ♦ more as an experiment than out of any genuine interest in Indigenous American music. Its melodies were taken from one of the first ethnomusicological texts ever written: Theodore Baker's dissertation, written in Leipzig. After a performance of the *Indian* Suite, MacDowell sneered in reference to the third movement (›*War Times*‹) and the very beautiful fourth movement (›*Dirge*‹), saying, ›Killed the Indian again last night!‹ MacDowell was considered one of the most

Bud Powell, around 1960

Amy Beach,
unknown date

Antonín Dvořák,
around 1884

influential early exponents of Indianism which sheds light on the fickle nature of the movement.

Charles Wakefield Cadman[7] vacillated between serious cultural interest and a desire to maximize musical effect. Unfortunately, he more often chose the latter, that is, entertaining, exotic-sounding kitsch. One danger that many Indianists could not overcome was the temptation to emphasize wild elements in their works, thereby reinforcing stereotypes.

Arthur Farwell[8] was different. From the beginning of his musical career, he felt called to renew American music with a democratic, grassroots spirit. With great idealism, he set out to collect indigenous, Black, and Hispanic folk music as building blocks for a future American national style. The Wa-Wan Press, which he founded, published the works, and he tirelessly toured the country from coast to coast, giving lectures and teaming up with local music societies to teach performers on how best to perform them. In this context, Farwell was primarily interested in Indigenous American music, as well as in its spiritual dimension. By approaching the spiritual element of music with an open mind and respect, he distanced himself from the Social Darwinist notion of a hierarchical world. For Farwell, social Darwinism was ›racism masquerading as Christianity‹.

As enlightened as this may sound, he also had his dark sides. He was very critical of his time, convinced that the onward march of industrialization was leading to sensory overload, disruption, and, ultimately, the spiritual and physical breakdown of civilization. In his 1903 *Articles of Faith* about Indigenous American music, he wrote: ›Indian music remains a great source of inspiration and a significant point of departure for the American composer who understands it in connection with its underlying wealth of mythical lore. For it springs from, and interprets in new colors, the 'great

---

7   Charles Wakefield Cadman (1881-1946) was an American composer. After his music studies, he followed the recommendation of Alice Fletcher, whose *Study of Omaha Indian Music* he had read, and traveled to Nebraska where he recorded and transcribed the melodies of the Omaha and learned to play their instruments. He often performed his Indianist works together with Indigenous American musicians.

8   Arthur Farwell (1872-1952) was an American composer. He studied composition in France, Germany and the US. In 1901, he founded the music publisher Wa-Wan Press with an emphasis on Indianist music. He later became a professor of music in California, Michigan and New York.

mystery›, the eternal miracle of natural and human phenomena, to which refreshing source American life is leading us back from the artificialities and technicalities which have latterly beset European culture.‹

This conviction continued to grow in Farwell. In the following years, he moved to California, where he developed esoteric ideas of salvation, with Indigenous spirituality as a basic ingredient. His goal was to escape what he saw as the ›Decline of the West‹. The key was held by the people of the American West, the prototypes of a ›new‹ kind of humankind, close to nature, trained in ›Indian‹ spirituality, and multiethnic—but led by whites. California became the center of an artistic and democratic movement of renewal, with Farwell as its prophet. In manifestos and newspaper articles, as well as in pageants in which Farwell himself took the stage as a ›seer‹, he spoke disturbingly of a ›new society‹ with ›new men‹.

Farwell's pageant works are largely forgotten. Compositions remembered from his California days include his Suite *Gods of the Mountains*, Op, 52 ♦, as well as his String Quartet *The Hako* in A Major, Op. 65 ♦, one of the most inspired of all his Indianist works. It can be considered the epitome of his Indianist style which he developed in his many early Indianist piano pieces.[9]

Farwell latched on to Indigenous spirituality as a pillar for a better world. Was it a romanticizing reinvention of the paradisiacal life of the ›happy savages‹—a relapse in the role allocation between the ›civilized‹ whites and the ›wild Indians‹ with which the Europeans glorified their colonial expansion? This would be particularly galling given that for many years Farwell, more than other Indianists, had been exemplary in steering clear of the hierarchies imposed by Social Darwinism.

In the second half of his life, Farwell fortunately moved away from the glorification of the American West. As a professor of music in Michigan and New York, he pondered the value of intuition, commented on the development of cultural life in the US, and developed a rather brittle polytonal style of composition, in which there was no trace of his once urgent search for a new American music. Ultimately, his work never gained the significance that it deserved.

---

9   Lisa Cheryl Thomas of the Cherokee Nation recorded a comprehensive, but incomplete collection of Farwell's piano pieces.

How did Indigenous Americans respond to the field research of white ethnomusicologists and composers? Were they pleased by their cultural interest, or disturbed or even threatened by the intrusion? Contemporary accounts vary. The fact is that the Indianists typically went about their research without first asking permission[10]. On the other hand, many Indigenous Americans were happy to participate in performances of Indianist music.

Not only Indigenous Americans were in danger of being taken advantage of by Farwell the Prophet, Cadman, or others. It was also a problem for composers and performers of African-American music, albeit in a different way. For them, the market was both a curse and a blessing. Recognition often came at the price of financial exploitation and perpetuated stereotypes.

African-American music continued to grow in popularity. Unlike the music of the Indigenous Americans and the Indianists, African-American music found more and more fans—not only millions of Blacks, but a growing white audience as well. In concert halls, in segregated clubs, on the radio, and on established record labels, milder forms of jazz received just as much attention as jazz works by white composers such as George Gershwin, Aaron Copland and Leonard Bernstein. White audiences wanted ensembles to put on a show and present themselves as choreographed swing bands with the obligatory Black jazz trumpet player who not only tooted his horn but also made silly faces and rolled his big eyes in a cute way.

Record companies that attempted to produce authentic Black music for a Black audience, such as Black Swan Records in the early 1920s, failed to gain more than a tiny market niche. They either folded or were bought up by larger record companies. Commercial success in the white-dominated mainstream music industry was the reward for perpetuating clichés.

Bebop ♦—a virtuosic and boisterous style of jazz played since the early 1940s by Charlie Parker, Dizzy Gillespie, Bud Powell, and others—

---

10 Today, Indianist works are often performed with the participation of Indigenous American artists or leaders. Examples include the recording of Arthur Farwell's piano works by Lisa Cheryl (see footnote 9) and the composer Curt Cacioppo (see footnote 6). On his website, he describes in detail the collaborative composition process he employed for his cycle of string quartets ♦ about the Diné creation myth.

emerged as an assertive insurgency against the white dominance of the music industry.

The reception of both African-American and Indigenous American music raises an important question: How legitimate is it to quote, borrow, adapt and reinterpret this music without belonging to the culture behind it? I don't mean to suggest that these are inherently disdainful acts—far from it. Traditionally, borrowing and reinterpreting music from other cultures has been considered proof of being knowledgeable and open-minded, of expanding one's horizons through artistic innovation. It was not seen as sacrilegious, but as a sign of appreciation and even of extending a hand in friendship (such as the Turkish elements in Mozart's opera *The Abduction from the Seraglio*). It was an attempt to compose an aural monument to another soundscape and to create an innovative artistic hybrid.

The list of composers who quoted or adapted others in the 18th and 19th centuries is endless.[11] When Brahms sought out new melodies and rhythms, he looked to Hungary. Rimski-Korsakov turned not only to the folk music of his native Russia, but also to Spain. And the Mexicans turned French wedding (›mariage‹) songs into their own mariachi music without triggering protests in France or copyright battles in the courts.

On the other hand, too many composers caricatured, stereotyped and mocked the music of other cultures in their own compositions.

Where is the line?

Before my trip to New York, I had read a lot about these issues.[12] In New York, I listened carefully to what Amy, Tony and Bob had to say about

---

11 The list extends into the 20th century, with Sergei Rachmaninov's *Rhapsody on a Theme by Paganini* for Piano and Orchestra, Op. 43 (1934), or Sting's Prokofiev quote in his ballad against the Cold War arms race, *Russians* (1985).

12 For example, Berndt Ostendorf in *Musik der USA*: »In the land of ethnic bricolage, the question of who, over the course of American history, stole which music from whom, is a topic of heated debate (...), and particularly difficult to answer. What is the role of the complicated interplay between white cultural norms, ethnic subcultures, and black folk culture? What about romantic projections on the supposed authenticity of Black culture? And what about the search of ethnically white people for unbroken primitivism, unencumbered sexuality, and joie de vivre, and the conversion of some Jews to ›Negroism‹ (as an alternative to passing as white Americans)? Aren't these specifically American versions of the pursuit of happiness?

them, and my own views changed significantly. But I'd rather let them speak for themselves.

This is the end of Petra's introduction. Now she feels ready to tackle the main part of her book for the second time:

How should the over-assimilation of Blacks in the white world (...) be evaluated? What role do exoticism and primitivism play as engines of the modernistic avant-garde? (...) Didn't representations of jazz go hand in hand with a progressive, civil rights-proclaiming tradition?«

By ›some Jews‹, Ostendorf presumably means George Gershwin, Irving Berlin, Aaron Copland and two music publishers: Isidore Witmark (1869-1941) whose interest in minstrel shows—despite his professed rejection of all kinds of racism—made him a pioneer in discovering Black talent and a supporter of Henry "Harry" Thacker Burleigh (see footnote 2); and Alfred Lion (1908-1987), co-founder of the legendary *Blue Note Records* label and Bud Powell's mentor, who had discovered his passion for jazz as Alfred Löw in 1920s' Berlin, before emigrating to the US.

GOIN' HOME

Every homecoming holds the chance of a new departure. Since we returned from New York exactly one week ago, this has become increasingly clear, even though both of us can still only guess where our departure will take us.

The day before yesterday, I sent a long email to my thesis advisor in Innsbruck. I'm sorry, I told him, but I won't be able to write anything good about our agreed topic in time. Antonín Dvořák and Amy Beach as opposites in the debate about a national musical style of the United States—a harbinger of today's identity politics?

I wrote him that I considered the topic to be problematic for several reasons. The controversy over the foundations of American music involved more musicians than just Dvořák and Beach. Furthermore, it was embedded in the ideological and cultural history of the United States from 1890 to World War II, a period too broad to cover in any great detail in a musicological dissertation. In addition, I wrote him, comparing debates about identity politics then and now seemed like apples and oranges because the discussions focused on different points. In Dvořák's and Beach's time, the core issue was finding identity in the shadow of nationalism. Today, in a world in which cultural life is defined less by nations and more by cultural communities, special interest groups and stand-out individuals, the debate is primarily about protecting identity from encroachments and ensuring cultural respect by negotiating the rules of interculturalism, I argued.

There's another reason for the length of my message. I like him. He's a nice, older guy who lives in his own world—the world of classical music. He once told me that he's worried that his world is gradually coming to an end. I guess that's why he gave me a dissertation topic that was related to a current hot-button issue. I had to be careful how I wrote my message to him so as not to offend his fatherly pride. He's not proud though, so it would be better to say ›fatherly aspiration‹—yes, his aspiration to be relevant in a time that is becoming more and more disorienting.

I tried to comfort him. Despite all the methodological doubts, the questions raised still seemed quite interesting, I said. That's why I'm writing this book instead, and will dedicate it to him. Of course, I'm also writing it for myself, too, if only to document the truly unbelievable insights I gained in New York.

Enough about my concerns.

For Bukar, things are more complicated. In the two years since we met, progress in his field has been so slow that it's actually regression. He works for justice in Nigeria, where conditions have been terrible for two decades. Hundreds of thousands of people have been killed; in some places it feels like civil war.

The Islamic terrorist organization Boko Haram is responsible for the lion's share of the atrocities, including barbaric murders and executions, rapes, forced conversions, the abduction of entire girls' school classes, lootings, and more. Boko Haram is the enemy of both Christians and mainstream Muslims, since the terrorist group ostensibly follows an old and outdated version of Islam[13]. To make matters worse, the Nigerian army and its allied paramilitary organizations and militias are also known for their brutality.

In 2013, the International Criminal Court in The Hague finally opened preliminary investigations. The testimonies sent to the ICC by victims and human rights groups were conclusive. One of them was Bukar's own eyewitness account of a massacre in Baga which could prove important in a trial. Nevertheless, it took another seven years for the ICC to determine that, while it could begin legal proceedings, it wanted to give the Nigerian justice system another chance to deal with the situation itself. Which, according to Bukar, it wasn't going to do.

Nigeria's justice system is not incompetent enough to force the ICC to take over proceedings, but it is too unreliable and fearful to launch a major trial against Boko Haram itself. Only a few minor Boko Haram perpetrators have stood trial in Nigerian courts which fear a backlash if they try to hold the terrorist group's leaders accountable. Similarly, the Nigerian army remains untouchable. How would it respond to closer examination? The unpredictability of its reaction is too great a risk.

---

13 The etymology of the word *boko* is unclear. It may derive from the English word *book* or from the Haussa word for 'lie' or 'deception.' Either way, Boko Haram takes a particularly radical view of Islam and fights against Western education, considering it un-Islamic.

Meanwhile, as Bukar and his fellow Nigerians wait for justice, they hear a constant noise. It's a kind of grinding. Not the grinding of the wheels of justice, ready to announce victory, but the sound of sand in the motor. Piles of painstakingly collected evidence are gathering dust. The victims feel that the national and international justice systems are either twiddling their thumbs or are incompetent or, even worse, are lacking the necessary political will.

Bukar's frustration is growing. He wants a trial to finally begin while the memories and evidence are still fresh, the witnesses are still alive, and the victims have not lost their last glimmer of hope in a functioning justice system. Despite his disappointments, Bukar always seems put together, optimistic, even funny. He's the most inspiring friend I've ever had. He's sharp as a tack and always up for an adventure—and he's good-looking, too. His mother, Fatima, took care of my grandfather until he died.

The story of how Bukar and I met is kind of complicated, but also simple. It started more than two years ago. I was frustrated with my dissertation, so I took a break and did an internship with a South Tyrolean Member of the European Parliament in Brussels. Fatima was taking care of my grandfather in Lauterbach (a remote village in South Tyrol), and Bukar had traveled from Nigeria to the International Nuremberg Principles Academy, an institution dedicated to enabling war crimes trials, to lobby for speeding up a Boko Haram trial at the ICC. Fatima told Bukar that I also had something to do with international criminal law, which was true. My South Tyrolean Member of the European Parliament had a special interest in international criminal law, and I still work for him as an assistant.

Bukar and I began to email regularly. Our emails quickly drifted from legal jargon to more personal stuff. I can't really say who made the first step. At first, it was just the conspicuously long replies, offers to help each other with our work, then the casual question of whether I'd ever eaten African food, whether we should visit the International Criminal Court in The Hague, what his vacation plans were (would he go visit his mother?).

Some of our remarks were subtle, others more direct. When the emails got too businesslike, we grew hungry, and nervous when it took more than two days to reply. Once, I sent him a photo of me with my grandfather with the explanation that he should have a look at the man his mother was taking care of. Of course, I figured that his mother had already sent him a picture of my grandfather, but I wanted him to see what I looked like. Seconds later, in the middle of the night, he replied with a photo of himself and his mother. I knew what she looked like, but I still remember my first three impressions of Bukar. His smile was incredible; thank goodness he didn't have a beard; and I was very disappointed that only his torso was visible in the photo.

When we first met in person, I was surprised to find that he was shorter than his long torso in the photo had suggested. His voice was a rich baritone, smoother than it had sounded in our few phone calls.

It didn't take long to arrange a meeting. After my grandfather had passed away, Fatima, a gentle and knowledgeable woman, moved in with me in Brussels. I enjoyed her presence and her wealth of African proverbs, and secretly hoped that Bukar would come visit her, which he did as soon as he could get a visa. We traipsed around Brussels together and sampled the city's cuisine, alternating between African food and Belgian chocolate. On the weekend, we took a trip to the coast, braving the strong winds for a long walk on the beach. For Bukar, it was a completely new experience. It was new for me, too, to listen to Bukar tell me about his family, as the wind whistled past our ears, as if he were offering me a place in it.

Ten days later, Bukar went back to Nigeria. Four weeks later, he quit his job at the *Lagos Herald* and moved in with me in Brussels. Even though the daily grind has taken over, the spark we felt at the beginning of our relationship still flickers warm and bright.

He chose to come to Brussels partly because of me and partly because conditions in Nigeria were getting worse for outspoken journalists like him. He didn't have a job at first, but soon found one in the English department of a news agency. The position pays poorly, but it gives him time to focus on his own work: justice for the victims of Boko Haram and peace in his homeland. Over time, I have come to understand how Bukar manages to live with the setbacks he has faced in his campaign.

His fight for a trial is more than the private cry for atonement and justice of a young man whose father was executed by Boko Haram for the unforgivable crime of coaching a women's soccer team. For Bukar, it's about more than his father, his mother Fatima and his sister Rehinat. Thanks to his eloquence and intelligence, he feels obligated to be a kind of spokesman for all the victims of Boko Haram. He wants to channel their grief and anger into a constructive project—a trial at the International Criminal Court—so that hatred does not have the last word. That's what he told me, and that's how he is. More hatred, even deeper divisions in Nigerian society, especially along religious fault lines, would go against his character.

One day in mid-August, Bukar surprised me with a wild suggestion. His persuasive words, his charm, and his undeniable logic left me with no choice but to agree.

»Petra, I know you are always ready for an adventure,« he said with a smile. »We have to go to New York. Yes, New York! Dvořák and Beach lived there. Maybe they left something behind that will help you. You have to find out. And I have to go there because that's where the UN Security Council is, and a bunch of NGOs as well. I have to get them on board if the Boko Haram trial is ever going to happen.«

I stood there speechless for a moment as he continued with his well-prepared proposal.

»We're both vaccinated, so we shouldn't have any trouble getting into the country. We can stay with Jiffy. You know, that distant cousin in Manhattan I told you about? I already asked him and he's cool with it. So don't worry about the money. And I talked to Ya, too. She'll be fine without us for three or four weeks.« Ya is the word for ›mother‹ in Kanuri, Fatima's and Bukar's native language.

»Okay,« I said. And so, on September 13, we flew to New York.

* * *

Our arrival in New York was more difficult than we'd expected. We were tired, the line for passport control was long, and Bukar had to answer a lot of questions when we finally got to the counter. It was cold and the taxi from JFK to Bukar's cousin in Manhattan was outrageously expensive. There were tunnel tolls, special fees, extra taxes—as newcomers to the Big Apple, we were easily taken advantage of.

When we finally arrived at Jiffy's, we quickly got the vibe that we weren't all that welcome, despite what he'd told Bukar. Jiffy was about to move in with his girlfriend and vacate his apartment, so we had only two days amidst a mountain of moving boxes to find another place to stay. We were lucky, even though high-level delegations from around the world were descending on New York that very week for the opening of the United Nations General Assembly. We weren't the only ones looking for a place to stay, but that only drove the prices up, albeit without drying up the supply in such a huge metropolis.

The furnished one-bedroom we found was located in a nondescript five-story building on the corner of East 16th Street and Third Avenue. There was no elevator, the pantry door didn't close all the way, and the lock on the sliding window in the bedroom (where we crammed our belongings onto a makeshift plywood shelf) was broken. But the important things worked: The shower was hot, the kitchen had a big fridge and a garbage chute built into the wall, and there was WiFi and a television.

We justified the horrendous rent by reminding ourselves that we were staying in the very neighborhood where Dvořák himself had lived and worked. Just a few days earlier, the corner of East 16th and Third Avenue had been renamed Harry T. Burleigh Place in honor of the African-American composer. If that wasn't a stroke of fate! We were in the right place, even if it did cost an arm and a leg. The neighborhood seemed to possess a special aura, we told ourselves, as if its streets, parks and courtyards had remained untouched by the 130 years that had passed since Dvořák's and Beach's era.

During our evening walks, we stood in awe before the well-kept brownstone at 327 East 17th Street where Dvořák and his family lived for two years. I couldn't find the bronze plaque I'd read about, which the Czechoslovakian government-in-exile supposedly screwed onto the house in 1941. Still, we enjoyed the feeling of seeing a monument that turned my abstract research into tangible reality.

In other cases, historical landmarks had been lost, bulldozed to make way for the ordinary, everyday life of a new era. Now replaced by a twenty-story cubic office building, the Hotel Clarendon at East 18th Street and Fourth Avenue, now Park Avenue South, was Dvořák's first residence when he arrived in New York. And where the National Conservatory of Music once stood at 126-128 East 17th Street, there are now apartment buildings with businesses on the ground floor in typical New York fashion: a parking garage, a shoe repair shop, a small hair salon.

It wasn't until later that we found out that Dvořák's house on East 17th Street was a fake. The original building had been landmarked by the City of

New York in February 1991. Four months later, they had a change of heart and, despite vehement protests (during which demonstrators sang *Goin' Home*), allowed the house to be torn down to make way for the expansion of Mount Sinai Hospital. The *New York Times* supported the house's demolition at the time with an article entitled *Dvořák Doesn't Live Here Anymore*.

A bust of Dvořák can be seen across from his former house, in the park formerly known as Peter Stuyvesant Park, but now called Dvořák Place. Was the name changed to make up for the embarrassing debacle with the Landmarks Commission? Or are Harry T. Burleigh and Dvořák placeholders after it became known that Stuyvesant, who founded New York in 1653, was a slave trader and deserved to be erased from public memory?

These isolated observations should have shown me how quickly and relentlessly the wheel of time turns in New York. But I was still searching for traces of the past. *Dvořák still lives here.*

During the day, Bukar headed down to the East River and the United Nations, while I spent my time doing research and reading biographies and essays in Pete's Tavern on East 18th Street and Irving Place, a block from where the Conservatory had stood. The bar was very old and had even been around during Dvořák's stay. Is it possible that he had walked into it from time to time after his lunch which he typically ate at Mrs. Wehrle's Inn across from the Conservatory? Perhaps Dvořák visited the bar on the days when work or bad weather kept him from lunching at Fleischman's Café at 10th and Broadway with the Austrian-Hungarian conductor Anton Seidl, who had conducted the world premiere of Dvořák's *New World* Symphony and always had something interesting to say about his idol Richard Wagner, the local music scene, or New York cultural life in general.

Did the spirit of Dvořák still lurk in Pete's Tavern? Indeed, it did, as I found out on my second visit, just four days after arriving in New York. I was sitting at a small, shiny table across from the bar which, at 4:30 pm, was still pretty quiet. Folk music was flowing from the loudspeakers above the counter. Was it Irish, Scottish or Gaelic? I wasn't sure; I wasn't listening very closely. My laptop was open on the table, waiting for me to type something. I hadn't touched a single key in the past fifteen minutes because I didn't know what to write. My head was empty; I was distracted by the rows of bottles on the mirrored shelves behind the counter. Then I stared again at Adrienne Fried Block's Amy Beach biography without knowing what I was looking for.

Looking up after taking a bite of my veggie burger, I saw an older woman standing in front of me. She had lively eyes, rimmed by faint wrinkles. Her jet-black hair was pulled into a bun at the back of her head. Her mouth was broad, her lips full, and she had a beautiful long nose. I guessed she was of Latin American or Indigenous American descent. She didn't wear makeup, or it was applied so well as to seem invisible. The simple black pantsuit she wore accentuated her slender, athletic build. It was difficult to guess her age, but I assumed she was around 80, although she looked much younger.

The woman looked at the two photocopied documents lying on the table next to my laptop and the Beach biography. One was Adrienne Fried Block's essay, *Amy Beach's Music on Native American Themes*, and the other the manuscript of a charming children's book that pianist Virginia Eskins had sent me while I was preparing for the trip. She may have been hoping that I could help her publish *Girl Genius—The Early Life of Amy Beach*.

»Are you a music student?« the woman asked. Her voice was so clear that I adjusted my estimate of her age down a few years.

I hesitated for a moment and she continued. »I'm asking because I see you're reading about Amy Beach. She's having something of a renaissance, you know, though there are still far too few people who know much about her.«

»Yes, you're right,« I replied.

»*Girl Genius*? I should know that one, but I don't. By Virginia Eskins? Hm, it must be lovely.«

»It is, but Eskins' book hasn't been published,« I said.

»And you?« She looked at me inquisitively. »What do you think of Amy?«

»Oh, I admire her very much. She is very interesting from an academic point of view. But, since you asked, I'm not a student, at least not anymore. It's a long story. I started writing a dissertation on her, but I got stuck and it's not going anywhere at the moment. That can't be Amy Beach's fault, can it?«

»Be patient,« the woman murmured, then she asked, »And you're from Germany?«

»Do I have an accent?«

»That's not what I meant,« she said. »No, no, you speak English quite well. By the way, my name is Calliope. But because it is so hard to pronounce, my co-workers call me López. I could pass for a Latina, don't you think?«

Had I heard right? If she had co-workers, then she was still working. Maybe she was a lot younger than I thought. »Hello, López,« I said. »Nice to meet you. I'm Petra. I speak German, but I'm from South Tyrol in Northern Italy.«

»South Tyrol? Yes, I've heard of it. Isn't that where Meran is located? Amy Beach once visited a spa there.«

López clearly knew a great deal about Amy Beach. Who was this mysterious woman? Before I could ask more, she spoke again.

»Come visit me, Petra. I work at the Ottendorfer Library, one of the many public libraries here in town. Actually, it's the oldest. It was founded in 1884, which makes it almost as old as I am,« she said, bobbing her head. »135 Second Avenue on the corner of 8th Street. Come by whenever you want.«

* * *

»Things are really buzzing at the UN,« Bukar said the evening after I'd met López in Pete's Tavern.

»The General Assembly's agenda is set. Hundreds of negotiations are about to begin. Everyone is buckling down and getting to work,« he said, and I could tell that he was happy to be a part of it. He told me enthusiastically about the people he'd met from non-governmental organizations who were working closely with the UN delegates in order to influence the debates and negotiations.

»This is civil society at its best!« he exclaimed. »They're knowledgeable, passionate, internationally minded, eloquent. You could say that these young people know exactly what a better world should look like and what needs to be done to get there, and they're all working together to make it happen.«

»Just wait,« I warned Bukar, telling him about my experience with NGOs in Brussels. »It's true that most of them have good intentions. But when it comes to getting funding from the European Commission or looking good for potential donors, then their true colors shine through.«

»That might be the case in Brussels, where there's a ton of money to be passed out,« Bukar countered. »But here in New York, it's all about lobbying the delegates of the UN member states.«

Bukar's idealism was endearing, but potentially dangerous. »Sorry Bukar, I don't want to be the doomsayer. You have to find out for yourself. But think about my words when an NGO representative talks down another organization or a colleague behind their back—›just between the two of you‹, of course.«

Bukar gave me a serious look that made me feel like I was letting it rain on his party. But later that night, he told me I was right to warn him. He had made that very experience with his third new contact. At first, though, he only said very little about June.

»Right off the bat I met a woman from ICTJ who spent several years in Nigeria herself,« he said.

»Wait,« I interrupted. »What's ICTJ?«

»Oh, you're right, I'm using too much insider jargon on the very first day! That must be a sign that I really enjoyed it. ICTJ stands for International Center for Transitional Justice. It's an NGO that steps in after a major conflict and conducts field studies and projects that help give victims access to justice.«

»Transitional…so they work toward transitional justice?« I asked.

»No, it's not the justice that's transitional, but the post-conflict situation. The projects are about first steps toward long-term justice. ICTJ helps give the victims a say in rebuilding the country's justice system and democratic institutions, and in negotiating new rules that will hopefully prevent a similar conflict in the future. The organization helps assess what kind of moral redress or reparations the various parties to the conflict are demanding from each other, and many other things, too. These are important pillars that need to be put in place, even though the official institutions are no longer functioning - or rather, because they don't work, or don't work yet, or never did work.«

»Now I remember,« I said. »I think there was an Afghanistan project that the ICTJ suggested Brussels should take on.«

»We sure could use an ICTJ project in Nigeria too. The people don't believe in justice anymore. They expect the worst from Boko Haram, but they know they're not going to get much better from the Nigerian army which is supposed to be protecting them,« Bukar sighed.

»Has the ICTJ made any suggestions about what should be done?« I asked.

»Definitely. The ICTJ representative handed me a draft of their proposal and asked me to tell her what I thought of it at our next meeting.«

That was only half the truth, I found out later. The whole truth was this: Just as Shanka, the ICTJ representative, was putting her draft proposal on the café table that stood between her and Bukar, a magnetic woman walked by. Her slim-fitting, knee-length, dark green cotton dress was both old-fashioned and chic. She had a tattoo on her ankle and painted toenails peeked out from her sandals, which looked like haute couture Birkenstocks.

The woman glanced at the paper on the table and said, »Oh, that again.« Then she handed Bukar her business card and muttered, »True peace comes from within.« Beaming at him, she added that it would be ›really nice to meet him very soon,‹ seductively emphasizing the word »very‹.

Bukar fell for it. Two hours later, he was in June's office. A poster on the door explained the acronym behind the NGO's name, JUICE:

JUstice through

Inner

Cleansing and

Empowerment

Bukar took a seat across from June who told him that peace and justice were not a matter for the ailing, fallible, biased, corrupt, and disappointing institutions in charge, but for the soul. She leaned forward, barely avoiding brushing Bukar's knees with her own, but placing her hand on his forearm.

»You know what I mean, don't you? Our inner selves and the cosmos need to find their way to each other,« she said without a trace of irony. »That's the only way for people to realize the Greater Plan without surrendering to false gods.«

Later, Bukar told me that he thought June's magniloquent words were just a bunch of hot air and esoteric mumbo-jumbo—especially when she made a twisted comparison between her theory of justice and COVID measures. »Your own immune system is stronger than the foreign entities that they want to inoculate you with,« she said.

Bukar assured me that he had left June's office as quickly as he could after that. I'm glad that he told me all about it two days after their meeting, including details like her tattoo and her hand on his arm.

Before I continue, let me say a few words about the problem I was having. It was the first time I had ever felt that something was wrong in our relationship. Fortunately, our little crisis ultimately had a happy ending.

When Bukar told me about June, I believed him when he said he was disgusted by her ideas. At the same time, I knew he was more attracted to her than he let on. But since I couldn't prove it, I had to deal with it. Why did he wait two days to tell me about his meeting with her? He probably realized that I wasn't immune to jealousy, no matter how much I loved him, and he wanted to allay my fears by describing his conversation with June as purely professional.

I also think it's possible that Bukar waited so long to tell me because he felt guilty about being under the spell of June. Oh, men, I thought. They're flattered when an attractive woman flirts with them. Then, with a bit of distance, they realize what their hormones have stolen: their brains and, more importantly, their control. For a man, losing control is even worse than losing his mind. Dear men, when will you ever learn?

That was the rhetorical climax of the conversation I had planned to have with Bukar, but it never took place. I tried to overcome my annoyance, keep a bit of serenity, and give Bukar the benefit of the doubt. Physical attraction is a powerful weapon. I certainly had fallen to it, too.

Then there was the psychological aspect. After his father's murder, Bukar had placed so much hope in real-world justice, but had been sorely disappointed. Wouldn't it be understandable if Bukar chose to put some hope in surreal powers, or at least wanted to test their potential?

* * *

The next day, the June thing didn't bother me yet. I felt like a bundle of energy.

The walk to the Ottendorfer Library took me just fifteen minutes. I headed down to Astor Place and then turned onto 9th Street toward Second Avenue, zigzagging across the intersections wherever the light was green. In New York, you have to be efficient, so I pulled out my phone and googled the library as I walked. Busy, distracted, and hectic—I felt like a real New Yorker, except that, unlike them, I couldn't find anything useful on the internet.

Then I found myself looking up at the Ottendorfer Library.

I had just passed the bright lettering on two Chinese mini-marts and J. Baczynsky's Ukrainian sausage shop and was surprised to see a third, more familiar language: German.

The words *Freie Bibliothek und Lesehalle* were worked into the bright red brick facade over a massive arch above the door to the library. Terracotta busts of Humboldt, Linné, Lavoisier and other scientists peered down at me from the very top of the building.

I was surprised. Not by the building's polyglot, philomathean appearance, but by the fact that it transported me to another era, one that I had come to know while I was researching my dissertation, though it had seemed distant and abstract. The end of the 19th century in the USA, which Mark Twain had called the Gilded Age. It was a time of contradictions.

Trade was booming, industrialization and cultural life were developing rapidly, and the elite believed that progress had no limits. This overshadowed widespread poverty, political corruption and an increasingly complicated demographic situation. The end of the Civil War was fresh in the collective memory and the African-American population were waiting to enjoy the benefits of a modern society—rights, education, prosperity. Instead, stuck in urban ghettos, upward mobility remained out of reach. They experienced racism, discrimination or, at the very least, paternalistic tutelage. Other ghettos were filled with fortune-seekers from Ireland, Italy, Eastern Europe, and, increasingly, Asia.

On the gilded side of this world, in upper-middle-class New York, the number of German-speaking immigrants was also growing. They upheld their education rituals in their new home, listened to Beethoven, Brahms and Wagner in the concert halls, and read news in German in one of the city's three largest newspapers, the *New Yorker Staats-Zeitung*.

In the Gilded Age, it made perfect sense for a philanthropist to fund first a hospital and then a library. After all, human beings needed both physical well-being and education.

It was at this time that Antonín Dvořák made his way to New York. He was unique in that he occasionally peeked over the fence surrounding his gilded world. At the Conservatory, he taught Black students, conducted all-Black orchestras, and was captivated by the sound of Black music. And then, I imagined, he would walk from the Conservatory down a block to the Café Boulevard (there is a pizzeria now at the corner of 10th Street and Second Avenue), read the Czech news in the *Národní listy*, drink a cup of coffee or two despite his chronic heart problems, and play a few rounds of darda, his favorite card game, with his faithful assistant Josef Kovařík.

During our evening walks, Bukar and I believed that this era, with both its gilded and its brutally bare sides, had long since vanished. But we were wrong.

Talking to López that morning, I learned more about the library which had been built in 1884, just a year after the German hospital next door. The funding for both institutions came from German-speaking Valentin Oswald Ottendorfer who made his donation to fulfill the wish of his recently deceased wife. I assumed that Dvořák must have walked the few steps from Café Boulevard over to the library to meet Ottendorfer, a man from Moravia in the eastern part of the present-day Czech Republic. After the revolutions of 1848-1849, he fled to New York and worked his way up to become the owner of the *New Yorker Staats-Zeitung*.

Dvořák and Ottendorfer must have come to know each other either in connection with reviews that Spanuth, the paper's music critic, had written about Dvořák's concerts, or while campaigning for the building of the Bohemian National Hall. Dvořák conducted a benefit concert, while Ottendorf did the publicity.

But the two men probably only spoke sporadically. Dvořák, a Bohemian with humble beginnings, may have eyed the wealthy German-speaking Ottendorfer with skepticism. Dvořák was notorious for shying away from social contact, particularly with the upper classes whose mundane small talk made him feel uncomfortable. He was also not one to pander to the press, speaking to journalists only when he had to. It is quite telling that it took a skilled journalist like James Creelman to pry Dvořák's recommendations concerning American music out of him. Once his words were printed, the composer was compelled to confirm them.

Everything I'd learned as a student and my first impressions in New York congealed in one phrase: Dvořák on every corner. While I'm too much of an academic to interpret history based on a series of coincidences, I couldn't ignore the fact that, in just half a day, many details had coalesced into a canvas, a narrative about the ties between Dvořák, Ottendorfer and 1890s New York. I felt sure that I would manage to paint my dissertation on that canvas, but I didn't yet know that it would turn out to be impossible.

But let me go back to the moment when I crossed the threshold of a new world and entered the Ottendorfer Library, a moment that gave me goosebumps. I walked up the four steps to the wooden door at the front of the building. The iron lattice that filled the entire arch at the entrance looked like a placeholder the way it was patched in. The paint was falling off the door, revealing coarse-grained wood underneath. Its handle could have been the cheapest model available at the hardware store down the street. The hinges squeaked when I opened the door and again when I closed it.

The squeak mingled with the voice of the doorman, who sat, hunched over, behind a semi-circular, cream-colored counter. He looked ancient, sitting there beneath a framed portrait of Ottendorfer himself. I would have overlooked him if he hadn't barked at me from behind a thick plexiglas panel: »What do you want?«

The doorman scared me. A few randomly placed curly hairs stuck out from his black, scarred head. A corona-era medical mask hung down from his left ear. His contorted mouth exposed the constant pain he seemed to be in, and his watery eyes gazed at me without focusing. The man must be very ill, I thought at first, then wondered how many broken years you had to live before you look like this.

»Good morning. Are you the doorman?« I asked him.

»Morning. I'm Bob,« he snarled, drumming rhythmically on the countertop with the fingers of his right hand, as if he were playing the piano. Then he snapped again, »What do you want?«

»I was invited by…Calliope. I met her yesterday,« I replied feebly.

»López? Hang on. Wait here,« he croaked.

With great effort, he hoisted himself up from his chair, plucked a small pink pill out of a bowl on the counter, swallowed it with a tired blink of his eyes, and shuffled toward the wooden stairway leading up to the first floor.

He clearly loathed each step, not only because of the pain, but presumably because he had to do a favor for a young, healthy, spoiled woman like me. There were other reasons why he went to get López so begrudgingly, but I wouldn't find them out until I got to know the library and its strange staff better.

»López? Visitor!« he called from halfway up the stairs.

López came down to the top third of the staircase. As Bob trudged back to the counter and heaved himself back onto his chair, she waved theatrically at me. With the light against her back, I could only see her outline. Colorful bars of light shone up out of the reading room on the ground floor and down from the first floor which, I would later see, held stained glass windows painted by children.

The reading room seemed huge, almost endlessly long, but only twenty feet wide. It contained several rows of two-story cast-iron bookshelves connected by aluminum bridges at about ten feet. They were chock full of books. A staff member about my age was stocking volumes on one of the front shelves. Neon lamps glared from above. Some of the light careened through the labyrinth of shelves and grazed the plastic book covers. The glistening tomes, the sparkling specks of dust in the air, the shiny hand-forged iron, the flickering of laptop screens, and the light falling on López from the first floor— all together it enveloped me in a gentle, fairytale-like iridescence, as if I were standing in the middle of an opera production.

When I saw López pause for a moment in the midst of this light show and solemnly stretch out her arm toward me, I spontaneously thought, here is the Queen of the Night standing in the Hall of Stars.

A tenth of a second later, I wanted to banish the comparison from my head. Why should I ascribe López any similarity with the dark, evil Queen of the Night? After a few more milliseconds, I understood. The comparison was about me, not her. ›Within these sacred halls‹ I was about to receive a magic flute from López that would help me get closer to my goal.

I snapped out of my daydream; López was standing next to me. She suddenly seemed completely normal and greeted me with an elbow bump, as was customary during the pandemic. Then she led me through the reading room on the ground floor, quietly, so as not to disturb the handful of readers I hadn't noticed before. We walked up to her office in the middle of the first floor, where a landing divided the staircase. From the last few steps, it was easy to overlook the reading room. Toward the back, over a sitting area, there was a sliding glass divider partitioning off the children's section. To the front, children had painted an eye-catching rainbow on a brick-rimmed arched window that overlooked Second Avenue.

Asking me to tell her why I had come to New York, I was astonished to find that López knew quite a bit about the musicological topics I was working on.

I was most surprised when she asked me whether I had any evidence that Dvořák and Beach had ever met in person. I said I didn't, but told her where a meeting might have taken place: at a concert in New York; at the Chicago World's Fair in 1893 where both of them conducted concerts; or quite possibly in Beach's hometown of Boston where Dvořák conducted three concerts. Certainly, Boston's musical elite, including Amy Beach, all made an appearance there to see and be seen.

»And you researched all of that?« asked López. »I think you have a lot of fascinating research ahead of you. One only ever knows as much as the sources reveal. And they always seem to have gaps at the most inconvenient places, as I'm sure you well know. Maybe their meeting was just a coincidence. Couldn't the two of them have met at a dinner party at the Ottendorfers', incognito of course? Or here in the library?«

»At Valentin Ottendorfer's? I don't think so,« I said. »Dvořák was known for mercilessly turning down private invitations. And here? Why here?«

López invited me to walk down a few steps with her and peer into the reading room below. »Look down there,« she said. »See those two elderly people? A man and a woman, a fuddy duddy and an old fogey. Perhaps they are conceited adversaries like Beach and Dvořák, but by all appearances, they seem quite friendly. Where would the two of them meet?«

I was dumbfounded. Her witty comment was a creative advertisement for the library's significance as a center of communication, but, historically speaking, irrelevant. Still, I looked down at the two old people sitting in the reading room and couldn't believe my eyes. Was I seeing ghosts? They really did resemble the portraits I'd seen of Beach and Dvořák on the cover pages of their biographies and in other publications. She was pudgy, had a big nose and her wavy hair was pinned back in a bun. His face was weathered, and he had small, probing eyes and longish silvery grey hair that fell in locks over his high forehead and crept down beneath his prominent cheek bones, covering his entire jaw with a full beard.

I refused to entertain the notion of ghosts. Instead, I turned to López and asked her about herself.

»Oh, that's a long story,« she began. Then she told me everything as I listened intently.

She was born to a Greek father (hence her first name Calliope) and a Navajo mother who was forced to leave her traditional clan of storytellers when she married an outsider. López wanted to continue the Navajo tradition of storytelling and to experience what they called K'é, or kinship, among clan members. Despite financial limitations and the racist policies of the time, she went on to study literature and became a reserved, but nevertheless moderately successful writer. She wrote two children's books with stories adapted from the Diné Bahane', the creation myth of the Diné, as the Navajo call themselves. This explained López's interest in Virginia Eskins's book about Amy, the wunderkind. Unfortunately, the success of López's children's books was short-lived, so she shifted gears and became a ghostwriter. At first, she was unsatisfied with the job, considered to be the lowest rung in the writing hierarchy, a profession that only offered anonymous success on the coattails of others. But her attitude gradually changed. As a ghostwriter, she realized, she had the chance to take on new perspectives and broaden her horizons.

»By continually changing my role, I learned more than ever before,« she said. But as a freelancer, she didn't have enough financial security to retire, so she took on the position as a librarian at the Ottendorfer Library.

I wanted to ask more about the storytelling tradition in her mother's family, but López said, »Another time. I have to go now.«

Okay, I thought. We exchanged phone numbers and promised to meet again soon.

After she'd left, I decided to go talk to the elderly couple in the reading room, but when I went downstairs, they were already gone.

* * *

The following weekend, we met every day for breakfast. First at Pete's Tavern, because I insisted on inviting López, and perhaps also because Pete's Tavern was so close to the site of the National Conservatory and a stone's throw from our apartment at Harry T. Burleigh Place. On Sunday, we met at the Ottendorfer Library, which was closed to visitors, before again breakfasting in Pete's Tavern.

During the first two meetings on Friday and Saturday, López listened closely as I told her all about my dissertation plans. In deep concentration, she rested a finger on the arm of her reading glasses which hung from a brightly colored braided cord on her elegant green sweater. A few times, she picked up the glasses and brought them to her nose, but never put them on. It seemed to me that she wanted to direct attention to her inquiring, dark brown eyes and their ability to see without glasses.

I was impressed by López's knowledge of music history, as I had been at our first meeting in the Ottendorfer Library. Still, our conversations didn't help me with my work. While I was interested in new analytical insights, she just wanted to tell stories.

Once I asked her specifically about my dissertation and whether she thought there were any parallels between Beach's and Dvořák's views on American music and the current debate over identity politics. As she thought about it, she pushed her reading glasses up her nose.

»You're searching for some grand, original thesis, am I right?« she asked, giving me a commiserative look over the rim of her glasses. »Anyone can come up with great theories. Theories that sparkle and shine as long as reality can be interpreted in such a way that it is compatible with the theory,« she continued. »Beware of such theories. When they start to crumble, you will have to reach a compromise—with your theory and with yourself. You will weigh what is of greater use to you: holding on to your theory or questioning yourself. And most likely you will find the middle ground.«

Her words were nebulous. Was she trying to caution me against choosing a thesis that was too construed? Or was she giving me an inflated reply to cover up the fact that she had no answer to my question?

The most eerie thing about meeting López was the presence (or absence) of the elderly couple from the library. During our first breakfast at Pete's Tavern, I noticed shortly after we'd arrived that they were sitting at a small table in the back of the restaurant, drinking tea and chatting quietly. I figured it was just a bizarre coincidence that I saw them for a second time, considering how many popular breakfast spots there must be in the East Village.

After our meal, López and I said goodbye at the front door on Irving Place and I went back into the restaurant to pay. I cast a fleeting glance at the table where the couple had been sitting, but they were no longer there, which was strange. While I had been standing on the street with López, I hadn't seen them leave, but maybe I'd just been distracted. Then I noticed that there was another way out, onto 18th Street.

During our meeting on Sunday in López's office, they were there again, sitting in the reading room, even though the library was closed. Weird. I began to doubt this was a coincidence.

When I saw them again at the back of Pete's Tavern during our third breakfast, I decided to get to the bottom of it. I got up and walked over to their table, introduced myself, and wanted to say something snappy or even distrustful, but I stopped short. The two of them bore such a strong resemblance to Dvořák and Beach that I felt a sudden surge of respect. Swallowing the lump in my throat, I finally said, »What a coincidence that we keep running into each other.«

They must have noticed my anxiety, but they remained calm and smiled, assuring me that it was indeed quite a nice coincidence. Their names, they told me, were Amelie and Tony.

López appeared next to me, and Amelie and Tony greeted her by name. They knew each other! This was getting even more confusing. If they knew each other, why hadn't López mentioned it when we were watching them from the first floor? Perhaps it was a one-sided acquaintance: They knew López because she was the librarian, but López didn't know them?

»This is Petra. She's from South Tyrol,« López told the couple at the table as my bewilderment grew.

»Oh, Meran, how lovely,« Amelie interjected.

»She's only been in New York for a few days. She's here to make progress on her dissertation on Amy Beach and Antonín Dvořák,« continued López with an unusual twinkle in her eye.

»I see,« said Tony as he rubbed his beard and smiled cheerfully. »They're not so easy to figure out, are they?« Then he chuckled abruptly several times until his laughs turned into long inhales and then contented snorts. »Keep at it, you're almost there.«

Tony seemed a likable kind of guy, uncomplicated, both grumpy and good-natured. I was fully disoriented. To save my sanity, I told myself to just accept the situation as it was. This was Tony Dvořák. He was flipping through a train schedule rather than a score, but it was definitely him, and he was sitting next to Amelie Beach.

Nice to meet you.

Was that possible? No. But never mind.

Tony and Amelie were only there when López was also there. Was that logical? No. But who cared.

Was López a medium that enabled real-life encounters with the dead, or was I hallucinating? Whatever.

Or did López facilitate these encounters because that was part of her job as a storyteller? That sounded like a nice explanation, but it wasn't logical. Completely unimportant.

It was what it was. My biggest chance. I had to seize it and stop asking questions. To further my research, I would have to accept a little hocus-pocus. Interdisciplinarity, you might call it.

It wasn't until later that I wondered how seriously I would be taken if I wrote in the footnotes of my dissertation: ›Interview with Antonín Dvořák and Amy Beach from September 2021.‹

Then something much more disturbing occurred to me. My academic self was about to do something that López had described as a human weakness. When your theories start to crumble, you will have to reach a compromise—with your theory and with yourself. Oh, Petra.

I sat there facing the two protagonists of my dissertation, bewildered, astonished, confused. And I was completely unprepared to make the most of the opportunity and ask them the right questions.

»You've known each other for quite a while, I take it,« I began timidly. »Are you still discussing what constitutes a national style of music in the US? And how do you view today what you said and wrote about American music back in 1893?«

After a brief pause, Tony inhaled with a long »Hoooh,« as if I'd asked a particularly difficult question, then twisted his face into a mischievous smile. He pulled on his beard, pinching the chin hairs into a point, then folded his hands.

»The answer is really quite simple,« he said demurely, pausing for dramatic effect. »Amelie is always right!«

He had barely completed his joke when he burst out laughing. Amelie interrupted him in a educational tone. »Tony, be serious. The young lady has traveled a long way to ask us this important question. We should make an effort.«

»Yes, Amelie,« Tony said, nodding like a school boy. »You're right again.«

Then he turned to me and whispered, »I told you she was always right!«

This time he stifled his laughter and suddenly became serious. »Petra, if I understand correctly, you have asked several questions. Three, to be exact. How long have we known each other? What is the fundament of an American national style of music? And what do we think now about the opinions we held one-hundred-thirty years ago? Hm. That's quite a lot for our first conversation, don't you think? Let me make a proposal: You will get a short answer and a long one. The short answer to all three questions is, I don't know. For the longer answers we will have to arrange another meeting. Would that be all right with you? Amelie, will you join us?«

Amelie looked offended. »Tony, that was not very charming of you. Miss Petra's first question was how long we've known each other. And you say you don't know?«

»But Amelie, of course I know. How could I forget? What I wanted to say was…« Tony stroked his beard and blinked, visibly grasping for a plausible excuse. »What I wanted to say was that I have met you so often over the decades and…each time you were someone different and each time even more enchanting than before.«

»Oh, you incorrigible charmer!« She looked at him in despair and shook her head, then continued matter-of-factly: »But it's true. We have been changing our whole lives. You have, in any case. Well, and me, too. That becomes increasingly evident the longer we are…here.« Was she avoiding the word ›alive‹? »We are becoming new and different time and again.«

Tony imitated Amelie's educational tone and quipped, »But tomorrow morning you will be the same one who signed up today to have breakfast tomorrow, right?« Then he reverted back to his own voice. »Ten o'clock in

López's office on the first floor of the library. Petra, would you be so kind as to organize some cake? I love poppy seed cake. You are all fine with that, aren't you?«

Tony stood up without waiting for an answer and headed for the exit, humming to himself. »I mustn't forget to bring some old documents with me. Amelie, you remember the letters from Fletcher, Farwell and the others? And do you still have the photographs? Petra will be amazed, I think. Yes, she'll be amazed. You know which photographs I'm referring to? The old ones from Chicago and the others too, if you can find them. And if you have composed something new…oh, never mind. The older stuff will do. Our time is up for now.«

* * *

Bukar grew hungry and curious as I told him about my unusual new acquaintances. He wanted to come with me to the next meeting.

»Sure,« I said. »It's not every day that you get to meet Dvořák and Beach.«

Bukar said little about his own encounters and kept quiet about June, his great nemesis, who remained nameless for the time being. He just mentioned a few NGO representatives who doubted the value of criminal law in addressing war crimes and crimes against humanity, like ›that woman‹ who believed that justice was something personal and spiritual. You have to look inside yourself and deal with your feelings of hatred, she had said.

As more and more details about this woman came out, my curiosity was piqued, but I wasn't suspicious yet.

As an African, Bukar should understand what she meant, she had told him, because her ideas about justice were in line with traditional African spirituality.

»No, not at all,« he had told her. »In my home in Africa, ideas like yours are not understood. Guilt and hatred are not private matters. They can only be resolved by the community.«

But the woman stuck to her psycho-crap. Bukar found it rather audacious how she tried to use African spirituality to back up her theories. When he reminded her that he knew better what made Africans tick, she dared to contradict him and brought up some random studies that were conducted by no-name researchers using unverifiable methodology.

Bukar was annoyed that the knowledge he'd gained of Nigerians' expectations of justice through years of personal interviews was being dismissed by someone who admitted she'd never been to Nigeria. Apart from her esoteric stuff and obscure pseudo-scientific studies, she had nothing else to go on. It was a situation Bukar was all too familiar with, the collision of white know-it-all arrogance with his authentic knowledge.

But then things took a turn for the better. Bukar told me about his coffee meeting with Walter, the legal advisor to the German UN Mission, who had listened to him carefully. Walter was an eloquent but quiet and humble guy well liked by his colleagues. He happened to mention, almost sheepishly, that years ago in an article in the International Law Journal of the University of Michigan he had called for expanding the jurisdiction of the International Criminal Court's to include acts of terrorism, in addition to the crimes already within the ICC's jurisdiction (war crimes, crimes against humanity, genocide, the crime of aggression).

»Our interests overlap,« Bukar concluded. »My goal of taking a terrorist organization to court is grist to his mill.«

Walter promised to organize a panel discussion where Bukar had the chance to explain to other legal advisors and NGOs why a Boko Haram trial at the ICC needed to be expedited. It was a good day for Bukar.

* * *

»Our relationship as musicians? Back then—my goodness, everything was quite different. My dear Miss Petra, you probably have no idea how things worked back then.«

Tony was sitting right next to me in López's office on the first floor of the Ottendorfer Library. Our chairs looked like miniature patio furniture, more for children than adults. Five chairs with small, hard seats and backs were arranged around a round table topped with green imitation leather. We had a direct view of López's plain, worn desk whose laminate surface had started to peel. Papers were chaotically stacked next to a computer screen, an oversized copier, and a tiny cactus. Built-in shelves filled the wall behind the desk, just below the stairs that led to the second floor. A paper cut-out of Eric Carle's *The Very Hungry Caterpillar* was taped to one of the upper shelves.

I thought of my grandfather who used to read *The Very Hungry Caterpillar* to me when I came to visit. It was fascinating how the caterpillar ate its way through the thick cardboard pages of the book after it had come out of its egg. The yarn that my grandfather pulled through the apples, pears, oranges and strawberries seemed to be alive. With childish fervor, I wanted to be a caterpillar too, and, when I'd eaten enough cardboard, to become a butterfly.

I looked around the room. At the far end of the tube-like floor, two steps and a sliding glass door led to a small room with a refrigerator and coffee maker and, past yet another glass door, a children's library. Before 1900, this space had been a private reading room for people in need of an extra measure of quiet; back then, that's how they circumscribed a room reserved for women.

On the other side of the floor, facing the street, I saw three tall, semi-circular windows set in mahogany frames. They overpowered the window-panes which children had painted with bright colors. The light that fell through these windows the day before had lent López's appearance on the stairs a magical quality. But today they just looked like ordinary windows. Just a little paint, nothing dramatic.

I was suddenly overcome by the impression that I was in a laboratory— in a surreal place where various times, generations and characters came to-gether to perform an invisible choreography. The child-like decorations— the painted windows, the shelves with thematically sorted children's books, the paper figures pinned to the wall—stood in meaningless contrast to the heavy grown-up world with its *Quiet Please!* signs on the shelves and child-sized tables. Meaningless because there was not a single child there to be quiet. This was no place for children, but for mummies, I thought, before pushing the image out of my mind.

Tony sat one side of me, Bukar on the other. I was amazed at how nor-mal it felt to be rubbing shoulders with none other than Antonín Dvořák himself. López sat on one of the chairs across from us and the other was reserved for Amelie, who had disappeared into the *Quiet Please!* area in the front of the children's section with the cordless telephone from López's desk.

Bob was there, too. After he'd brought Tony a large beer and watery coffee in paper cups for the rest of us, he'd found a smaller chair at an even smaller wooden table covered with salmon-colored faux leather. He was off to the side, but still close enough to hear us. Bob lowered himself onto the chair, pressing his palms down on the table with a pained expression on his face. I wondered if he would have smiled if he'd noticed the irony of the big, bright, hand-written sign hung on the bookshelf just behind him: ›Non-fiction‹.

»No, I can hardly imagine,« I said in response to Tony's question about what it was like back then. »Tell me. What was it like?«

»Didn't you want to know how Amelie and I met? And weren't you curious about our views on American music?« countered Tony, turning his small dark brown eyes to make sure Amelie was still out of earshot. »Amelie is a wonderful person. I've known her long enough to be able to say that. But—and please don't tell her I said this—when I first met her, I didn't really like her. She was quite eccentric, if you ask me. Just twenty-five years old, but she acted like an old maid. Which she was. Or do you think that Henry, her dear husband, who could have been her father…«

Tony stopped short when López cleared her throat and gave him an accusatory glance. He couldn't help but grunt merrily before he kept talking. »Forgive me, López, but you know what I wanted to say in my own way. You also know that, later on, I completely later changed my mind. I swear she knew every trick in the book! Her escapades with Arthur Hyde and then with David Williams who she wanted to convert to heterosexuality…«

López cleared her throat again and rolled her eyes. »Tony, that sounded pretty voyeuristic, didn't it? We really don't need to know all the details, now do we?«

»Not to change the subject,« I interjected, »but how did you manage to follow all the Boston gossip from Bohemia?«

»From Bohemia?« asked Tony.

It was easy to become disoriented in such unusual company. I recalled that Dvořák was buried in the Vyšehrad Cemetery in Prague. But there he was, sitting next to me. »I mean, I just thought…,« I began, squirming in my seat.

»I know what you were thinking,« Tony said, sounding all fatherly. Then he looked at me as soberly as if he wanted me to take an oath. »Do me a fa-

<50>52</50>

vor. Never ask me where I've been over the last one-hundred-twenty years. I've been everywhere and nowhere.« He patted me on the shoulder, as if to seal our little agreement, and the ice between us was broken. Then he turned to López.

»Don't be so strict,« he told her. »I just wanted to make up for what I'd said earlier about Amelie being an old maid. But nothing is enough for you. As I'd said, I didn't know much about Amelie when we first met, but my first impression was that we were opposites. I think it was in February 1893, during my second visit to Boston. My first had been in November 1892, when I conducted my Requiem. In any case, it was before May 1893 when my recommendations on American music were published. My reputation as a composer of national music had preceded me in Boston and I wanted to live up to it. After my Second Symphony, Nikisch[14] conducted *My Home*.[15] Everybody loved it, including me. Maybe it had to do with the fact that William Apthorp described me in the program notes as the epitome of the American dream: the poor kid who pulled himself up by his bootstraps and made it. That sounded really nice. In Europe, my background always served my critics as a reasonable explanation when they wanted to carp at some missing spark in my work. And I suddenly found myself among people who saw it the other way around, which was refreshing. After the concert, we all stood together. Everyone was in a good mood. None of the Brahmins[16] had any reason yet to dislike me, since my views on Black music hadn't yet been published,« he added sarcastically.

Amelie finished her phone call and came back. »Tony, are you talking about that night in Boston again?« she asked as she sat down.

»Yes. As you can see, I haven't forgotten how we met,« he replied.

»I certainly hope not. But please be fair this time.«

»Of course. Anyway, we stood there, the Brahmins and I, and those whose affinity for the arts had earned them the privilege of standing next to

14 Arthur Nikisch (1855-1922) was a Hungarian conductor who conducted the Boston Symphony Orchestra from 1889-1893 and later the Gewandhausorchester in Leipzig and the Berlin Philharmonic.

15 Antonín Dvořák: *Můj domov* (*My Home*), Overture for Orchestra, Op. 62, B. 125a

16 Patrician families in Boston at the time were known as Brahmins. They were direct descendants of the Mayflower pilgrims which, along with their wealth, gave them considerable influence in Boston.

the Brahmins. By the way, isn't it great that art can make you an aristocrat in Boston? A topic for another time. And, of course, there was the enchanting Amelie who stood out from all the others. She would have deserved to stand there with us twice. Once as a Brahmin and once for her extraordinary talent. But then she would have talked twice as much nonsense!«

»Tony, stop,« snapped Amelie. López also looked upset.

»Okay. Then there was Apthorp, the friendly program notes writer. And especially George Chadwick[17] and Edward MacDowell, the bigwigs among the local composers. They had returned to Boston after studying music in Germany. They could speak German quite well, but I'm sure you know all that, being a music student yourself,« said Tony.

He took a sip of beer and went on before Amelie could interrupt him. »And then there was this giant of a man. He wasn't a real Brahmin, but he was a Civil War hero and a generous philanthropist, so he could easily pass for one. Colonel Henry Lee Higginson[18] was so wealthy that he founded and paid for the Boston Symphony Orchestra out of his own pocket. His equally wealthy cousin Thomas had welcomed me as a second Columbus when I arrived in New York in October 1892. Now that the campaigns to conquer the West had been successfully completed, he told me then, I should help the country with the artistic battle. Somehow, Higginson managed to take over the conversation. He told me about his cousin Thomas who had commanded a Black regiment during the Civil War and fought for the abolition of slavery. An ideological fad, he said, but still the right thing to do. A struggle for people forced by fate to be cruel. ›And they're unmusical at their core,‹ interrupted journalist Philip Hale.«

I felt Bukar's torso twitch and thought I saw him make eye contact with Bob for a millisecond.

»Stop bad-mouthing Higginson and Hale,« said Amelie. »I know you detest them both. But things were different then.«

»I'm not bad-mouthing Higginson. And I don't detest him at all. Higginson was a godsend for Boston. He was a perfectly decent man. But Ida, his wife, and especially Hale—let me bad-mouth them. They weren't inno-

---

17 George Whitefield Chadwick (1854-1931) was an American composer at the New England School of Music which drew on autochthon music.

18 Henry Lee Higginson (1834-1919) was a Boston banker and philanthropist.

cent, and besides, I'm doing it for you. Otherwise, I'd have to come straight to the point of my story. And I'm sure you wouldn't want that.«

»If things keep going like this, one point is enough,« Bob interjected unexpectedly from the background, but Tony did not seem to notice.

»The point is that just then in the discussion, dear Amelie, you said something for the first and last time that evening. ›Have you read the *Boston Herald* lately,‹ you piped up. ›It would be wrong to think that plantation songs are representative of Black music. They are the result of what the slaves did with the white hymns that they heard in church.‹ Something inside me rebelled. I thought of Harry Burleigh, my assistant. When he used to visit me at home, he would sing plantation songs with that beautiful baritone of his. He'd learned them from his blind grandfather who'd been a slave. That was my first step into the movingly beautiful and lyrical world of Black music.«

»Tony, stick to the point. After mentioning the article in the *Boston Herald*, I was about to add that there are other opinions and that I also disagree. You may recall the first words of my article in the *Herald*. You know which article I mean—my commentary on your proposals. ›Without the slightest desire to question the beauty of the negro melodies…‹ But the gentlemen in attendance prevented me speaking again.«

»That's what you say today,« said Tony. »But don't you understand how disappointed I was back then? Mrs. Beach, the wunderkind celebrated far beyond her native Boston. I was very curious about your work, and then, at the first chance you got, you went and agreed with Hale!«

»Henry Krehbiel, too, whose opinion you always respected, said that…« began Amelie.

»I know what you're going to say,« interrupted Tony. »Before you quote him incorrectly, I'll do it. ›A voice harkening from Africa can be heard in the plantation songs, one that was shaped to become a unique African-American voice. It was shaped by the social and political circumstances in America and predominantly by shared suffering.‹«

»But that wasn't the correct quote,« said Amelie.

»No, that's what I said. Before you quote him incorrectly, I'll quote him incorrectly. But it's more or less correct. As a composer, I know what he meant. And, be honest, so do you.«

»What do you mean?«

»Art is not the result of literal transcription, but of reworking. Contemplating, feeling, inhaling, exhaling, empathetically coalescing.«

»Yes, indeed,« agreed Amelie.

»Anyone can write down a Black or ›Indian‹ melody…«

»Don't underestimate that, Tony. ›Indian‹ melodies are not tonal. There are quarter-tone increments.«

»Are there? Well, you know more than I do,« admitted Tony.

»I'll be frank: I do. You always lumped everything pentatonic and syncopated together.« Amelie seemed to enjoy having the upper hand over Tony. She remained friendly, although there was a hint of meanness in her words. She rubbed her nose delicately with a small lace hankie, put it away in her purse, and spoke much more openly.

»But you're right, Tony. What counts is not copying, but…you said it best: inhaling and exhaling.«

»I always imagined that the organ that inhales and exhales was my lungs, and they are Bohemian. And what I inhale is Black, ›Indian‹, or Slavic air, or something else. If the Tartar air were good, my lungs would inhale and exhale it, too, But what I exhale has the taste of my Bohemian lungs on it,« said Tony thoughtfully.

»Tony, let's not discuss your bad breath, please. Those pipes…« This time it was Amelie who got an accusatory glance from López. Amelie bowed to her without complaint. López seemed to be a person of authority for both musicians.

»Okay, Tony, apart from your bad breath, it's a lovely image, the inhaling and exhaling. It applies to my work as well. You know what I've written. Gaelic, 'Eskimo,' as it was called back then, Balkan, Tyrol—I soaked it up and reworked it. Even the voice of the hermit thrush outside my window in Peterborough, in the MacDowell Colony. Nevertheless, as far as Hale is concerned, let's be fair. What you just said about your Bohemian lungs are the words of an old man. You spent your whole life watching cultures give and take and learn. Hale didn't have that perspective. Give him a break. Maybe he just spoke too hastily.«

»Oh, I don't think so. Remember how he tried to bash MacDowell for his *Indian* Suite? He wrote that he didn't give a damn where MacDowell got his musical material. When he went to a concert, he wanted to listen to music and not a course in folklore, he said. He could just picture Mac-

Dowell sitting with a plug-hatted chief, the firewater beginning to work, and old Chief Triple Tone chirping like a cricket. And about my *New World* Symphony, he wrote that it would appeal only to an audience of intelligent negroes and well-dressed Indians—both sheer impossibilities for him. No, Amelie, Hale's comments were not spur of the moment. Nor was his criticism that Blacks were unmusical. These were premeditated insults that revealed his ugly, racist core. And you and the Higginsons kept your pretty little mouths shut.«

»You're really good at simplifying,« Amelie replied. »I was also the object of Hale's criticism. He liked my symphony because it sounded so ›masculine‹. But the orchestration, he said, was ›typically female‹—too noisy. But Higginson was a good man, as you say.«

»He sure was. Except that on that evening he was full of praise for his father-in-law, Harvard professor Louis Agassiz, who taught his students that Blacks and whites came from different species,« Tony said.

»I remember that differently. Higginson had simply said that Louis had been a wonderful father to Ida, my even more wonderful wife. Not more. He didn't make any comments about the origin of humanity and his father-in-law's theories.«

»Why did you say that he ›had been‹ Ida's father?« asked Tony.

»Because he'd died twenty years before. Didn't you know that?«

»No. Why were people in Boston still talking so much about his ideas twenty years later?«

»I don't know. Maybe because in Boston nobility and haughtiness go hand in hand,« said Amelie. »But let me ask you something. Why did you say that during our first meeting you were bothered by Agassiz getting a brief moment of praise even though, first of all, you didn't even know he was dead, and second, you didn't know back then what his views were. You didn't learn about them until the summer of 1893 in Chicago when Alice Fletcher gave me and then you a copy of her *Study of Omaha Indian Music*. She made it clear to everyone that she was furious with people like Agassiz because she believed in the unity of humanity and he didn't. Be honest, Tony. You're telling stories again.«

Tony was clearly agitated. »If that's the case... But why did Higginson have to say that Ida was even more wonderful than her father, just after she had tearfully explained that she had been to Cottonham, the Higginsons' plantation in Georgia, the week before. It was hard to imagine, she said, how difficult it was to work with those freed slaves, and the more she saw them, the less she liked them.«

»I've had enough of your dogmatism, Tony! You may be right about Agassiz and his daughter. But I don't buy your attempt to hold Higginson responsible for their views. I remember him as a musically trained, generous and socially minded man. Why did he buy Cottonham? Not to make money—he had enough of that—but because he saw it as an educational project. And as a temporary New Yorker you may not be able to admit it, but the fact is that the best symphony orchestra in the US was in Boston at the time, thanks to Higginson. He used his money and his taste to make sure that only the very best musicians and conductors were recruited. You must know that his funding came with the stipulation that ticket prices be kept as low as possible so that the less privileged could also attend concerts and have the opportunity to expand their horizons…«

»I can guess what you're going to tell me next,« Tony interrupted. »That Higginson organized inexpensive concerts for the large Black population in Boston, the poor Italians, and the Portuguese whalers?«

»Tony, that's not fair. You know it wasn't that simple back then.«

»But was it really that complicated? At the Conservatory in New York, things were easy. We had scholarships earmarked for African-American students, Black composers received support, and I once conducted an all-Black orchestra…«

»I know, but that was New York.«

»That's what I said. And it wasn't Boston, which I didn't like, no matter how good its orchestra was. And you were a part of it.«

»And that's why you took me to task in public?« asked Amelie.

»What do you mean?«

»Your interview with the *Boston Post*,« she explained. »You wrote that there were many talented composers in the United States. How generous of you. But then you added that none of them were women, because women lacked the intellectual capacity, or something along those lines.«

»I said that?« asked Tony in disbelief.

»Oh yes.«

»My goodness, I wouldn't say that today.« Tony's guilty look was fleeting; then he defended himself. »But you of all people disagree with that statement?«

»Of course I do.«

»Then let me remind you of your reply ten days later in the *Boston Daily Traveler*. It was quite well done. I was too busy or too new to this country, you wrote, to know about the work of women. Otherwise, it would have occurred to me that between 1675 and 1885, they had written no fewer than 153 works including 55 operas, 15 operettas, six cantatas, and so on. Incredible, I thought. Mrs. Beach had done so much work researching and adding up all those works so accurately. I was amazed, but then you went on to say that the achievements of women composers were even greater, relatively speaking because, compared to their male counterparts, they lacked the life experience, physical stamina, and endurance necessary for the nerve-wracking process of composition. I thought: so where's the disagreement?«

»You thoroughly misunderstood me!« exclaimed Amelie.

»Why?«

»What I meant back then was that women were in a disadvantaged position, but with hard work they could catch up with men or even surpass them.«

»The only problem is that none of what you just said was actually published in the *Boston Daily Traveler*. You're reading into it retrospectively,« said Tony.

»I'm sure I would have expressed myself more clearly later on, or even changed my argument completely.«

»Sure. Later. Later I wouldn't have said anything about a lack of female talent.«

»Later I would have emphasized what I'd always said about myself: that I want to be judged based on my artistic ability and not on my gender,« Amelie said.

»But back then, in the *Boston Daily Traveler*, all you wanted to say was that, all things considered, men were right. Women were at a disadvantage when it came to ability, with only one exception: you, the brilliant Amy Beach,« argued Tony.

Amelie was at a loss for words. Was she annoyed? Did she feel caught? She folded her hands on her lap and paused briefly. »Tony, if Hale and Higginson bothered you so much, why didn't you contradict them yourself, instead of expecting me, the weakest in the group, to do it?«

»As a guest of honor, I felt obligated to be cordial, you see,« Tony said. »Besides, think about how important it was for me professionally to make contacts in Boston, especially with a music critic like Hale. I was the Bohemian farm boy, you were the Brahmin. You could have said so much more.«

»Balderdash! You were a coward, that's what you were. And an opportunist. You needed Hale's applause and Higginson's money.«

»Pardon me, but I supported myself and didn't live off my spouse's income like you did,« Tony retorted.

»I know enough people who live off their own earnings without being opportunistic. What was it like for you to want to please both the Bohemian and the German audiences? You always wanted your name printed on the program as 'Ant. Dvořák' so that no one would know whether you were an Austrian Anton or a Bohemian Antonín. Was that not opportunistic?«

»That...no, that wasn't opportunism. You wouldn't understand. My music and the political question of my position in a multiethnic monarchy were two different things. It was easier for you. You belonged to the elite in Boston and you could have used your situation to your advantage,« Tony said.

»Used my situation? You mean as a woman?«

»Would you just drop the whole women's issue and stop claiming you were oppressed? That wasn't something you thought or said back then. The role of the helpless lady seemed to suit you just fine. Capricious Amy Cheney became Mrs. Henry H. A. Beach. Do you think it would have occurred to Clara Wieck to compose or perform as Mrs. Robert Schumann?«

»You're such a macho!« exclaimed Amelie. »When I said that I did not want to be judged based on my gender, that didn't mean I accepted the stereotypes of the time. Quite the contrary! I wanted to break free of them. But in the interest of propriety...«

»Yes, yes, in the interest of propriety. What a quaint excuse.«

»You were no different, my dear Tony. You worried about what other Bohemians would think of you if you became music director in Vienna, or if you left for New York without your wife, or if your music became too American. You were constantly concerned with what people in Prague thought about you. A matter of propriety, was it not?«

López interjected before Tony could throw another punch. She had been quietly observing the duel, hunched in her chair, her eyes darting from one opponent to the other. It apparently wasn't the first time she'd witnessed such a heated exchange between the two.

She had had enough. López sat up straight, stretched out her forearms in front of her, folded her hands and let them drop slowly and dramatically onto her lap. She had such an authoritative presence that the bickering ceased, and the room fell silent.

»May I?« López asked, making it clear that she wouldn't take no for an answer. She seemed to have shed her role as librarian and transformed herself into some kind of mythological authority. »You're getting nowhere. None of the people you've been fighting about, including yourselves, are without fault. From our current perspective, all of them have plenty of room for improvement. Don't forget that you are squabbling about things that happened one-hundred-thirty years ago. Let me give you a few examples, starting with Professor Agassiz, because his case is multifaceted and instructive. Could he have known, ninety years before the discovery of DNA, that all humans have the same genetic roots? No, he could not have. But maybe it wasn't about what he knew, what he didn't know, or what he could have known. Maybe it was about how much responsibility he took for what he knew. Did he knowingly misuse science in order to make his racist attitudes appear more respectable? He had no proof that all people belonged to the same species, but also had no proof that they didn't. And he was familiar with something that was held in even higher esteem than it is today—the biblical passages that claim that God created all people in his image. Anyone who questioned that must have been aware that he was playing with the devil. Today, we can evaluate everything through the lens of history and then, only then, can we pass judgment on it. Or let's take Higginson. We can't deny that he was empathetic with Black Americans. Otherwise, he wouldn't have praised his cousin Thomas for leading an all-Black Civil War regiment, even though he risked the disapproval of Boston's high society. He wouldn't otherwise have tried to excuse the cruelty he attributed to Black people with the suffering they had endured. He argued paternalistically that Blacks were lacking certain virtues because they had not received sufficient education—a situation he believed could be remedied. What does this mean for us today? Should we condemn him today for subscribing to the paternalism that well-meaning whites saw back then as their responsibility? And as for you two—Amelie, should you have been more of a feminist back then? More than your upbringing and survival strategy in the male-dominated music world would have allowed? And you, Tony, should you have been harder on people like Hale who could have shred you to bits? Should you have endangered your reputation as the son of a Bohemian butcher who'd risen to transatlantic fame? Why am I saying all of this? Because it's important to approach these stories—and history itself—fairly. We can't twist the past to suit today's tastes. We can't erase people and events from the past, as Stalin tried to do when he erased Trotsky from official Bolshevik photos. No, we have to deal with events and people from the past as they were, with their problematic elements. We can only judge them in the context of their epoch. If there is a discrepancy between what was back then and what we think should be now, then we can use that very discrepancy to learn more about the passage of time and the evolution of identities. People change. I don't only mean in general, but specifically in the case of how you, Tony and Amelie, deal with each other and your acquaintances. It is not the saints, but the average, imperfect people who have the most to teach us about history. Think about it. I, your friend Calliope, know what I'm talking about. I, too, am a changing woman in the midst of eternal change.« With that, López sank back into her chair.

A changing woman. At the time, I didn't grasp the full significance of her words.

As López spoke, Tony's mood changed dramatically. He withdrew from his cheeky garrulity and fell deep into reflective thought and self-doubt. Visibly touched by López's speech, he grasped Amelie's hand and squeezed it briefly but affectionately.

»If I could talk like that…« he said. There was nothing left of the playful mudslinging from just a few moments earlier.

»Calliope! You do justice to your name,«[19] Tony said to López, then bobbed his head as if he had more to say but no words for it.

---

19 With a name literally meaning „beautiful-voiced" (from kallós, meaning „beautiful," and ops, meaning „voice"), Calliope was the most prominent of the Muses—

López agreed with a silent nod.

»She's right, isn't she? How different we were back then,« Tony said to Amelie. »Me, the Czech romantic idealist from Nelahozeves. You, the caged nightingale from a mansion in Boston. We were so blind to what was truly important, and full of prejudice, too. Your appearance and your clever oratory skills made me biased at first. An upper-class Brahmin woman! I should have known better. The dear Lord gave me the same special talent with which he has blessed you as well—the ability to listen deeply to music. After reading your scores I should have known that there was something extraordinary behind your tidy facade, that you were able to see beyond the glitz of Boston's well-to-do, that there was a hungry fire burning beneath your sense of propriety. I understood you better after hearing your string quartet ♦. But in the years after we met—no, I underestimated you. I was too consumed with myself.«

Amelie put her hand on Tony's, first touching it with her fingertips, then enveloping his whole hand in a heartfelt squeeze. She looked at Tony and I noticed that his eyes had grown moist.

»Thank you for saying that, Tony. You're right. I was very preoccupied with myself then, too. I wanted to be a composer! And a pianist! But I knew all too well that these ambitions conflicted with my comfortable, sheltered lifestyle. And I'll admit, I was happy with that lifestyle. You never met Henry, my husband. He was a good man. He loved me. And he was an attentive sounding board for all the plans I had. He did his best to support me, he made music with me, and he wrote poems for me to set to music, all within the limitations of what was considered decent and proper. He told me that I should compose more big works like the Mass or the symphony. That was not considered appropriate for women back then. The conventional wisdom was that women could be good performers, but they lacked the intellectual depth to create their own significant works. But Henry encouraged me anyway. In retrospect, I believe that he pushed me to compose because it kept me at home and limited my public appearances as a pianist. They were embarrassing to him. He wanted the best for me, but being so much older, that often meant picking up the supervision where

---

the nine sister goddesses who in Greek mythology presided over poetry, song, and the arts and sciences

my mother had left off. Yes, he was more of a father than a husband. Just now, as we were talking about Higginson, I was thinking of Henry and of a comparison that suddenly occurred to me. Henry's positive, loving attitude toward me was similar to Higginson's attitude toward the Blacks. Henry liked me, but he did not see me as an equal. From his point of view, I was by nature weak, but capable of growing with his help. That's how Higginson viewed the Blacks. Henry didn't realize that his protection and support confined rather than liberated me.«

»Interesting, Amelie. That's really very interesting,« replied Tony, still deep in thought. »You say that his care was a hindrance. I had a similar thought earlier, but in an entirely different context. You know that I recommended that Americans base their national music on African-American and ›Indian‹ music. Why did my recommendation come true for African-American music, and why did it fizzle out after thirty or forty years for ›Indian‹ music? And that, even though Arthur Farwell explicitly declared that he was doing nothing but working day and night to fulfill my recommendation? Did you ever think of that?«

»My goodness,« replied Amelie, »We've known each other for so long, but that's a new question.«

»I think I have the answer,« announced Tony. »African-American music fended for itself, despite all the hurdles. Nobody needed a white filter to listen to African-American music—especially not jazz!«

Bob chuckled in the background. He'd been silent for so long that we'd practically forgotten about him. »Yeah, man! You said it. It's time that Amelie got that into her head.«

His comment seemed aggressive, and I couldn't understand why, but Tony ignored him and went on. »Things were different for Indigenous music. It remained behind a curtain of protection and was only made accessible to audiences after having been filtered by the Indianists,« he said.

Tension still hung in the air from Bob's interjection and I tried to cover it over. »That's very interesting,« I improvised. »A common paradigm in music history, the humanities, interpersonal relationships…«

»What?« asked Bukar. »Can't you put it in layman's terms?«

»Okay, I'll try,« I replied. »What I'm talking about is paternalism. Henry Beach screwed up by treating Amelie in a fatherly manner. The Indianists screwed up by only allowing ›Indian‹ music on stage after they'd filtered it. And then they screwed up again. Stylistically, they were riding on an old, clapped-out ship, namely the German Late Romantic period of music, and when that ship sunk and times changed, it was adieu to ›Indian‹ music, while Black music sailed into the avant-garde on the winds of popular music.«

»Gotcha. That makes a lot more sense,« said Bukar and gave me a fist bump.

Tony was not amused. »Maybe we should discuss it again. Your summary was a bit simplistic and unfair,« he said with a frown. Perhaps he'd expected something more complex from a PhD candidate. »Sailing into the avant-garde on the winds of popular music, that's not what really matters. If that were the benchmark, most of my compositions could be thrown away. Both kinds of music are justified, side by side, right? And please also keep in mind that the Indianists, at least Farwell, weren't as influenced by the Late Romantic tradition as you imply. Farwell was adamant about freeing himself from the influence of German music. You also mustn't forget that some of the Indianists composed very significant works. Think of Amelie's String Quartet, Ferruccio Busoni's *Indian Diary* ♦, Charles Tomlinson Griffes's Two Sketches Based on Indian Themes, and, of course, Farwell's innovative piano music and his *Hako* String Quartet.«

»That would be worth discussing,« Amelie said enthusiastically. »Was Arthur's String Quartet really an Indianist work? If I'm not mistaken, he didn't use any original Indigenous melodies at all in the quartet. Instead, he said his intention was to capture the voice of a Great Plains ritual…«

Bob interrupted before Tony could reply. »Listen, listen! What a miracle, Tony. Three string quartets on the Best of the Indianists list. Put together by whom? Of course! By the master of the string quartet. Is that a musical Mount Everest or something?«

Tony groaned. »Bob, just drop it. I also mentioned Busoni's and Farwell's piano pieces. And, really, I'm getting tired of all the senseless labels. Master of the string quartet? No! I wanted to be master of the opera, but it never happened. I should have finished *Hiawatha*.[20] But back to Farwell.

---

20 During his time in New York, Dvořák intended to write an opera about the life of the historic Indigenous leader, Hiawatha, which would span his childhood, marriage

Amelie, what you just said seems like nitpicking. Even if Farwell didn't use any ›Indian‹ melodies in his String Quartet, that doesn't mean he didn't make a serious attempt to capture an ›Indian‹ spirit.«

»Yes, yes, Arthur did like to track down spirits,« Amelie said. I was surprised by her comment.

»Petra, Tony,« she continued, »don't misunderstand me. It's indisputable that Arthur was enormously talented. But I don't see him as the great, ingenious guiding light of the Indianists. For me, he was more of a dreamer. He started projects that he never completed and proposed theories that he didn't think through. I once spent a whole night with him talking about his wild theories.«

»You knew Farwell personally?« I interrupted.

»Yes, of course,« said Amelie. »We got along well. Before the World War, he traveled through the US giving lectures on Indianist music and often played my *Eskimo* pieces for his audiences as examples. We didn't see each other often, but we wrote a lot. López, do you still have the letters?«

López noticed that Bukar and I were astounded. Correspondence between Amelie and Farwell—here in the Ottendorfer Library? That would be fodder for my dissertation. But why here? Bob sat up, his eyes darting anxiously between López and Amelie.

»The Ottendorfer is full of surprises,« said López. »When Valentin Ottendorfer planned the library, he wanted there to be safes on the ground floor. Where the reception is now, there used to be a brick vault housing numerous safes with fireproof, burglarproof steel doors. According to Ottendorfer, that was one of the important functions of a library.«

»I didn't notice the vault or the safes,« I said, puzzled.

»Of course not,« López said. »The vault was removed when the reception area was expanded decades later. It was already gone when I started working here. But a few safes are still here. They're hidden behind a bookshelf. They're not very accessible, but that doesn't matter. Apart from Amelie's correspondence, there's nothing left inside.«

---

and death. Dvořák was inspired by the heroic poem *Song of Hiawatha* by Henry Wadsworth Longfellow (1807-1882). According to Michael Beckerman and Joseph Horowitz, there is evidence that Dvořák wrote the second and third movements of his *New World* Symphony as templates for the opera music. The project was never completed because Dvořák never found a libretto to his liking.

»And how did the letters get here?« I asked.

López and Amelie looked at each other cluelessly, until Amelie finally said, »I honestly don't know anymore.« López nodded in agreement.

»López offered me the storage space during one of my many moves, but I can't remember when that was,« added Amelie.

Another strange coincidence. Correspondence between Amy Beach and Arthur Farwell, which was potentially important to my dissertation, happened to be in this very library, which I found by coincidence after meeting López (by coincidence) in Pete's Tavern, where she'd approached me for no other reason than having seen the Amy Beach texts randomly spread out on my table.

»And no one has read these letters? I mean, no one from academia?« I asked.

López and Amelie looked at each other helplessly again. »No,« said López, »but I was sure that, one day, someone would come for them.«

»I'd always hoped that would happen,« said Amelie.

»You knew that I would come?« I asked incredulously. Were López and Amelie pulling the strings of fate? The supernatural events of the past few days were getting to be too much. I had come to New York to work on my dissertation, not to play with Ouija boards.

»We didn't know that you would come, but that someone *like* you would come,« López clarified, which only partially relieved me.

»And what did you write about in the letters?« I asked Amelie.

»I haven't read the letters in fifty years. As far as I can remember, we wrote mostly about folk music—European and African-American folk music, the music of the white settlers and cowboys in the West, and especially about ›Indian‹ music. I learned a lot from Arthur. Take Inuit music, for example. Don't linger on expressing intonation and rhythm with Western notation, he said, but try to understand the essence of the music and then convey it authentically.«

Tony agreed. »Well said, Amelie. And let's forget the rest for the time being.« It was a clear message that our meeting was over for the day. He asked if my questions had been answered.

»Yes, for today,« I said, although I would have liked to continue our conversation. »But it would be nice if we could talk more some other time.«

Tony nodded and went to the kitchen to get another beer, while Amelie asked me if I still thought that the Indianists had screwed up.

»I'm sorry I expressed myself poorly,« I said. »I didn't mean to make such a sweeping generalization. Musically, I think they're interesting. Well, not all of them. Some of the works are kitschy and some of them use questionable methodology. But I like others. To answer your question, my explanation of why the Indianists basically evaporated after the 1930s wasn't entirely wrong. They embedded Indigenous music too much in the Late Romantic and didn't manage to make the leap to modernity. Bartók was different. That's why he managed to transport Hungarian, Romanian and Bulgarian folk music into modern times.«

»We can talk about that, and about Béla, later, if you like,« said Amelie.

I was surprised that Amelie used Bartók's first name, but I didn't mention it. Did she know him?

Suddenly Bob called from the corner, »I'll be there! And let's talk about why jazz did not disappear. And what is truly authentic.«

Amelie seemed slightly annoyed. »Yes, okay then.«

I wondered if the two of them had ever talked about music before, or about anything at all.

López said she had to go, but told me first where in the library I could find literature on American music and New York during the Gilded Age. When she left, Amelie and Tony were suddenly gone. This time, I wasn't surprised.

While I followed López's instructions and started searching the library's painfully slow database for useful titles, Bukar sat down with Bob and began talking to him. It was Bukar, however, who did most of the talking, while Bob mostly used body language. From a distance, it looked to me like his voice was causing him pain, but later that evening, as Bukar and I sat at the kitchen table in our tiny apartment, Bukar told me in yet another magical story that this wasn't the case at all. Magic was becoming a leitmotif of our New York adventure.

* * *

Bukar dropped two paper bags onto the kitchen table. They contained the sushi he'd picked up on his way home.

»Bob isn't who we think he is,« he told me.

Nothing could shock me after all that had happened, but I was still curious. »Is he a zombie, too?«

»No, a living human,« said Bukar. »But he's really old, like almost a hundred.«

»So that would make him The Hundred-Year-Old Man Who Climbed Out of the Window and Disappeared Into the Library?«

»I don't know. He says 'Bob' is his pseudonym because he needs his peace and quiet. His real name is Bud Powell. That doesn't ring a bell.«

»*The* Bud Powell?« I must have missed something, because the real Bud Powell had been dead for a while. »You've never heard of him?«

Bukar said no, he hadn't. I figured that maybe jazz didn't play quite the same role in Nigeria as it did in my parents' house when I was a kid. I quickly explained off the top of my head what I knew about Bud Powell.

»Without exaggerating, he was one of the most important jazz pianists of his time, the 1940s and 50s. Ever heard of Charlie Parker?«

»Yeah, he sounds familiar.«

»Okay, same time, same style. Bud Powell was doing on the piano what Charlie Parker was doing on the saxophone. They created a new style of jazz with fast and dynamic solos with incredibly complicated out-of-the-box rhythms and harmonies. They were the rebellious counterpart to big band jazz and what they played was known as bebop,« I said. ♦

»Right,« Bukar interrupted. »That's what he called it. ›My life was bebop,‹ he said. But he explained bebop in a totally different way than you just did. To be honest, it all sounded kind of scatterbrained to me. It was really hard for him to talk. He'd say a short sentence, then pause and look around furtively, almost fearfully, and then say something else that had nothing to do with what he'd just said. ›Bebop, becop, mob, bop,‹ he said, or something like that. ›That's the sound of the policeman's club when it pounds the notes out of a Black head and straight into the piano,‹ he said.«

I cringed at the brutal image. But then, irreverently, a sense of relief came over me. Bukar and Bob were pulling me out of the Late Romantic haunted house I'd been stuck in with Tony and Amelie. Jazz was a breath of fresh air compared to the exquisite yet macabre odor that Amelie and Tony emitted.

I knew that the comparison was faulty. Nearly a hundred years old and visibly damaged, Bob was a monument to morbidity. But the music he held within him was young and fiery.

I'd always had a weakness for jazz, despite my classical training. In my opinion, jazz and classical music are quite compatible. Of course, nothing can match the rich timbre of a symphony orchestra, but in other areas jazz has the upper hand. I don't just mean *what* we hear—like the freedom of improvisation, one of the most attractive features of jazz, a skill that fell by the wayside in classical music after the Baroque era. I also mean how we listen—more relaxed, more physical, less ritualized. No one will raise an eyebrow if you clap after the first movement or—heaven forbid!—in the middle of a piece. No one will be bothered if you drink wine and eat a sandwich during a concert.

I was also glad that Bukar had taken on more than a backseat role. He and Bob had started out as outsiders in my conversations with Tony and Amelie. Bukar was kind of bored. Bob always seemed to be listening carefully, but sullenly kept his distance; he bridged the gap only by tossing in an aside now and then. Now the two of them had come together, and I sensed that over time they would get to know each other better, man to man or great-grandfather to great-grandson.

If it were true that Bob really was Bud Powell, it would be just as fascinating as my unlikely encounters with Amelie and Tony. His story didn't apply to my dissertation, but he would have a lot to say in a broader discussion on musical identity in the United States.

Besides, I thought, the old man can't have spent fifty years in the library as the doorman without getting wind of the odd meetings that took place there. Bukar would be helpful in finding out more about what Bob knew, he just needed a lesson or two about jazz. I opened a bottle of wine and poured each of us a glass.

»Bukar, if it's true that Bob is Bud Powell, then you should find out more about him. Come, I'll tell you a bit more about jazz. Would that be okay?«

»No lectures, please. Wait until dinner, then you can play me a few pieces,« he said.

He didn't sound very enthusiastic. Where was Bukar's usual curiosity? While he disappeared into the kitchen to transfer the sushi from the Styrofoam boxes to the plates and drizzle the dressing packets onto the salad,

I racked my brain. How could I get him excited about Bud Powell and jazz without a lecture? I thought of the movie *Round Midnight*, about a drug-addicted jazz musician who was supposed to be a cross between Bud Powell and the saxophonist Lester Young. The movie was based on the book *La danse des infidèles* by the Parisian Francis Paudras. As a young man searching for the meaning of life in 1950s Paris, he found the answer in the music of Bud Powell who was also living in Paris at the time. Paudras managed to befriend his idol and help him rid himself of drugs, alcohol and an exploitative mistress named Buttercup. With a superhuman willingness to sacrifice, he was able to stop or at least slow down Bud's self-destruction—but only for a while.

I looked online to see where we could stream *Round Midnight*. It was the best jazz movie I'd ever seen, mostly because of Herbie Hancock's fantastic soundtrack which earned him an Oscar for Best Film Music in 1987. But, I quickly realized, that was the problem. Bukar needed to learn about Bud Powell's music, not Herbie Hancock's.

Then I stumbled upon a French documentary movie on YouTube called *Inner Exile*. When Bukar came back from the kitchen, I turned it on. We sat on the couch and were spellbound by what we saw. The movie was mainly about how the highly sensitive Bud Powell, as a Black man, found refuge in bebop. Refuge from a world not interested in his skill as a (Black) classical pianist. And, especially, refuge from a cycle of police brutality, psychiatric wards, personality-altering electroshock treatments, and a constant flow of alcohol. Ultimately, each attempt to turn his life around ended in even more abuse and yet another stay in a psychiatric institution.

Though I was familiar with most of the story, I couldn't have explained it to Bukar as well as the movie did. Sometimes a picture is worth a thousand words. There was Bud's face before and after he first became the victim of police brutality in Philadelphia in 1945: feisty and ambitious, then fearful, disturbed, empty. There was the way Bud chewed his own mouth while he played the piano, the inward concentration of an artist who didn't give a damn what anyone else thought. And there was the suffering in his pained eyes. He was in his late 30s but, with a scar on his head, he looked decades older.

When the movie talked about the cops' clubs falling mercilessly on Bud Powell's head, Bukar turned it off. »Bob told me about the billy clubs, the

Black skull, bebop. Now it makes sense. Unbelievable. Bob doesn't say much, but what he does say runs deep,« said Bukar.

Later, we found out that Bob's etymology of ›bebop‹ was not his own invention. He'd borrowed it from James Langston Hughes,[21] the writer behind the Harlem Renaissance, a movement among Black artists in Harlem in the 1920s and 30s. Their goal was to support Black culture and build self-confidence in their work. It was a protest movement that served as fertile ground for bebop to flourish as a counterpart to more traditional jazz. I wasn't surprised that Bob had adopted Hughes' explanation of the word bebop. It interwove art with the everyday, including the pervasive racism that tragically affected Bud Powell and became an integral part of his music.

We kept watching the film until I was compelled to pause it again. A young French jazz pianist was trying to define bebop but was rather technical about it.

»Bebop is not only about what melodies are virtuosically played over what bass lines,« I told Bukar. »It's about living in Harlem at a time when Black boys could die for their country in World War II but not sit at the front of the bus in their own city. And it's about a time when mainstream jazz lined the pockets of the white music establishment, while the ingenious, down-home jazz musicians met on empty stomachs for jam sessions in cafés and cheap clubs. Bebop was born at the intersection of resistance, traditional authenticity, and the quest for freedom.«

»You sound like you've spent time in Harlem,« said Bukar, nodding.

»C'mon Bukar, you know this is my first time in New York. As a musicologist I have to be able to put myself in other people's shoes and broaden my South Tyrolean horizon. But back to bebop. Yeah, I'd say it's two-thirds quest for freedom and one-third tradition. It was too traditional to stand up to the free jazz avant-garde twenty years later, but too free to be accepted by fans of traditional jazz.«

In the movie, we watched Bud become involved in the bebop subculture at a young age, particularly at Minton's Playhouse. It was there that he met

---

21 James Langston Hughes (1901-1967) was an American writer and a pioneer of
    Black cultural self-empowerment.

virtuosos like saxophonist Charlie Parker and trumpet player Dizzy Gillespie. I hit pause again.

»Sorry, Bukar, I have to give a lecture now, but I promise it will be short and to the point. As a musician, I have to explain something that isn't mentioned in the movie but is essential to understanding Bud Powell as a soloist. When brass instruments land in the hands of good musicians, they can be played with incredible virtuosity. They are predestined for the turbulent bebop melodies. Bud's ambition was to transfer the breakneck speed and conspicuous passing tones of bebop brass to his instrument, the piano. His role model—not stylistically, but in terms of tempo—was jazz virtuoso Art Tatum, fifteen years his senior.«

»And the club was called Minton's Playhouse?« asked Bukar.

»Yep.«

»Is it still around?«

»Yep,« I said, unaware that this was only half true. I later found out that Minton's Playhouse was still there, but it had been totally renovated after a fire in 1974 and now bore little resemblance to the original club.

»Then I know what we have to do.« He had that same adventurous look in his eye that he'd had when he told me we were going to New York.

»I'm in.« I didn't need any further explanation. »But before we go, let's listen to some more music. That was your original plan, wasn't it?«

»Sure, okay.«

We started listening while Bukar refilled our wine glasses.

»Don't you think we should invite Bob and López? I'm sure Tony and Amelie wouldn't mind staying home to listen to classical radio,« Bukar said. »You're listening to WQXR!« He skillfully mimicked the overly enthusiastic station ID.

A good idea all around, we both agreed. Then we listened to a few more titles that Bud had recorded in 1949 with his ensemble, The Modernists. All of them were bebop legends: Sonny Rollins on tenor sax, Fats Domino on trumpet, Tommy Potter on bass, and Ron Haynes on drums. Bukar was impressed by the fast piano runs in *Wall* and *52nd Street Theme*. Finally, *Round Midnight* ♦, one of Bud's lesser known but grippingly beautiful ballads, led us back into his sublime but painful world.

* * *

Meeting Bob was a highlight, but Bukar's main interest was still his campaign for a Boko Haram trial at the International Criminal Court. He was under pressure to prepare for the panel that Walter had promised to organize. It was a unique opportunity to speak with legal advisors from other countries and numerous NGO representatives.

I haven't met many journalists, but those I do know are night owls, including Bukar. When he has something important to do, he pours himself a karkadeh tea after dinner, sits down at his computer, and types up a storm. At some point, usually around two or three o'clock in the morning, he'll indulge in a glass of whisky.

At the beginning, I was annoyed by this work habit, because it didn't leave much room for us. Occasionally, Bukar felt bad and skipped his late shifts for a few days to spend the evenings with me, dining out or doing puzzles at home. But then he went back to his old ways. I've since come to accept his routine because it's how he does his best work.

This morning, he had been sitting at the computer since breakfast and had already announced that he would be busy until the following evening. Day shifts and night shifts. Bukar had decided that his strategy for Walter's meeting had to be based on facts, facts and facts. No tear-jerking personal stories, although he could tell plenty of those, starting with his father's murder. No, Bukar said, you can't play the emotional card with legal experts. They want facts. Facts that prove that crimes have taken place and that a trial is both necessary and possible.

Bukar used me as a guinea pig for his line of reasoning. He had already worked it all out in his head—the facts, his information strategy.

»I need at least four slides. I'll have to prepare them by tomorrow,« he told me right after breakfast.

»You mean you're going to do a PowerPoint presentation?« I asked.

»Yes, and I also need to print it out. That's always a good idea, so people have something to hold on to, something to take with them. And they don't have to write down the statistics and facts they see on the slide.«

He sounded set on his plan, but then he added that finding a printer was actually quite complicated. »Yesterday I saw online that there is a Civil Society Resource Center where the UN provides meeting rooms and computers with access to its database. But when I went there yesterday, a sign said that it was closed for renovations. So I walked down another block to the Church Center at 777 UN Plaza on the corner of 44th Street. It's not as well equipped as the Civil Society Center, but it's the gathering spot for all the NGOs,« he said.

»You mean for all the accredited NGOs, right?« I asked. Bukar nodded.

»But you're here on your own. You're not with an NGO,« I reminded him.

»Yeah, but…well, I got some help. June gave me access as a JUICE representative.«

»June?«

»The esoteric woman I told you about.«

Alarm bells went off in my head. The woman you didn't tell me everything about, my intuition told me. »What's really going on here?«´

That was when he confessed what was going on with June. I was angry with him for not being more upfront with me, but also relieved that the cat was finally out of the bag.

Bukar looked at me silently for a while. »Do me a favor,« he finally said. »Come with me to the Church Center tomorrow. That would make it clear to June that I'm not up for grabs.«

»Absolutely not. That would be acting, wouldn't it? An invitation to play with secrets behind the facade of a functioning relationship. No, Bukar,« I said categorically. »If you're not into June, then tell her yourself. Don't make me do your dirty work.«

Bukar nodded. He had heard me loud and clear. But apparently, he could also read my thoughts and knew that I was wondering why he'd accept help from someone like June, his esoteric antithesis, who categorically rejected the role of criminal law? Would Bukar really manage to outdo good old Tony in his opportunism?

Bukar repeated himself for the hundredth time that there was no way he could possibly be interested in June because they were such polar opposites, but he added that it was tempting to pit his strength against hers for that very reason. Were these the blunt words of someone obsessed with the will to prevail, or was it the chutzpa of a flirtatious gambler?

»Don't you understand the appeal of paradox?« he asked. »My worst enemy helps me print the presentation that I'm going to use to refute her.«

Despite my resentment, I got it, but still felt like sparring with him. »Make sure that the paradox works to your advantage.«

Bukar smiled with calming self-assurance. That was the beginning of my (short) path to overcoming my anger. I let him give me a reconciliatory hug. Then Bukar insisted on describing the PowerPoint slides he was planning to make.

»First I need to prove why a criminal trial must focus on the massacre in Baga in January 2015—the type and magnitude of the crimes, the accountability, the clear violation of the law of armed conflict.«

»Law of armed conflict?«

»Yeah, it also applies to internal conflicts. I'll be happy to explain it to you another time. The legal advisors know what it's about. So, on the first slide, I'll show a map of the locations of war crimes that took place between November 2014 and January 2015, each with the number of victims. Potiskum, November 10, 78; Dogon Fili, November 20, 56; Kano, November 28, 200; and so on, ending with Baga, January 3-9, 2,000. Then on the second slide, I'm going to put a video clip from December 21, 2014. It shows Boko Haram militants in Bama executing in cold blood dozens of people lying on the ground. The speaker in the video looks into the camera and says that even though the Prophet commanded them to take prisoners and not to kill them, they don't believe it's a good idea to take prisoners in their current situation. He actually said they wanted the blood of the prisoners to turn the ground red. Can you believe that? It's crazy that the speaker so cavalierly contradicts the Qur'an but still considers himself its greatest protector. It says a lot about their messianic mentality. At the end of the presentation, I'll show a video of former Boko Haram leader, Abubakar Shekau, screaming as if possessed, ›We'll kill them! We'll take them as slaves and sell them!‹ Legally speaking, there are two points to be made: First, he clearly announces his plan to commit a war crime. And second, he is proving that the highest level of leadership is accountable for these crimes.«

»Boko Haram made international headlines not with the Baga massacre, but with the abduction of schoolgirls,« I pointed out after listening quietly. »Wouldn't it be better to focus on that?«

»If it were only to impress the Western media, then yeah,« Bukar said. »You mean the mass kidnapping in April 2014 when 276 schoolgirls were abducted in Chibok. You're right, the media was all over that primitive, brutal crime. It showed just how much Boko Haram was against women and education. But—and I'm speaking as a Nigerian human rights activist—it was also a case that made me tear my hair out because the Western media only saw and published what they wanted to, not the whole reality. Chibok was just the tip of the iceberg. Boko Haram has been kidnapping schoolgirls all along, and they're still doing it. Should I tell you what just happened in September? Every month for the past two decades, Boko Haram has murdered a large number of people somewhere in the country. The international press is used to that. The Baga massacre came two days after the Charlie Hebdo attack in Paris which was one reason why the Western media ignored it, just like our former president, Goodluck Jonathan. He offered his condolences to the French, but said nothing about the massacres in and around Baga.«

I began to see how passionately Bukar was going to address the human rights advisors. I felt rather overwhelmed by all the facts he'd just laid out, but I figured his audience would be more familiar with the topic.

»If you want to focus on the mass abduction of schoolgirls in Chibok in 2014, then that would be worthwhile for another reason,« Bukar continued.

I looked at him expectantly.

»Chibok is a good example of how our government deals with these kinds of crimes. Shekau…«

»Who?«

»Shekau. He was Boko Haram's leader at the time,« Bukar said. »Remember his name. I'm amazed he's not better known here. It's like his name just goes in one ear and out the other. Shekau confessed publicly to abducting the schoolgirls but still managed to avoid arrest. Instead, the government agreed to a ceasefire with Boko Haram in October 2014, three months after the Baga massacre, and announced that the girls had been freed. Boko Haram denied it, saying they had no intention of releasing the girls and even if they did, it would be impossible, since many of them had already been taken as wives by the militants. Some others were also free, having managed to escape, albeit without the government's help. A few others were released in 2016 as a result of negotiations, and a few more in 2017. One hundred girls are still being held by Boko Haram or are considered missing.«

»Isn't that also a crime worth prosecuting?« I asked. »I'm sure the international community would…«

»Yeah, the international community would be on your side,« Bukar interrupted. »But the international courts? You can't win a case with outrage, even when it's justified. You can only win it with precedents, and the legal situation surrounding the premeditated execution of prisoners of war is a hundred times clearer than kidnapping girls and forcing them into marriage.«

»And you think that's okay?«

»No. But it doesn't matter what I think. Of course I don't think it's okay, but that's how international law works. Since its inception at the International Criminal Tribunal for the former Yugoslavia, sexual crimes have been swept under the rug because of plea bargains between the perpetrators and the prosecutors. A blind eye is turned to sexual crimes if the defendant is willing to confess to other crimes that are less damaging to his reputation. You know what I mean? As frustrating as it is, the prosecution of sexual crimes is on shaky ground and I don't want to take any chances.«

I shook my head. Bukar's logic was understandable, but I feared he might run into trouble in a public presentation.

»Let me explain my last two slides,« he said before I could express my misgivings. »On the third slide I will describe in detail how the Baga massacre came about. Day one, January 3, Boko Haram launched a multi-pronged attack on the regional headquarters of the MJTF in Baga.«

»You'll have to explain what that is,« I pointed out.

»Sure. The Multinational Joint Task Force is the joint unit that protects the border region between Nigeria, Chad and Niger and is supposed to prevent Boko Haram from moving. But you already know that. You also know that on January 3, there were only Nigerian troops in the barracks, and they fled after putting up only a short fight. The residents of Baga also fled. When Boko Haram attacked the neighboring village of Doron Baga, near Lake Chad, more people had to flee. On January 4 and 5, Boko Haram destroyed every house in the villages within a 40-kilometer radius. Many of those who fled were butchered. I saw the corpses with my own eyes, stacked twelve deep in the grass along the foot paths. At least fifty people tried to escape in fishing boats across Lake Chad. Boko Haram shot most of them from the bank. The rest reached a small, mosquito-infested island. They were near starvation when the Chadian army rescued them a few days later. Then, on January 6, Boko Haram returned to Baga and Doron Baga, shooting and beating anyone who was still there. All remaining houses were destroyed with explosives and petrol bombs. Aerial photographs taken a few days later showed that 3,100 houses had been leveled. I'm going to put all this on the slide, with arrows to show the movement of the militants, little bomb icons to mark the sites of the worst destruction, and info boxes with the number of victims at each spot.«

Bukar had told me about the Baga massacre before, but I was shocked again by the brutality and at a loss for words. He seemed to notice how distraught I was and continued even more matter-of-factly.

»Before I get to the last slide, I need to add two important pieces of information. The first is, what motivated Boko Haram to completely destroy such a large area around Baga? Maybe I should make an extra slide on that.«

He took a piece of paper and drew a rough sketch. »Here is Dongola in Sudan. Omar al-Bashir, Sudan's dictator at the time, allowed Boko Haram to store weapons there. They were basically lying around in the Libyan desert, waiting to be picked up, after Gaddhafi was defeated. Some of the weapons were supposed to be brought to the region between Bama and Gwoza, about 50 kilometers southeast of Maiduguri where Boko Haram wanted to set up its Nigerian headquarters. From Dongola, the transport route to al-Fasher was fairly straightforward, but from there they had to cross the Chadian desert to a geographical curiosity. Can you see it? Here, near Lake Chad, not far from the capital, Ndjamena, the western part of Chad almost touches Nigeria, but a piece of Cameroon is stuck between them like a raised finger. This area was the most difficult part of the transportation route. It is the only more densely populated region, and border troops from three countries are busy checking weapons shipments and putting up a stink whenever they feel like it. Boko Haram had only one card to play: maximum terror. For the people on the western bank of Lake Chad like Baga and Monguno, that was a death sentence.«

I was horrified that anyone would devise a corridor of death across three countries just to transport weapons more easily. »And what's the second thing you wanted to add?«

»I feel like I should explain why I know what I'm talking about,« Bukar said. »It's not typical to be able to collect untainted information in the middle of a bloodbath like this one. I've thought a lot about how to discuss that, since I have to protect my sources. As a journalist, it's my right to use anonymous sources as long as I protect them. But I also want to be credible; I want to prove that my story is not second-hand, but that I actually experienced it. That's also something I will have to demonstrate in court if need be.«

I saw in Bukar's face that he was reconsidering the points that he must have already thought through so many times.

»I'm still not sure how to tell my story to the legal advisors and the NGO representatives,« he finally said. »But you—I'll tell you the whole story. Back in 2013, a good year earlier, I was in Monguno doing a story on smuggling across the Nigerian-Cameroonian border. The town used to be on Lake Chad, but the lake had dried up so much that the water was five kilometers away. The people there couldn't fish for a living anymore, so they had to turn to other sources of income, like smuggling. At that time, they weren't smuggling weapons, but things like cattle, alcohol, cigarettes, and French luxury goods from Cameroon. I met a really nice, talkative, wiry guy around the age of 40, I'd say. He was pretty tight-lipped about his job, but he seemed to have a lot of them, or at least he was wealthier than the other residents of the town. Although in Monguno, that wasn't saying much. I'll call him Mr. Monguno. We became friends, first in person, then through text messages, especially after I helped his son get a job in the cafeteria at the *Herald*.«

Bukar noticed that I had raised my eyebrows. »Petra, don't look so critical,« he said. »It was a win-win situation. In a nutshell, a year later, after the Boko Haram attack, I wanted to write a follow-up to my smuggling article, so I visited him and also went to Baga. When it all went down on January 2, I was really glad to have his help. He drove me around in his Toyota pickup so that I could watch the events unfold, but we always went at a time when it wasn't dangerous. He seemed to be having fun, as if telling death to kiss his ass was his favorite hobby. In the middle of it all, he would make phone calls in a local language that I didn't understand. I didn't know who he was walking with. Maybe with his informants on the other side of the border? I didn't ask. Once he pointed to a cardboard box on the back seat of the pickup and said, ›If things get dicey, this is our life insurance.‹ I lifted the lid and saw a black jihadist flag. I asked him how useful it would be when we ran into a military checkpoint. He played it cool and proudly replied,

›Then I'll show them the holes in the flag and say we'd just killed the bastards and took it.‹«

»Are you still in touch with Mr. Monguno?« I asked.

»No,« Bukar said, his tone suddenly dry. »Three weeks later, when Boko Haram humiliated the President… Did I ever tell you this? Our dear President Goodluck Jonathan went to a campaign rally in Maiduguri on January 24 with a huge military contingent in tow. He promised that victory over Boko Haram would come very soon and that the situation would then stabilize. Right after Jonathan left the city, smaller Boko Haram groups attacked the lone army post of Jimtilo west of Maiduguri and a few other towns. All the soldiers who had gathered in Maiduguri rushed to Jimtilo, giving Boko Haram the perfect opportunity to invade Maiduguri with no one to stop them. The army had trouble getting back to Maiduguri from Jimtilo because the only main road was full of refugees fleeing the surrounding villages. For two full days, Boko Haram wreaked havoc in Maiduguri, burning houses and killing anyone who resisted, including two imams. By the evening of the second day, Boko Haram withdrew, knowing that it wouldn't be able to control a city of two million people for long. But they had won their propaganda victory against Jonathan. During all of this, Mr. Monguno drove a journalist from the *Vanguard* to the frontlines. Both were killed by one side or the other.«

I couldn't understand how Bukar could recount these horrible things so stoically. »And you?« I asked.

»Rehinat and I hid in my apartment in Maiduguri. We used what we had to build a hiding place at the end of a long corridor, in case Boko Haram came and wanted to kill us or kidnap my sister. We heard gunshots and screams in the street—screams of people dying. It scared us out of our skin. But we didn't want to be heroes and we never dared to look out the window to see what was happening on the street. Instead, I sat at my computer and sorted through the hundreds of photos that I had taken with my phone during the Baga massacre. I added descriptions to the photos and emailed them to my mother so they wouldn't get lost in case something happened to me. It was pretty macabre.«

»Fatima knew about it?« I asked.

»Yes. She must have been so worried knowing that we were in a lot of trouble and not knowing when—and if—we were going to get out.«

Fatima had never told me about all she'd had to endure from afar. My respect for her inner strength grew even more.

»Are you planning to include some of these photos in your presentation?« I asked.

»Yeah, I think so, but maybe not the most brutal ones. Which brings me to my last slide. I'm not interested in spurning outrage or turning people's stomachs. I want to channel their anger and disgust by convincing them that we must have a trial soon. The perpetrators need to be brought before a judicial authority that applies legal standards objectively and investigates crimes meticulously so that the catastrophic spiral is broken and Boko Haram and the army stop justifying their own extreme violence with the extreme violence on the other side.«

»Does that mean you see Boko Haram and the army as equally guilty of violence?« I asked.

»No, that would be unfair,« said Bukar. »Both are at times excessively violent. But Boko Haram is motivated by a pseudo-Islamic disinhibition while the army is just completely overwhelmed. You can't compare them. But what I was getting at is that each side is feeding the other, and this dangerous dynamic must be stopped and justice must finally have the last word.«

I understood Bukar so well and wished I could carve his words in stone.

»In my last slide I need to show how the impunity to which Nigeria is subjected continually leads to more violence, and how this dynamic is driving our already weak democracy into the ground,« Bukar continued. »You may remember the election in March 2015, right after the Baga massacre and Jonathan's humiliation in Maiduguri, when Muhammadu Buhari won. He was a military general, a former rebel, and a real hawk.«

»I see what you mean,« I said. »It's the same in Europe, too. Far-right politicians draw on unresolved conflicts and stylized culture wars. But how do you put that on a slide?«

»I don't know yet. I have to think about it. Maybe as a chronology of events that led to the spiral of violence and contempt for democracy? I don't know.«

I didn't know either, but I had a suggestion. »I have no idea how legal advisors and transitional justice NGOs tick. But could it be that slides with graphs and numbers aren't the only thing they want? Maybe they'll also need a powerful, morally moving, upsetting personal story?«

I was surprised by Bukar's reply.

»I am so sick of constantly being told we need more cheap emotions. Should I talk about the girls in Chibok again for the hundredth time just because the feminist West is more appalled by the kidnapping of three hundred girls than by the murder of a thousand worshippers or five thousand farmers and fishermen?«

I was moved by Bukar's strong reaction, but also hoped that he would behave differently during his presentation. »What if instead of telling the story of the Chibok girls for the hundredth time, you told the story of the Doron Baga fishermen for the first time, and the fathers and mothers and children in Maiduguri who feared the worst when Boko Haram attacked?«

»Yeah…«

»The more objectively you tell it, the more powerful it can be…«

»Yeah. But it's going to be a long story. The meeting with the legal advisors is only scheduled for two hours—one hour for my presentation and one for Q&A.«

»Let's talk about it over the next few days,« I said. »You'll find a way.«

* * *

It wasn't easy to convince Bob to spend an evening at Minton's Playhouse. López proved very helpful, especially in pointing out that it wasn't the Minton's he knew, but that it had been completely renovated.

We—that is, Bob, Bukar, López, and I—took the subway to 116th Street at six-thirty on a Thursday evening. From there, we walked one block to St. Nicholas Avenue and then two blocks up to Cecil's Steakhouse on the corner of 118th Street.

Minton's Playhouse, the birthplace of bebop, was located there in what used to be Cecil's Hotel. Founded in 1938 by saxophonist Henri Minton, it suffered a devastating fire in 1974. Before the fire, there had been a bar at the front of the hotel which was attached to a restaurant with a dance floor. And right at the back, there was a club with a stage.

Today, the spacious lounge at the front opens into a modern, Afro-Caribbean steakhouse. At the rear, where the stage used to be, there is a door leading to a club in the next building.

It was a cold, wet evening. Fall was marking its arrival. The weather app predicted a downpour and we'd planned to hop into the steakhouse just before the deluge, but the app was wrong. The rain came earlier. When we finally arrived at Cecil's Steakhouse, soaked to the underwear, we huddled around a bar table in the lounge and waited for our clothes to dry off a bit before heading to Minton's.

I noticed that the servers were mostly Latino or European, a concession to the gentrification of the steakhouse that now pops up in every guidebook. We ordered three beers and a soda water for Bob.

We were unlucky with the weather, but we'd picked the right day of the week: *Jam Thursdaze*. Every week, Minton's house band plays first and then invites visitors to jam with them on stage. According to online reviews, the house band was supposed to be pretty good, featuring both amateurs and a few bigger talents.

»So what's it like to be back at Minton's?« I asked Bob, hoping to coax a few words out of him.

He surveyed the room disapprovingly, looking at the brightly lit, mirrored bar shelves overflowing with bottles, the modern bar furniture, the tennis match playing silently on an oversized TV screen, the nostalgic pictures on the wall. Bob tossed up his hand as if to throw it all away, a gesture that said it all. But then he began to speak.

»People used to come here to eat good, simple food. They'd do themselves up a bit if they wanted to cut a move on the dance floor after dinner.« Bob ate some peanuts from the dish on the table. He was beginning to thaw. »Fat Adelle did the cooking. Old Minton made sure there were always flowers on the table. And if things were tight that month, Minton would help you out. Musicians only had to pay when they sat at a table. Two dollars. Otherwise, we could jam in the back when it got late. We played whatever we wanted.«

»We? Who else was there?« I asked.

»Well, pretty much everybody. Thelonious Monk, Charlie Parker, Dizzie Gillespie, Oscar Pettiford. And of course Mary Lou Williams and Kenny Clarke.«

»So it's true that bebop was born here during the jam sessions?« I asked.
»Mary Lou had a story of her own.« Bob sipped his soda. »Apparently Thelonious said, ›Hey, if you don't want the other guys to steal your numbers, make them so hard they can't be stolen‹. That's how bebop was born. Would be a nice story if it were true.« Bob smiled. »It could be true. Those guys who played here were really good.« He paused to sift through his memories. »Dizzy once said that it was easy to play on 52nd Street. That's where all the famous bebop clubs were—Onyx, Downbeat, Three Deuces, the original Birdland. ›On 52nd Street, you play for money, but it's here in Minton's where a musician really cuts his teeth. Here you play to make a reputation among the other musicians.‹«

»And did you have a good reputation with them?« asked Bukar. »If my math is right, you were just a teenager.«

»Oh yeah,« said Bob. »And I acted like one too. I was a rascal!«

»I heard a story that you put your foot on a white tablecloth but Thelonious Monk saved you from being kicked out. Where was that?« I asked.

Bob shifted his eyes to a table just six feet from ours. »Over there, by the window.«

»And…?«

Bob rubbed his bare head slowly as if he had to carefully herd his memories, like lost sheep. »Thelonious…I liked him. And he liked me.« Bob stared silently into space for a few seconds. »I owe him a lot. Yeah, it was there by the window. ›Leave him be,‹ Thelonious said, ›the kid's got talent.‹ And then they let me go.«

As he spoke, he moved his fingers quickly along the edge of the bar table. »I'm not bragging. That's what Thelonious said.« He paused again, seeming to crawl deeper into the past behind his closed eyelids. »He said that no one played his pieces as well as I did. Thelonious was incredibly musical. He knew the sound he wanted and always nailed it. As a boy, he accompanied gospel songs at church. That's how he learned. He never missed a note.«

Pause.

»Later he would pound on the keys in wide, rhythmic clusters,« Bob continued, whacking the tabletop with his forearm. »It caught on slowly. At some point people called it free jazz.« Bob looked at me with his tired, swollen eyes. »Musically, I understood what he was trying to do. But technically—ha! I thought, why are you pretending you can't play the piano. You can! You learned classical music like me. Later, I guess he went his own way. But we stayed friends.«

»Even in difficult times?« I asked.

Bob nodded and squinted at me. »Petra, you know everything. You prepared for this, didn't you?« He inhaled slowly. »Yeah. The drug bust.« He hesitated.

Was he going to tell us about the arrest seventy years ago and everything that happened afterward that ruined his life? He started chewing on his own mouth, as he did when he played the piano. Then his jaw stopped moving and he collected himself.

»In August 1951, not far from Blue Note, Thelonious and I and two other guys were sitting in a car, chatting. We saw the drug police coming. I panicked and threw a bag of heroin out the window. Unfortunately, it landed right where Thelonious was sitting. They arrested us and took us to The Tombs.«

»The Tombs? What's that?« asked Bukar.

»It's a huge prison in Lower Manhattan, so corrupt and bloody that no Black man would ever want to land there.«

»But why were all four of you sent there?« Bukar wondered.

»So they could post a hefty bail bond. I told you they were corrupt to the core. Thelonious didn't have 1,500 dollars. He could have said he didn't do it, that I was the one who threw the bag out. But he sat in The Tombs for six weeks instead of ratting on me.«

»And you?«

»I didn't even thank him. Man, I was broken. I flipped out. Like I always did with just one drop of alcohol. I panicked. Would they hit me on the head again like they did in Philadelphia? Would they send me back to Pilgrim State for electroshocks?«

Bukar looked confused, but before López had a chance to jump in and explain, Bob spoke first. »Pilgrim State Hospital on Long Island. Electroshocks were the new fad. They used them to reprogram depressed folks, schizophrenics, homosexuals, hooligans like me.«

»Hooliganism is an illness?« asked Bukar.

Bob drank his soda water. The lines on his forehead seemed to say that he was done answering personal questions.

»I mean, do you think anyone would have seriously diagnosed that?« asked Bukar.

After a long pause, Bob put his hand on Bukar's forearm. Good, I thought, he trusts Bukar; he's opening up more.

»Now I know that I had schizophrenic tendencies. And I couldn't tolerate alcohol. One sip and I completely lost control. But the doctor at Pilgrim State said I was hyperactive, that my mind was running away with me. They asked me about my job and I said I was a jazz musician and had written 150 pieces. That only made them more convinced that I was crazy, that I had lost touch with reality. Poor Black kid, they thought, let's give him a few more volts to keep him in line.«

I couldn't imagine what it must have been like to be treated with electroshocks for weeks on end. Inhumane. A nightmare. It was appalling that something like that could be considered standard practice in a civilized country. I felt helpless and didn't know what to say.

»Can you tell us what it was like?« I asked, quite embarrassed by the voyeurism of my question.

»Yeah. Very painful,« Bob said. »But not like pulling out a fingernail. That hurts like hell and then it's over. No, getting shocks is like they're amputating your brain, your emotions—taking out everything that makes you human.«

»You were scared…«

»You bet I was. When I was in The Tombs, I was sure I was going to die. They're going to kill me, I thought. I didn't just tremble with fear, I screamed, I fought, I totally flipped out.«

»And then?« I asked.

»And then the vicious cycle began. When I flipped out, they threw ammoniac water on me and took me to Belvedere Hospital to be examined, then to Pilgrim State, and then to the Creedmoor Psychiatric Center in Queens, where the really tough cases go. They didn't have enough staff, so they got creative. We inmates had to do everything ourselves. Cleaning, cooking, growing vegetables in the garden. We were basically left to live out our symptoms as we pleased, until we were magically healed. You can imagine how terrible things were. When the staff thought they were losing their authority, they'd use a few straightjackets as a last resort. And a few of us were punished by being strapped to a radiator next to a mattress that reeked of piss.«

»That's horrible,« said Bukar, lowering his head. »How did you survive?«

»The truth is, I almost didn't. Later in Paris, Francis told me I would just have to endure the withdrawal symptoms after getting off the Largactil that Buttercup had gotten me on. And I did what he said. What else could I do? Before that, none of the psychiatrists in New York had told me to bear it. Fran could have told me…«

»Fran was in Paris, wasn't he?« interrupted Bukar.

»No, not Francis,« he said, pronouncing the name with his best French accent. »I'm talking about Mary Frances Funderburk. I always called her Fran. She was a wonderful woman, Celia's mother. Maybe my only true love.« Bob furtively wiped a tear from his reddened eyes. »You should know that I wasn't a ladies' boy like the others. But then, around 1949, my tantrums drove Fran and Celia out of my life. Goddammit! I never wanted that to happen. Fran loved me, I know she did. She was so thoughtful. In the mid-60s, just before I became terminally ill, she took care of me like an angel.«

Bob pulled a thick black wallet from the pocket of his suit jacket and pulled out a couple of bills. Then he found what he was looking for: a frayed black-and-white photo.

»Fran,« he said, showing us the picture.

She was a beautiful, young woman with big dimples. Her curly hair had been pulled back from her face and her expression shone with warmth, despite the artificial photo pose. The same lady as in *Inner Exile*, but much younger.

»I didn't deserve her love. She was the woman who could have told me to endure my pain—and all the humiliation.«

»She looks very nice,« said Bukar. »Don't be so hard on yourself, Bob. It's been over for a long time.«

»Oh no, it's not over! Do you know what it's like to find out you're the electroshock guinea pig just because you're Black? When white patients experience pain, doctors care. They pump them full of psychotropic drugs. But nobody cares about a Black man's pain. I did not endure it. After a while, I was released and went back to play in the clubs. I recorded a couple of albums, snuck away to get some booze, and the whole shitty cycle started all over again.«

It felt like a rendezvous of extremes. Here in Minton's, where Bob's career had begun with so much hope, he sat like a scraggy, old, sweaty, shaking, fearful pile of suffering, telling of his trials while drinking water because anything else in the glass would have been a death sentence.

I remembered my first impression of Bob a few days earlier at the Ottendorfer. I'd wondered what a person would have to go through to end up like him and how long a body could take it. Now I had an answer to the first question.

»But the shit must have stopped at some point, right?« I asked. »I mean, otherwise we wouldn't be sitting here together.«

»Yeah, you're right. The shit stopped at some point. In installments. Installments of shit. The last one was the best.«

Was he being facetious?

»In 1964, I said adieu to Paris. My comeback in Birdland was so-so. The old pals took good care of me, but I didn't live up to their expectations. Oscar Goldstein, my manager, who'd screwed me over ten years earlier, had me followed everywhere by a babysitter. Don't even think about having a drink, he said, that would be bad for business. But I was enough on the fence to slip away. Hell, I was just thirsty. After I butchered a show at Birdland, Oscar fired me. Francis wanted me to come back to Paris and sober up. He came to New York, bought me a ticket and waited for me at the airport. But I didn't come. He must have flown back alone. Then Fran took me in. Things could have gotten better. She did everything she could, but I relapsed again and again. My friends tried to get me out of the hole I'd fallen into. They dangled a big carrot in front of my nose—Carnegie Hall in March 1965! And then Town Hall in May! Both concerts were a disaster. In June 1965 I went back to Cumberland Hospital with lung problems and jaundice. In August I was discharged, but three months later I was admitted to Kings County Hospital. I played in the hospital band while my teeth rotted. Who cares, I wasn't a trumpet player. Things got better when I was with Fran. But in July 1966, I was sent back to the psychiatric ward of Kings County Hospital. Fran knew that I couldn't take another round of electroshocks. One evening after an appointment with the psychiatrists at Kings County, we were taking the A line back home. I had an inkling that it would be my last appointment before I was admitted for good. Then we met Charlotte.«

»Charlotte Hubach,« López added. »She was a wonderful woman. Unfortunately, everything she did has since been forgotten.«

»Yes, Charlotte Hubach.« Bob's eyes clouded over for a moment. »I'm sure she was over 70. When she saw us huddled on a bench in the subway, she was grave but kind. She could see in Fran's and Celia's faces that something was wrong. I can remember that even though I was high. She asked if we needed any help. I'll never forget Fran's answer. ›Please help us,‹ she said. ›My husband is a great artist. But he's about to be admitted to Kings County and that would kill him. To save him, I must hide him in the most remote place in the world.‹ Charlotte asked a few questions. She must have figured out who I was. She liked my music. She said, ›Let's get off at the next stop and take a train to Astor Place. We're going to the Ottendorfer Library in the East Village. I'm the librarian there.‹«

López interrupted. »She probably said that she *was* the librarian. She retired on her 66th birthday in 1957. I know that because that's when I took over her job. I didn't need the librarian's apartment on the second floor of the library, so Charlotte kept living there. She had lived there for thirty years. But when you met her in the subway, she was about to move in with relatives in New Jersey. She had gotten old, and she passed away the following year.«

»She was fantastic,« said Bob. »I didn't realize it until later. Fran accepted Charlotte's offer. First, she asked if I'd really be safe there. Charlotte told us to trust her. So we changed trains and went to the Ottendorfer.«

»Wait a minute. That's a wild story,« I said. »There is a librarian's apartment in the library? And what else do you know about Charlotte?«

»You can get to the apartment by taking the stairs to the third floor, right behind the office,« explained López. »I'm sure you saw the stairs. What was so special about Charlotte? A lot! She was the last librarian to make the library a German meeting place. This part of the East Village used to be called Little Germany, but after World War I, it quickly disintegrated and the Germans moved uptown. Ukrainians and Poles took their place. The library's collection had always been half German and half English, but then it became increasingly international. When the Nazis came to power in Germany, thousands of German-speaking immigrants fled to New

York. Charlotte saw it as an opportunity, and started a lecture series on German exile literature. It's hard to believe, but greats like Bertolt Brecht, Lion Feuchtwanger, Oskar Maria Graf and others spoke right there where we were sitting just a few days ago. And she also organized an exhibition on painting in exile that drew names like Marc Chagall, Max Ernst, George Grosz, Jacques Lipschitz, Maurice Utrillo… Charlotte was incredible. She was well-connected and politically savvy. And she had her heart in the right place.«

Bob wasn't listening. Maybe he already knew the stories about Charlotte, or maybe he was still thinking about the subway trip that saved his life.

»I could barely hear what Fran and Charlotte were talking about,« he said. »But I remember bits and pieces. No access to alcohol, they said. Damn, I thought. And a doctor she trusted from the German Hospital would come by periodically to check in. Okay, I thought, as long as he's not a psychiatrist. Charlotte was very clear about one thing. Fran couldn't stay with me in the library. She and Celia could come visit, but not more. Fran and Charlotte didn't agree on this at first. Fran was so soft-hearted, she would have let me do anything. But Charlotte was insistent. First of all, there wasn't enough room for three people in the apartment. Second, only one person was allowed to stay there, because there was no fire escape. And thirdly, Charlotte said, my life could only be saved if I realized that I had to make some serious changes. This was something I had to do on my own. She was right about that. I can remember it all very well, and by God, it worked. I disappeared in order to finally live again. A few weeks later I read in the newspaper that I had died on July 31 of all kinds of things, but mostly cirrhosis of the liver. No problem, I thought, and heard on the radio how beautifully my friends had bid farewell at my funeral without knowing that my urn was full of air. That was the legend that let me survive.«

The story sounded like straight out of a spy novel or a witness protection program. But it was really quite simple: If there are programs to protect people from other people, then why not have a program that protects someone from themselves? That's what Charlotte did.

It was the most I had heard Bob talk, and he wasn't finished.

»There was something else. Fran once asked Charlotte why she was doing this for us when she didn't even know us. Charlotte said she didn't really know, but that the Ottendorfer was committed to helping people. Valentin, the founder, was a refugee, she said. Then there were the German immigrants. And then me. So, now it's my turn to give back to the Ottendorfer, as long as I can, even if it's just as a doorman.«

»I knew Charlotte for a short time,« said López. »In 1957, when she passed her post on to me, she talked a lot about her work ethic. Then she visited me again to ask my permission to let Bob live in the apartment. Of course I agreed.«

Bob shivered. He wiped his hands across the bar table, as if he wanted to clean it, almost knocking over our glasses.

»Yeah, and now I have to shower you with gratitude for that,« hissed Bob. He sounded annoyed and aggressive and not at all thankful. »Even though I don't want to. How *noble* you are!« he said mockingly.

López gave us all a puzzled look. »You sound like... It seems there are things you've left unsaid. What's going on?«

Bob looked at López furiously and barked, »You *noble Indian*!«

López jumped. Bob's exclamation was like a bolt of lightning, not only for her, but also for Bukar and me. López pressed her back against her chair, inhaled deeply, and seemed to focus inward. I could tell that it took a great deal of effort for her to maintain her composure. Later, I told her how much I admired her calmness in the situation. She told me that, while she was listening inside of herself, she experienced a rare encounter with her maternal grandfather. He had been a *hastói*, a respected storyteller for the Diné who were not yet as worn down from living on the Navajo Nation Reservation as they are today. When Bob suddenly snapped at her, she heard her grandfather quietly tell her, ›Hózhó is our way.‹ She told me that *hózhó* was one of the three fundamental principles of the Diné and meant something like balance, harmony and beauty.

»Pardon me, Bob,« López said composedly, »Why did you say that? What's wrong? Let's talk about it.«

Bob suddenly frightened me. Whatever it was that had made him so difficult sixty years ago was bubbling up to the surface—the unchecked rage that drove away Fran and many of his friends.

I looked around the bar. It would have been embarrassing if the patrons had noticed the sudden change in mood at our table, but they hadn't. Then I saw the television. Instead of the tennis match, Amelie was on the screen.

She was standing at a stove in a kitchen and talking. A cooking show, I thought at first, but no, it really was Amelie. The TV was on mute, so I didn't notice her right away. She was chopping a bouquet of garden flowers as if they were parsley with practiced seesawing movements of the knife, and she was looking straight at us.

I realized that López had also seen her. I poked Bukar and pointed to the TV, then put my finger to my lips so he'd keep quiet about it.

Bob didn't seem to have noticed Amelie yet, but his ire had faded, at least for now.

»I'm sorry, López,« he said. »I didn't mean to offend you, but don't you understand? From my point of view, you have always been and still are on the other side. My music, the music of the ruffian Black slaves—you don't give a damn about it. As an Indigenous American, allied with prominent whites like Amelie and her crazy friend Arthur, you concern yourself with higher things—with the oh-so-intellectual music of the ›noble Indian savages!‹«

»Please, Bob,« said López. »That's unfair. In my modest understanding of music, there are no such categories.«

»Just think about it.«

Bob closed his wrinkled eyelids, then opened them and said, »And not just you, López. You too, Amelie.« Without missing a beat, he raised his eyes to the TV screen. He'd known she was there all along.

»Where did your interest in ›Indian‹ music come from? You, López, from your ancestors? And you, Amelie, do you think that ›Indian‹ music is less primitive than Black music?«

»Excuse me, Bob, but what makes you say that?« asked Amelie indignantly.

I looked around the bar again, worried that we were drawing attention to ourselves, but for everyone else the TV still seemed to be on mute. Only we could hear Amelie.

»What makes me say that? I'll give you a clue.« I felt unsettled by the stream of pent-up anger flowing out of Bob. »1893, Chicago. You were at the World's Fair, right?«

»Right.«

»The exhibit was called the Columbian Exposition in honor of the man who had initiated the subjugation of America four hundred years earlier.

In the middle of the exhibit was the White City, a vision of a shiny future. Right?«

»Yes, that's right.«

»Pay attention to the details. What was the city? White! And what was in the middle of it? The statue of a Harvard graduate—the crowning glory of creation. Then, at an appropriate distance, a statue of a Radcliffe graduate. A bit further, the Midway Plaisance began. Remember? The beautiful promenade that led from the shiny white center to the increasingly darker periphery. It was the perfect image of the Social Darwinist hierarchy. The two Teutonic and two Irish villages were closest to the White City. Then came the Middle Eastern, the West Asian and the East Asian exhibits. Finally, as the catalogue promised, visitors would come to the ›savage races‹ at the end of the promenade. First to the North American Indians who were referred to as noble savages, then to the Africans from Dahomey who were supposed to represent the repulsive kind of savages. Amelie, do you remember?«

Amelie looked uncomfortable. »Of course I do. But my perception was much different. I wasn't at all interested in the political significance of the Midway Plaisance. I didn't catch the intention to arrange the villages in some kind of cultural ranking. Maybe it said that in the catalogue, but I didn't read it. I was only interested in the music that was presented in the villages. To be more exact, I wasn't interested in the question of which type of music was more primitive or more developed—a question that cannot be answered anyway. I was interested in their differences.«

»So you only paid attention to the music?« asked Bob.

»Yes.«

»Also to the music of the Africans of Dahomey?«

»Oh yes. I can remember that very well.«

»You remember it very well? And do you remember that the Africans, forty women and sixty men in grass skirts, were described in the catalogue as ex-cannibals?«

»Really?« interrupted Amelie. »That…then that definitely went too far.«

»And you didn't see the sign at the entrance to Dahomey Village asking visitors not to ask the Dahomeyans about their cannibalistic past because that would have bothered them?«

»No…oh God, my musical curiosity must have blinded me.«

»Then you also didn't notice how the former slave traders patted themselves on the back. Compared to these wild Africans, a little slavery sure did our Blacks some good, ha ha! They actually published things like that in newspapers and books after the World's Fair.«

»Bob, I can only say it again: I truly did not see it. Or I forgot.«

»Of course! Irrelevant details are easy to forget.«

»Please, Bob, don't be so polemic. I went to the fair for the music. The drum rhythms were very sophisticated. They were polyrhythmic. I wondered back then how they could possibly be written down.«

»Have you ever wondered what a Black person might have thought after visiting Dahomey Village?«

The expression on Amelie's face made it clear that she had never considered the question. »Explain it to me,« she said.

»Total disillusionment. And anger,« Bob replied. He rested his head on his hands and breathed heavily as the memories flooded back. »My grandfather was at the World's Fair. He was a bright guy. Like a lot of other Blacks, he thought at first that the Fair would give them an opportunity to present themselves as part of the general wave of progress that was rising in the country. But then he heard that Blacks were kept off the fair's preparatory committees with all kinds of nasty tricks. The ringleader was the chairwoman of the Board of Lady Managers, Mrs. Bertha Palmer. The very same fine lady who helped you premiere your *Festival Jubilate* ode in the Fair's Women's Building. My grandfather was worried about other things. He bought a book by the anti-lynching activist Ida Wells, *The Reasons Why the Colored American Is Not in the Columbian Exposition*. I still have it on my bookshelf. He learned that there had been more lynching victims in 1893 than in the previous years. What a coincidence! He went to the exposition anyway because he believed in social progress—in spite of everything.«

»And that social progress did come about, don't you think?« asked Amelie.

»My grandfather lost his belief in progress the moment he entered Dahomey Village. He understood that the purpose of the exhibit was to prove that he and all Blacks lacked any capacity for culture. He was so bitter about it that he became obsessed with the idea that he was one of the poor, humiliated people put on display in Dahomey Village.«

Amelie was visibly moved by Bob's words.

»My grandfather's stories became part of our family tradition,« he continued. »They took on a life of their own. As children, my siblings and I were convinced that he had been part of the exhibit, even though he always told us that he wasn't, that he just felt that way. Still, we imagined him as a cannibal pounding on his drums, not knowing what that meant for us, his grandchildren. We didn't know whether we should laugh or cry.«

Amelie was even more disturbed. »That's horrible! I'm so sorry.«

»That may be. But you weren't sorry back then. You came and stared. And you were so full of your musical interest that you forgot that you weren't watching some kind of drumming half-monkeys, but real, flesh-and-blood people. That's what makes me so angry.«

»I'm sorry Bob. I didn't realize that.«

»No? How is that? Oh wait, I know. You were thinking of the ›Indians‹. Their music is so interesting because they are a tragic but necessary pawn in the tapestry of heroes that celebrates your glorious conquests. Black music, on the other hand, the music of the former slaves, only conjures up uncomfortable memories. Memories of suffering and injustice, of civil war. Your generation was still dealing with the aftermath of that bloody mess. Whites just wanted to sweep the memory of racial strife under the rug.«

I watched López give one of the servers two discreet signals. One meant, *the bill please*. The other, combined with a quick glance at the television, meant, *change the channel*. The server took her cue, grabbed the remote that was lying next to the cash register, and turned it back to the tennis match. Amelie was gone.

I just barely caught Bob's comment to López. »I saw that,« he whispered. »It's uncomfortable, is it? You just want it to go away? Protect your sister? Just you wait.« His tone was threatening.

»Your table in the club is ready,« the server said as he returned López's credit card and receipt. He ushered us to the back of the restaurant and opened a large fire door upholstered in magenta leather. Then, we were inside Minton's Playhouse.

* * *

My first impression of Minton's Playhouse was disappointing, but it was my own fault. I had secretly hoped to enter a magical place, like the cave where Ali Baba pulled bebop out of a bottle. Instead, we found ourselves in a totally normal club. Red, yellow and purple neon lights shone down on the small stage. The wall behind it had been painted with a fresco that resembled Mexican *murales*. It depicted three musicians, all white or Latino, leaning against a boudoir or lounging on a bed with a Black woman.

It was only later that I learned more about it. *The Lady Sleeps* was painted in 1946 by a man named Charles Graham. The Black woman lying on the bed was another star from Minton's heyday: Billie Holiday, sleeping off a hangover. The fact that she was doing so in the company of three light-skinned men made the picture somewhat unfitting. It seemed like a tasteless commentary on a strong woman who had been raped as a child, was addicted to heroin, and courageously sang against lynching and other racist violence. It's a good thing I didn't know all that at the time. But back then, unburdened by these later insights, I continued to look around the club. There were tables and functional chairs set up in straight rows. A few historic photos hung on the brick walls which were bathed in blood-red light.

The good thing about the plain ambience was that it didn't even try to imitate the original Minton's. As I took in the room, I watched to see how Bob would react to it. There was no trace left of his outburst in the bar. Did the change from the bar to the club also change his mood? Could I read his reminiscences in his eyes or in the wrinkles on his forehead? Did his restlessness conjure up a stage with a piano in front of him?

None of that. He looked bored as he sat on his chair. Instead of nervously practicing his fingers on the table, which was right in front of the stage, his hands lay flat. He looked tiredly around, from the stage where the house band was setting up, to the walls that displayed photos of artists who'd played in Minton's. I couldn't find any of him, and I was sure that he'd already noticed the absence of his photo. A very young Thelonious Monk was the most prominent musician pictured. With his beret and oversized sunglasses, he looked like Che Guevara. There was also a photo of John Coltrane, another product of Minton's, playing his tenor saxophone with a scrunched-up face. No Bud Powell. How strange.

I hoped Bob wasn't offended. He later told me that he was actually quite glad not to be represented in the gallery. That way he could stay unrecognized and anonymous. Bob had spent the last fifty years in absolute anonymity, and I sensed how important it was for him to keep it that way. Was he still afraid of saying yes to a drink in the company of other players or fans? Or had he gotten used to being non-existent for others and to working everything out inside his own head?

The house band began to play a bebop revival. The pianist and the trumpet player delivered nice solos that merged into cumbersome *tutti* sections. The occasional musical weaknesses were covered up by the band's positive vibes. In clubs, it's not just the music that counts, but the whole show. This was especially true for pianist Mathieu Ricard, a French-Malagasy who must have been around thirty years old. With his lanky build and bandana tied over his curly hair, he looked like a piano-playing pirate. His hands and arms mimicked Thelonious Monk's characteristic movements. His fingers were stretched out like claws that ambushed each chord, then hastily pulled back, as if the keys were on fire. With each retreat from the keyboard, his elbows swung up behind his back.

After a good hour, the house band invited members of the audience onto the stage to jam. Three or four of the volunteers played with such ease that they were clearly regulars at the 'spontaneous' jam session. Two saxophonists and two gender-neutral singers took to the stage, along with an adolescent from the Netherlands who was there with his parents. It must have been the highlight of his New York vacation to sit behind the drum set on stage at Minton's, although he played so shyly that he could hardly be heard. Mathieu, the pianist, responded to the boy's hesitancy by playing more percussively. Then there was a Korean on bass who played quite well. Instead of presenting some show-off number he'd memorized, he listened to the others and responded to their rhythmic and harmonic shifts, while still managing to squeeze in a respectable solo now and then.

»I like him.« It was the first thing Bob had said since the concert began. »He feels the jazz.«

»Really? A Korean?« I asked.

»Yeah, why not? If you feel it, play it,« Bob said. He shook his head like someone who is longing for something. »Ever heard of white negroes? That's what we called them. Niels-Henning Ørsted was my bassist in Copenhagen in 1962. He was sixteen, but already into it. He was a good kid. I was glad he made it big later on. Then the five years in Paris. Where would I be without Pierre Michelot? We got along. When I was so stoned I could hardly see the keys, Pierre would guide me with his bass.«

Bob suddenly stood up and walked to the stage. Mathieu asked with his eyes which instrument Bob was planning to play, and Bob responded by wiggling his fingers. Mathieu raised a hand in feigned protest. Another pianist had already volunteered. »Wait a few minutes,« he said. But then he seemed to take pity on old, hunched-over Bob.

»Name?« Mathieu welcomed Bob onto the stage.

»Bob.«

»Oh, a new face.« Mathieu winked at the audience to emphasize his play on the word ›new‹, since Bob's wrinkled face obviously wasn't. »Well then, good luck.«

Bob walked over to the Korean bassist and asked whether he knew *Willow Weep for Me* ♦. He nodded.

»Okay,« Bob said. »Then let's go.«

What followed is hard to describe. What would you say if you had heard Chopin play one of his Polonaises for you live, in person, and you had to tell someone exactly what it was like?

Bob sat down at the piano, just like in the old videos of his concerts that I'd seen. He sat there very still, his eyes raised toward the ceiling. Then he started to play without cueing the bassist. After he'd played the theme with a few embellishments, the bassist joined him, timidly at first, then with more and more self-confidence. The two quickly harmonized with each other. Instead of the original swinging rhythms, they agreed on a slowly trodding blues beat. Bob tottered with his upper body. His fingers seemed tired. He didn't look at them at all while playing, which made it all the more impressive when they suddenly broke into lightning-fast arpeggios. It was hard to believe that those speedy fingers were nearly a hundred years old. If playing was difficult for Bob, then he didn't let on. His face remained stoic, engrossed in the music, although the chewing movement of his mouth and the beads of sweat running down his cheek suggested effort.

I looked around and noticed that the other patrons in the club were spellbound by the two nobodies on stage, one of whom was so old that his age alone was enough to draw attention. The music arose out of Bob and the bassist delicately and calmly—a stark contrast to the coarse blocks of sound produced by the house band.

In the second half of the piece, Bob and the bassist switched roles. Until then, Bob had been gently dabbing the melody, but then he restrained him-

self and started repeating the main chord progression with flat fingers, giving the bassist something to build his solo on. The bassist seemed grateful for the invitation as he gave the anonymous man at the piano an emotional, affectionate look.

I recalled a recording I'd heard of a concert Bud Powell had given in 1960 in the Grugahalle in Essen, Germany, together with two of his oldest friends, bassist Oscar Pettiford and drummer Kenny Clarke. They were among the remaining few who were willing to take a risk to help their buddy get back on track, even though he was chronically sick, grumpy and unpredictable.

In Essen they also played *Willow Weep for Me* ♦. Bob limited himself to a minimalistic accompaniment, while Oscar Pettiford plucked a long and quiet but impactful and mysterious solo. In the lonely abstraction of his chord progressions, Bob expressed the extent of his suffering: He was physically broken, introverted, silenced. *Sad as I can be, hear me willow and weep for me.*

How different the number sounded tonight. Instead of weltschmerz, I heard detachedness with a dash of dreaminess.

While I was thinking of the concert in Essen and wondering if Bob also compared the then with the now, he stopped playing. Suddenly, in the middle of a phrase, after the last run to the top of the keyboard, Bob played several syncopated chords that cadenced in a refined ending. Then he stood up, walked over to the confused bassist, patted him on the shoulder, and nodded a couple of times. It was a wordless gesture of thanks and recognition. A server helped Bob down the steps from the stage and he came back to our table.

It all happened so quickly that the audience sat in a bewildered silence, as if hypnotized. It seemed like forever until the tension released. Finally, they broke into applause mixed with whistling and calls for an encore. But Bob had already signaled to us that he wanted to leave the club immediately.

* * *

We took the subway back from Minton's Playhouse, first half an hour on the C line to 14th Street before we changed to the L line. Our train wasn't full. A Black man got on, wearing a heavy down jacket, a dark blue bobble hat and shiny chrome headphones. Without paying attention to us, he hunkered down on the wooden bench across from where we were sitting. Two stops later, we were at the northwestern corner of Central Park, the beginning of New York's most expensive neighborhood in. A few young revelers filled the train with their alcoholic presence; they got off after two more stops. Then we were speeding underground beneath some of the city's most important music hubs: Lincoln Center, Sony Building, 50th Street Station, just a block or two from Carnegie Hall and some of the finer jazz clubs, and then the theater district on Broadway and Off-Broadway. The train shook violently; that alone was enough to awaken anyone who'd dared to doze off in the city that never sleeps. Even the man with the bobble hat woke up for a few seconds.

López was still recovering from the intense discussion she'd had with Bob and Amelie. To avoid another outburst, she'd been trying to send Bob positive signals since the beginning of the subway ride. For her, Bob's behavior had been nothing more than an extreme outburst of emotions. No intentional malice, but another one of Bob's out-of-control moments, which were typical of him, although they had become much less frequent over time. López praised Bob's short performance in a few brief but sincere words. Then, to keep the conversation flowing, she turned to Bukar and asked whether he'd enjoyed the show and how he liked jazz in general.

What was Bukar supposed to say? »Yeah, I really liked it. It was my first jazz concert—what an experience! Bebop? It was interesting, but I guess I'd need to listen to more of it to understand it better. It was really cool how well Bob can still play at his age,« Bukar said dutifully.

He knew that his little speech sounded canned, so he started over. »Okay, let me tell you the truth. Honestly, I wasn't really listening most of the time. But, Bob, when you played, I felt totally awake. It was really good and I'm really going to try to warm up to bebop. But there were these long parts that were annoying. First, your absurd argument about who's lower on the social ladder, Indigenous Americans or Black Americans. As if it mattered! You take flak from the top whether you're on the last rung or on the second-to-last one. And then the question of whether a ›white negro‹ or a Korean can play jazz? Why the hell not?«

Bukar was spot on, I felt intuitively, even though he oversimplified a big, controversial issue. Music is not just a matter of technique, but of the meaning within it, of the feeling it conveys, which can't always be imitated or explained. Musicians can only express a feeling with the vocabulary they have under their belt. So the question of how much of Harlem's vocabulary a Korean can understand is not completely irrelevant. Once, Bukar had taken me to an African dance club in Brussels. It wasn't very likely that I would pick up the African rhythms, he'd said—they weren't in my blood. Didn't that opinion apply now?

»So you believe that every Korean, or whoever, can play Highlife or Afrobeat?«

»Touché!« He laughed as he recognized my nasty rhetoric. »The question,« he said, growing serious, »is whether a Korean can play jazz or a white person can play Highlife. The word *can* is the key here. Do you mean every white person or Korean or whoever *may* play, or is *able to* play? Of course anyone may play. That's what I meant when I said, why the hell not? But are they able to do it well? That's tough. Nobody plays Highlife as well as a Nigerian. Okay, maybe someone from Ghana or the Congo. But a white guy? I guess he could at least try to learn it.«

Bob nodded in agreement.

The man in the bobble hat, sprawled out on the bench across from us, suddenly cut in.

»Hey, you from Nigeria, man?«

»Yeah,« said Bukar, his curiosity awakened. »You too?«

»Yep.«

»Whereabouts there?« asked Bukar.

»Near Ibadan,« the man replied. »You?«

Bukar went over and sat down next to him. »From Maiduguri. I'm Bukar. What's your name?«

»Maiduguri. Oh man, crap town.«

»I think the city is okay.«

»But it's a Boko Haram city, isn't it?«

»Yes, unfortunately,« Bukar admitted.

»Sorry, I forgot to introduce myself. I'm Lucas.«

»Hey, Lucas. That's my girlfriend over there with some friends of ours,« said Bukar, pointing to us.

»Your girl is white?«

»Man, Lucas, don't you start, too.«

»With what?«

»Why is everybody always obsessed with just two things? One, she's white. Second, she's female. As if that proves you have a good eye for people. Her gender is pretty obvious, so that only leaves the other important trait, her skin color.«

»Gimme a break. That's important, isn't it?«

»Anyone can see that she's a white woman, just like I can see that you're a Black man. Tell me something else about yourself? What are you doing here? Do you have a girlfriend? Or maybe a boyfriend? Do you believe in God? What are you listening to on those headphones of yours?«

»I'm a taxi driver,« said Lucas.

»You look more like a subway rider,« countered Bukar.

»Yeah, I'm about to start my shift.«

»At this hour?«

»Yeah. Guess why,« Lucas challenged.

Bukar shrugged.

»Because I'm a Black man.«

»Listen, Lucas,« Bob said out of nowhere from our side of the train. »I've been around a lot longer than you. Yes, you're right. Sometimes it's tough being Black. But don't make yourself a victim.«

Lucas sat up straight and stared incredulously at Bob. When a man of his age dished out wisdom, it was only proper to sit up.

»The better part of my life began when I stopped feeling like a victim,« continued Bob. »You're not the only one who drives a taxi at night around here. The Indians do it, the Mexicans, even white guys like the Russians and Ukrainians. They're all victims, but not just because of their skin color. The social system here craps on everyone, not only us Blacks. ›Because I'm a Black man‹—you can say that when the police beat you like they did me. Have you ever felt their clubs on your skull?«

»No, sir.«

»So don't act like you're a victim of a racist system.«

Bukar came to Lucas's defense. »But maybe Lucas is a victim of the system. Lucas, why are you in New York and not with your wife and kids?«

»It's all messed up. After the divorce…« Lucas began.

A now abandoned wing of the
Creedmoor Psychiatric Center

Birdland's original site: Broadway and 52nd street

Minton's Playhouse, around 1940

The Ottendorfer Library (2022)

...its book shelves (2002)

...and the librarian's office on the
second floor (around 1940)

»All messed up. Yeah, I'm sure it's a fucking mess. But it's your own fucking mess. Not the system's. You know, I screwed up in my life, too. My wife, my daughter. But it was on me, not my skin color,« Bob said.

»Man, I don't know what got me down,« replied Lucas. »Was it me or the system? Back home it was my problem. Here it's the system.«

»Do you miss them?« asked Bukar.

»Who?«

»Your wife, your kids.«

Lucas thought for a moment. »Yeah, man, I miss them.«

»A lot?«

»Yeah. A hell of a lot,« Lucas admitted.

»Do you have anyone here to talk to about it?« asked Bukar.

»I guess not.«

»See. That's what I mean. You're an exploited Black male victim of the system. Okay, screw it, fight back, I'm with you. But you're much more than that. You're dealing with your divorce. Maybe you regret it. It's none of my business, but maybe you do. Maybe you're homesick and you want to see your kid again. And did you always want to be a taxi driver?«

Lucas wiped his left eye with his finger. »I went to architecture school. I wanted to be a draftsman.«

»I understand. You must be disappointed that it didn't work out.«

»Yeah.«

»And be honest. Your disappointment doesn't have anything to do with being a Black man, does it?« argued Bukar.

»No, of course not. I know what you're getting at, and you're right.«

»Now about my white girlfriend who has a Black boyfriend. Do you know how much it bothers me when her colleagues say, ›Petra has a Black boyfriend,‹ instead of saying that Petra has a smart boyfriend and he's such a good journalist, or even a terrible journalist, but he's a good dancer, and on Sundays he makes the best pancakes, or whatever. But no. The only interesting thing about him is that he's a Black man. And I don't want to be indiscreet, but I'll say it anyway, Petra will forgive me. When you live with a white woman, you think, oh, today she is as beautiful as the first time I saw her, or today she is in a bad mood, why won't she toss those worn-out pants she keeps wearing, damn, that was not her best cooking tonight, but I really love to smell her hair. You never think, oh, she's white, just as white as she was yesterday and I, goddamit, I'm Black! The more time we spend together, the less important it becomes until you completely forget about skin colors. Unless, of course, little peepers come along and remind you.«

»Ha! You're pretty funny, man. I get you. That helps me.«

»No, brother. I don't know how to help you. But WhatsApp me and we can talk. That might help, don't you think?« offered Bukar.

»Yeah, man, it would.« Lucas glanced out the train window. »I have to get off at the next stop.«

While Lucas plucked a cigarette from his bent-up package, Bukar wrote down his number on a slip of paper and handed it to Lucas as he stepped off the train at 42nd Street. Bukar sat on the bench across from us, his chin in his hands, for a good two minutes before coming back over.

»That's how it is in Nigeria. There are more problems than we know can solve,« he said. We were silent. »The system, the religions, people's personal problems—they all gang up and choke you.« Bukar squeezed his own neck to emphasize his point. »Who has time for a luxury like justice?«

The group remained quiet again. I was about to say something encouraging, but Bukar raised a hand to silence me.

»I was thinking about these things during the concert, too« he said. »I'm sorry for that. Especially sorry to you, Bob. You deserved my full attention. But I can't help it. The day after tomorrow I'm giving a presentation to the legal advisors and NGO representatives. I'm really hopeful. But what if all my hopes are dashed?«

López saw how despondent Bukar was. She went over to him and put her arm around his shoulders. »You'll give your very best presentation. You'll do a good job. And if it's not good enough, you've always got us.«

It was the first time I remembered López approaching Bukar so personally. Her gesture was very kind, and I had the impression that she meant it—that Bukar could count on her.

* * *

The next morning, as I stopped at a bakery on my way to the Ottendorfer, I had a magical, almost embarrassing thought: The future of my dissertation depended on my choice of cake. Would one piece of poppy seed cake and two pieces of fresh fruit cake encourage Tony and Amelie to be patient, open and talkative during our interview on the relationship between music and nationalism—an issue I considered to be very important for my dissertation? But then I reminded myself that Amelie and Tony didn't need to be bribed to engage in a blithe and stimulating discussion, even if they turned snippy and cranky at times.

Amelie and Tony are lucky, I thought as I walked toward the Ottendorfer with the box of cake in my hands. With their immaterial existence, they are free to observe time taking its pickaxe to other people's bodies and minds, without having to worry about age-related ailments themselves.

Tony struck me as particularly warm-hearted. Most of the Bartók biographies I'd read agreed with that. But some also said that he could be much different: shy, pedantic and, most of all, insecure. He was constantly worried about being cheated, they said, about not understanding something or grasping it too late, about being seen as boring or shabby by the upper-class on whose money he depended. They were his main source of income with their commissions, purchases of scores and concert attendance. He was well aware that his hobbies were a source of mockery, particularly his fascination with trains (in New York he also loved steamboats and their timetables) and the Bohemian card game darda. To his critics, these interests were proof of his simple-mindedness.

My experience with Tony was different. I didn't see him as insecure or simple-minded. Perhaps he had grown increasingly self-assured over the years and, as his music became more successful, had freed himself from his dependence on applause.

His upbringing as the son of Bohemian butchers was enough to make him down-to-earth. His music is unmistakably rooted in folk music. Even the most sophisticated works sound simple and natural, not like the laborious result of hard work. Does his naturalness flow effortlessly from his pen as a result of his groundedness, or is it a fancy trick?

And then, the most important question of all: Bartók's sentiments about national music. From my perspective, he was full of contradictions. He was invited to the United States because of his reputation as a nationalist composer, but by the end of his tenure in the United States, one could argue that he was one of the first creators of world music. How ironic. His music does not divide, it brings people together and does exactly what world music is supposed to do: It takes you out into the world and teaches you something about yourself. It shows you how good it can feel to recognize that foreignness is a part of you.

On the way to the Ottendorfer, I also thought about Amelie. She was no less cheerful, but in a very different way. She was warm and caring and tended to reach out to people more than Tony did. I mention that because I didn't expect it. What I'd read about Amy Beach suggested that she was very educated, amicable and interested in nature, but that she was also a rather frumpy daughter of Boston's high society. One biographer suggested that her undeniable talent had been subjugated by the constraints of her social position. Had she been allowed to experience all that she was sheltered from in the early part of her life—namely, academic training and worldliness—then her compositions would have been more original and artistically daring. This judgement applies to Amelie's early work, I think, but less so to her later phase, particularly after the death of her husband. Amelie's musical style evolved considerably over the decades, even though she was only limitedly impacted by major milestones in music history, such as impressionism and atonality. Did her views on music and her outlook in general develop side by side? A difficult question. Amelie tended to oscillate between very pointed, direct comments and thoughtful, but elusive answers.

These thoughts swirled through my head as I walked to the Ottendorfer in preparation for what would be an important, perhaps decisive conversation.

* * *

Neither Bob nor López were there to greet me in the Ottendorfer. Instead, I met Gladys, the intern. I'd only seen her once or twice before, shelving books.

»Hello,« Gladys said with a friendly smile. »Bob's upstairs and López isn't here yet.«

If López wasn't there, then Amelie and Tony obviously weren't either.

»She'll be here in ten minutes,« Gladys assured me, her warm, deep brown eyes telling me not to worry.

I introduced myself, since we hadn't spoken to each other before. She said she knew who I was, while I confessed that I didn't know anything about her. It was embarrassing, actually, since I'd spent so much time in the library already.

Gladys pulled up a chair. »Come, let's chat for a few minutes. I like to talk about music.«

She had studied flute, she said. As she spread out her dark brown fingers on her light blue jeans, they did indeed look delicate and suitable for a flutist. A typical cliché for musicians, I thought, but before I could decide whether the cliché was justifiable or silly, Gladys started telling me her story.

The internship at the Ottendorfer Library was hopefully only temporary, she said. Working together with López was intellectually enriching, she found, and she was getting along better and better with Bob. But at heart, she was a musician. She didn't study music for years to sit at a computer and check the availability of books, fill out forms, write overdue notices, and shelve returned material. She had developed a kind of manic aversion to the latter task because it reminded her that she, too, had been shelved.

Six months ago, at the end of her probationary period, the orchestra management said they had to let her go. I shouldn't believe she was arrogant and thought she was better than she was, she told me with a pleading look, as if she truly feared that I would think poorly of her. She had always known that newcomers to the orchestra didn't have job security. Sometimes it was difficult to fulfill the high expectations. On the other hand, it could be that a player was so good that the orchestra members viewed him as competition or as a threat to the group's routine of inconspicuousness. Their contracts were terminated with polite excuses like ›challenges aligning with a homogenous orchestral sound‹. But in Gladys's case, the story was straightforward. She had overheard two colleagues in the ladies' room saying that she had to leave. She was another one of them who thinks she's untouchable just because she's Black, they said. Grants must have been thrown at her like plastic beads on Mardi Gras, the women complained. The madness had to stop, and the Black girl had to go. Let me handle this, one of them said. She would talk with the others.

The politically correct justification for ending Gladys's probation period was that a critical number of orchestra members felt she lacked the necessary trust and collegiality. In an orchestra that values teamwork, this was a crucial argument. It had nothing to do with her performance, of course. And certainly not with her skin color. They wished her well.

Before I could respond to Gladys's story, she preempted my show of anti-racist indignation. I should avoid generalizations, she said. The days when Blacks like Marian Anderson[22] and Shirley Verrett[23] were openly discriminated against because of their skin color had passed. Progress had been made. No one in orchestras was openly racist anymore, and she knew other female musicians who felt that discrimination against women was a bigger problem these days. Auditions were held anonymously, so it wasn't until the final round that skin color was even revealed—and at that stage it was all about the quality of the playing. And a lot had changed since funding from public and private donors became tied to inclusivity.

But, Gladys added, that didn't mean everything was okay. No, things had become a lot more complicated. Cast in the shadow of visible racism, the kind that led to protests like the murder of George Floyd, there were many situations where racism wasn't overtly apparent to a white person, but was still perceptible to Black people, whom everyday life had equipped with a sixth sense for it. This kind of racism was hard to prove, and therefore all the more perfidious. She said she could tell me dozens of stories about it.

Gladys had done what she could to avoid subtle racism. She had managed to secure a first chair post in a famous ensemble in Switzerland. Europe was more relaxed about race than the United States, but her illusion

---

22   Marian Elina-Blanche Anderson (1897–1993) was an internationally celebrated American alto. In 1939, the conservative women's organization Daughters of the American Revolution prevented her from performing in Washington's Constitution Hall due to the color of her skin. In response, Eleanor Roosevelt, then First Lady and co-author of the Universal Declaration of Human Rights, left the Daughters of the American Revolution and organized an alternative concert. Anderson sang the spiritual *My Soul's Been Anchored in the Lord* at the Lincoln Memorial, in an arrangement by African-American composer Florence Prince, for an audience of 75,000.

23   Shirley Verrett (1931–2010) was an American mezzo-soprano. In her memoir, *I Never Walked Alone*, she described how conductor Leopold Stokowski had to cancel her performance as the Wood Dove in Arnold Schoenberg's *Gurre-Lieder* because the Houston Symphony Orchestra was opposed to having a Black singer. Stokowski went on to support Verrett all the more in other concerts.

was shattered. She watched as influential members of the orchestra's board and their allied media partners accused a Jewish conductor of playing too much Jewish repertoire, such as Ernest Bloch and Leonard Bernstein. That was when Gladys had decided to take advantage of the next opportunity to return to the US, which she did. But when her contract wasn't renewed at the end of her probationary period, she was in despair. She'd been put in the box labeled *Black* and shelved.

A guest in the library interrupted Gladys's emotional monologue. He knocked on the plexiglas divider and gestured that he had a book to return. Gladys wiped her face with her hands, stood up, greeted the customer cheerfully, and said to me, »Go ahead and go upstairs. I'm sure López will be here in a minute.«

»Good. Next time you can tell me more, okay?«

I headed for the stairs.

* * *

We finally found each other on the second floor of the Ottendorfer. López arrived first, then Amelie and Tony came through the sliding glass door that led to the back room where the refrigerator and coffee machine were. Tony was holding a glass of beer. He and Amelie sunk down into the faux leather armchairs next to me. López buzzed around in the background.

Bukar wasn't there this time. It was the day before his talk with the legal advisors and NGO representatives and he was working on his final preparations. He'd told me beforehand that he'd be working day and night.

Bob was neither present nor absent. After bringing us coffee and forks for the cake, he told Gladys he was going to take a break and withdrew to his usual spot—the tiny wooden chair next to the red children's table in the corner.

Our interview began differently than I'd anticipated. I'd just served the cake when Tony dove right in. »Petra, you wanted to hear my advice on developing a national American style of music,« he said.

»Yes, I do, I...« Before I could specify my question, he cut me off.

»Tell me, Petra, what exactly is American music—or, to be more precise, the music of the United States?« He drew out his words and gave me a clueless look, as if he was asking this question for the first time in his life. Baffled, I was at a loss for words.

»If I asked you to name a typical piece of American music, what would you say?« he reiterated.

It felt like a quiz. I hadn't expected the great Bartók to put me on the spot like that, and I searched helplessly for an intelligent answer. »I don't know…from a contemporary perspective …maybe jazz? Or *West Side Story*? I'm sure you mean classical music. Otherwise, Jimi Hendrix would be a candidate. What about your own *New World* Symphony? Then there's Copland?«

As I scrambled for words, an old trick occurred to me. I asked a question in return. Old men love to be seen as a source of knowledge and wisdom. »How about you? What do you consider to be typical American music?«

Tony thought for a moment. »Stephen Foster.«

»Who?«

»Stephen Foster.[24] You know him even though you don't know you do. That's true for most Americans. You are perhaps not aware of my arrangement of Foster's *Old Folks at Home*,[25] but how about *Oh! Susanna* or *Old Black Joe*—do they ring a bell? Foster composed nearly three hundred folk songs. They were simple, respectful tunes written for hard-working white people and Black people. They had a huge impact, even though he remained unknown. Have you ever paid attention to the lyrics of *Old Black Joe*? It's a hymn to the noble spirit of an aging slave. I wasn't the only one to like Foster. Charles Ives[26] often quoted his songs as well. Ives—he would be another quintessentially American composer.«

»So Foster and Ives would be your best examples?« I asked.

»No. Actually, they wouldn't. Foster died young. The Civil War ruined him. He drank too much and died impoverished before the age of forty.

---

24 Stephen Foster (1826–1864) was an American songwriter.

25 Stephen Foster: *Old Folks at Home*, arranged for soprano, baritone, choir and orchestra by Antonín Dvořák (B605, 1893). Dvořák conducted the premiere on 23 January 1894 at a benefit concert organized by the National Conservatory.

26 Charles Ives (1874–1954) was an influential American composer.

And Ives—I don't know. I never met him. I was fascinated by him—posthumously, I guess you could say—you're aware of my, ah, situation. He also subscribed to my vision of a style of music that was deeply rooted in America. But as much as I respect him, I don't see him as a composer who represented the America of his time. He was a remarkable, but also peculiar eccentric. In the end, he only reached his own faithful followers.«

»I understand what you mean. To be the all-American star, Foster lacked commercial viability and Ives was too unconventional,« I summed up.

»Petra, you use harsh words sometimes. But unfortunately, you're right.« I'd passed Tony's exam and felt relaxed enough to make a joke. »So, who's the typical American? Maybe Deems Taylor?«[27] ♦

Tony pounded his thigh and snorted. »Ha! Deems Taylor? My goodness! He was all icing and no cake. What made you think of him?«

»Exactly that. His music—pure sugar, made for the masses. He didn't really have a style of his own, but if you make something sweet enough, it will taste good to anyone. And well crafted, from a technical point of view. Isn't that American?«

»Well, I know what you mean, even though it's not a very nice thing to say,« Tony said. »There were other, more sophisticated composers that were very American. Particularly among the Black community, whose growth and influence I had predicated and supported. Harry Burleigh, William Dawson[28]…«

Amelie interrupted Tony. »Don't forget Arthur Farwell! And especially not Griffes!«[29]

Her comment surprised me. I'd never expected her to be interested in an outsider like Charles Thomlinson Griffes ♦. With his penchant for impressionist music, he was light years ahead of her. But I agreed with Amelie. I, too, held Griffes's work in high esteem.

---

27 John Deems Taylor (1885–1966) was an American music critic, radio presenter and largely self-taught composer.

28 William Dawson (1899–1990) was an American composer and music teacher. Along with numerous works for choir, his *Negro Folk Symphony* (1934) is his most significant composition.

29 Charles Tomlinson Griffes (1884–1920) was an American composer and leading representative of American Impressionism.

»Yes, of course. Griffes too. But the best answer was Taylor,« said Tony, chuckling at our baffled reactions. »And do you know why? Because his terribly commercial, shallow music, his technically perfect kitsch, as you say, is proof that American music does not exist.«

»Jazz?« called Bob from the background.

»Yes, Bob. But I'm talking about classical music. We can talk about jazz another time. Until then, try to pick one of your two versions.«

»What do you mean?« asked Bob.

»Whether jazz is very American, or very Black.«

»Yeah, yeah, another time,« grunted Bob. »When the discussion starts with that kind of either/or, nothing will come of it anyway.« He headed for the coffee maker.

»As I said, there's no typical American classical music,« commented Tony. »And why not? Because, musically speaking, there is no America. America is a melting pot. A huge stew with whites, Blacks and Indigenous people swimming in it. No, seriously, it's even more complicated than that. Not just white and Black people swimming around, but Irish and Italian and Jewish white people, plus African-American and Cuban Black people, and many kinds of Indigenous people. Not to mention, from today's perspective, the Mexicans and Puerto Ricans and Indians and Chinese. People used to put them all in the same box. So did I. My goodness, how uninformed I was. When I met the ›Indian‹ musicians on vacation in Spillville, Kovařík told me they were Kickapoos from the Iroquois tribe. He didn't know what he was talking about, even though he was born in Iowa! I figured it out later. The Kickapoos aren't Iroquois, they're Algonquian, and the Iroquois aren't a tribe, they're a confederacy and besides, the Indigenous people in Spillville came from many different groups. But that's America. Endlessly diverse and endlessly complicated in its diversity. Am I right?«

Amelie and I nodded in agreement.

»And, honestly, when I came to New York, I didn't have any idea how diverse America was,« continued Tony. »I was pretty naive and I thought that I could just transfer European ideas to this country. My home, Bohemia, is culturally homogenous. I assumed that Americans wanted to learn from me what their best, most fruitful common denominator was. And my Bohemian common sense told me that the common denominator is always folk music. I got to know American folk music and found out that I quite liked it. Black and Indigenous folk music have interesting pentatonic melodies, syncopated rhythms, and speak to a broad spectrum of emotions. So, I told them that was the treasure they should nurture. But I wrongly assumed that there was a common denominator among the many different kinds of folk music in America. It wasn't until later that I realized I'd opened a colossal can of worms. Especially in Boston...«

»In Boston? A can of worms makes me think of the Bohemian plums I was served in Munich,« Amelie said disgustedly.

Tony insisted, ignoring her nasty remark. »Especially in Boston. In complacent Boston where choosing the right kind of music was not only a matter of good taste—something that Bostonians certainly had—but also a matter of defending the dominance of the Brahmins. Once at a meeting in Fleischman's Café, Seidl couldn't help but read me what Bülow[30] had to say about Boston after his concert tour. ›Puritanism has frozen art in New England. The Bostonians openly display their apathy. Presumably they reckon it as one of the Fine Arts. But that it is not. It is simply a form of paralysis.‹«

»Tony, don't be so dreadful,« interrupted Amelie.

»But I have to be, Amelie. Refined Boston was on very shaky ground. The cultural dominance of the Irish and the befriended Anglo-Saxons crumbled when a lot of Blacks and Italians and Portuguese suddenly came to Boston. You must have noticed that. And what did you do? You defended your dominance. Black music? No thank you. It had to be Gaelic music. Anglo-Saxon, northern, and with a diploma from Germany. Like the Italians or Swedes or Russians, African-Americans hardly qualified as original Americans, you once said. True. But the Anglo-Saxons, who best suited your view of American music, hadn't they also immigrated at some point, or had they always been in the United States? Do you understand what I'm saying? You were interested in defending the dominance of your ethnic group.«

»How many times must we discuss it? I've already told you a hundred times that I didn't see it like that. I never made a case for a generally accept-

---

30 Hans von Bülow (1830–1894) was a celebrated German pianist and conductor in his day. In 1875, he embarked on two concert tours through the US and Canada.

ed basis of American music. I only said what I considered to be the basis for me. And that's why I wrote my *Gaelic* Symphony.«

While Tony and Amelie were bantering, Bob had pulled his child-sized chair up to our table.

»Ah-ha,« he snarled. »You wrote your symphony for yourself.« He scowled and rubbed his nose. »And the edification of three hundred thousand Irish and Anglo-Saxons was just a coincidental byproduct of your personal project.«

»Bob, composing was always personal for me. I don't believe in composing political manifestos,« Amelie said.

»But when Tony composed his *New World* Symphony as a homage to Black Americans, you had to add your two cents. Stop it, you said, those Blacks don't deserve it. They're not true Americans.«

»Well, I didn't say it like that. And I explicitly added that I did not want my comments to be misunderstood as a criticism of African-American music. On the contrary, I held their melodies, rhythms and expressivity in high regard. I simply found it malapropos that Tony…«

»…as a white guy, interjected Bob.

»Exactly. That he should make use of music from a culture that was not his own.«

»But it was okay for you to make use of ›Eskimo‹ music a few years later?«

»Yes. Because it is indisputable that ›Eskimo‹ music is Indigenous American music.«

»Or because you'd been talking to your friend MacDowell about national music?«

»Edward? What's wrong with Edward? He was completely opposed to national music. Nationalism had no place in music, he said.«

»Yes, he said that. But since he was the only one with that opinion, he also said that if music must be nationalistic, then priorities must be set. ›Why cover American music with the badge of slavery rather than with the stern but at least manly and free rudeness of the North American Indians?‹ That's what he said, isn't it?«

»Well, yes.«

»And what were your thoughts when someone, in his capacity as a cultural insider, that is, a Black person, finally wrote a symphony as an homage to Blacks? After everything I've just heard from you, namely that you like Black music in general and that cultural insiders write better music—wouldn't it have been logical that you'd react positively?«

Amelie paused. »Who do you mean? And which piece?«

»I mean William Dawson's *Negro Folk Symphony* ♦. It's a work that poignantly combines recollections of slavery with the hope of a better future, isn't it? And it was written in a harmonic language that you must have enjoyed, since it is so European.«

»Yes, of course I'm familiar with the symphony, and I like it very much. The end of the second movement is quite creepy. Amidst the muffled, distant pulse of African drums I can almost hear a belly rumbling with doubt about whether the future will ever get better. It's really very moving. And besides, Tony, if you'll allow me a little aside, it goes well beyond your *New World* Symphony in one point. Back then, I had said that it was out of place to write African-American inspired music and make it sound so Romantic. The suffering of the slaves should be audible as well.«

»Well put, Amelie. But the question was how you reacted when Dawson published his symphony. He met all your criteria, didn't he? He was a real-live Black person and wrote skillfully in a Late Romantic style.«

Amelie hesitated. »Actually, I didn't say anything at all. I wasn't aware of it for years. I didn't get to know it until much later.«

»Ah-ha. I sense a contradiction between your noble comments and your behavior.«

Amelie seemed annoyed. »And I sense that you are very unfair and, in the name of your untouchable morality, want to accuse me of something that is not my fault but the fault of our music industry. As you surely know, it has long treated the music of Black composers as second-rate. I can't be blamed for the fact that, back in the 30s, it took some time to get to know the work of a Black composer. Do you think I could have listened to Dawson's compositions back then on the radio or come across them on Idagio or Spotify?«

I appealed to Bob: »Isn't it more important to find out what Amelie would say about Dawson's symphony today?«

Bob swept away my question with a wave of his hand. He still seemed agitated with Amelie, but he dropped their conversation and I changed the topic.

»Let's let bygones be bygones and focus on today. There's something else I've been wondering,« I said. »What role did nationalism play in music and what can we learn about it from today's perspective? That the musical nationalism at the end of the 19th century was on the wrong track?«

»We're much wiser today,« Tony said. »Now we know how catastrophic nationalism can be. But back then? We had no idea how horrible and destructive, both physically and morally, both World Wars would be.« Tony contemplated the past for a moment and shook his head in disbelief. »We believed in nationalism as an organizing principle. A system that guaranteed the self-determination of ethnic groups but also kept a balance between competing nationalisms. I was a citizen of a monarchy in which Austrians and Hungarians held special roles as regents of one half of the empire or the other, and the subordinated Czechs had to please the rulers. It was pretty unfair considering that we were the economic motor of the whole empire. I belonged to a disadvantaged group of people and couldn't help but become a nationalist. I'm sure you, as someone from South Tyrol, can understand how a minority group that feels short-changed clings to nationalism—even to a fault. Nevertheless, that was my political stance, and I don't think I was overly nationalistic. On the other hand, I was always suspicious of aligning music with nationalism. Why? Please be patient—I have to give a bit of background. Why do people make music? Because in music they experience community. People make music when they're celebrating, working or worshipping together. Hermits do not make music. And if they do, then to remember a community they once belonged to. That music is the starting point of my work. The music of the people coming together spiritually. Like the music of Stephen Foster. Honest, open-hearted music that refuses to be shackled by politics.«

I wanted to interrupt Tony, but he kept talking.

»I know what you want to say. Yes, music can be taken captive. There are national anthems, military marches and of course war songs. The *Indianists*, if you'll allow me a side comment, were often overly interested in this kind of music, for whatever reason ♦. But believe me, when simple people sing about war, it's not because they're excited about the next slaughter, but because they're mourning the dead. Again— yes, you're right. Music can be used for nationalistic purposes. I cannot

prevent that. But I can distance myself from it and resist it. Even as a good Czech.«

»Have you always distanced yourself from the use of music for nationalistic purposes?« I asked.

»Unfortunately, not. It wasn't always as easy as you might think. But if I had to live my life over again, I would. At least I would try. Others have managed to.«

»Whom are you thinking of?«

»I'll give you an example. You know Brahms's *German Requiem*. It's called *German* because the lyrics are in German. During Brahms's time, that stirred up a controversy, because German was spoken in the Protestant churches, while the Catholics used Latin. But Brahms's Requiem wasn't meant to be political. Now imagine that Wagner had written a German requiem. With Wagner, I wouldn't have been surprised if the term German had been used to invoke some convoluted idea about the rise or fall of the German people. That's the difference between Brahms's German and Wagner's German.«

That was an interesting example, I thought, but Tony didn't give me a chance to comment.

»You know, Petra, my artistic ambition was always to find recognition as a musician because I am good and not because I am Czech. Consistent, wasn't it? But in the real world, things were often quite complicated. After one of my first successes, the *Slavic Dances*, my publisher Fritz Simrock wanted to market me as a Slavic composer. Okay, good, I thought in my typical naïveté, then let's do that. When the political conflicts between the Austrians and the Bohemians made it opportune to downplay my identity, I went along with that, too. But when my fellow Bohemians started accusing me of kissing the Austrians' asses, well, then I felt I needed to polish my Slavic identity a bit. I was constantly walking on eggshells.«

»And here in America, you were neither an Austrian nor a Bohemian,« I pointed out, cutting off Amelie as she tried to interject another argument. »Was that a remedy, a kind of redemption for you? Is that why you were so happy here?«

»Yes and no,« said Tony, rubbing his forehead thoughtfully. »I could live here without the complicated squabbling in the Austro-Hungarian monarchy. That was a relief. But when I published more works in an American style after my *New World* Symphony, particularly my *Humoresques*, my *American* String Quartet ♦ and my *American* Suite for Piano, the Bohemians accused me of being a traitor! The Bohemian String Quartet, which was one of the best ensembles in Prague at the time, didn't mince words when they told me they would not play my *American* String Quartet. That upset me quite a lot, since I knew its members well and, perhaps more importantly, I had always considered myself a good Bohemian. And that is why, as wonderful as my experience was in the US, I decided to do away with national labels. I am no longer the American. The switch worked. I returned to Prague and America was passé. Black and ›Indian‹ melodies, *Hiawatha*—it was all over.«

»Just as your identity switches had always worked?« I asked.

»Yes.« Tony squinted, looking like he felt obligated to explain himself. »Petra, I understood that your question contained a hint of criticism. But changing identities interested me from an artistic perspective. Politically speaking, I had to be a nationalist. Artistically, I have always been a vagabond. And that's how I still see it.«

I had been waiting for a statement like that one. A vagabond. Yes, a vagabond. In the best romantic sense. A pinch of worldly experience in the footsteps of the poor but free journeyman, and a pinch of Bohème. A bigger picture that I could convincingly work into my thesis.

»Allow me to say something from an entirely different perspective,« López said out of the blue. We all nodded politely. »I already mentioned that my grandfather was a Diné storyteller.«

»Diné?« Tony looked clueless.

»Navajo. We call ourselves Diné. My grandfather used to tell the Diné creation myth, the *Diné Bahane'*. It's completely different from the creation story in the Bible. It revolves around a process of growth. People, or rather the original beings, come into existence by laboring through four different primeval worlds. I say labor because they keep running into trouble along the way. They are chased from one world to the next because of their vices. But here's the interesting part. In the first world, which corresponds to the first day of creation in the Bible, a Holy Wind blows in the darkness, the *Nilch'i Diyin*. It brings about the 'meaning', which will later guide the four early Holy Peoples. So, 'meaning' existed before humans were created in physical form. Hegel would have called it the 'world spirit,' and he would have been thrilled, if I'm not mistaken, but I'm not a philosopher. Now what does all this mean for music? We surely agree that music is a part of the human spirit, a part of human longing that cannot be explained in a material sense, a vehicle to fulfill the human need to communicate things beyond rationality.«

Amelie, the well-read geek, started to quote Arnold Schoenberg.» ›Music can express what words…‹« Tony gestured to her with a discreet wave of his hand that she shouldn't interrupt López.

»Let's stay with Diné mythology for a moment,« continued López. »Music, you might say, is metaphysical and precedes matter. What does that mean? The New strives for the Old, like children do with their parents. The real, material world strives for music, or, I should say, the real world finds symmetry in the aesthetic rules of music. In the Diné culture, symmetry is tantamount to perfection. Conversely this means that music does not strive for the real world, or, to put it more clearly: Music should not allow itself to become a servant of ever-changing political trends.«

I kind of understood what López was trying to say with her intricate imagery. Music should not allow itself to serve the political trend of nationalism. But, to be honest, we were all a bit overwhelmed by the complexity of López's thoughts. Her assumption that the spirit—and with it, music—preceded physical existence, seemed very speculative. Where would this spirit exist if not in a body equipped with senses and intellect? A spirit cannot exist without a body. But I had to admit that people who believed in souls probably had less of a problem with her theories.

I also disagreed with López's implication that music should not serve political trends. I thought of Bertolt Brecht and Kurt Weill. Why should I have a problem with this team using music as a means of mobilizing for a good cause?

And then, pondering what a ›good cause‹ is, I remembered that right-wing rock bands also use music as a tool of mobilization, like Frei.Wild from South Tyrol. There are no steadfast rules for good and bad mobilization through music. It's a matter of political opinion which can and should be discussed.

Despite my misgivings, I was glad I got to hear López's excursion into Diné mythology. Though abstract, it contained a measure of truth that resonated with me. Music, in my opinion, is two things. It is pre-personal. I mean that the most basic forms of music—tone sequences and rhythms—are intrinsic to being human and exist inside of us without training, before our personalities take shape. Second, music is pre-political. Music existed before humans began to organize themselves in political entities.

As a result of these two characteristics, I believe that music is predestined to unite people from the most diverse backgrounds. Everyone likes to sing; everyone likes to tap their foot; everyone likes to dance. And everyone likes to sing, tap or dance with someone else. In other words, excluding others from participating in music would contradict its very nature.

* * *

López had agreed to give Bob a morning off so that he and I could have a longer talk. We'd made an appointment for the morning of Bukar's big presentation to the legal advisors and NGO representatives in the German UN Mission.

I had planned to look over my notes and go over my questions for Bob while I walked the fifteen minutes to the Ottendorfer Library. Instead, there was one question I couldn't get out of my mind. Should I talk to Bob about the strange thing Bukar and I had observed the night before?

Here's what happened. Bukar had been working on his presentation until late in the evening, until his head was spinning. He suggested we take a walk to get some fresh air, so we set off down Second Avenue, then across Astor Place and back via Union Square.

As we approached the Ottendorfer at around eleven o'clock, we saw a small delivery truck parked in front of it. A man was walking back and forth between the truck and the library, struggling to carry heavy boxes of books and load them into the vehicle. He made three trips while we were standing there, but he could have been schlepping for much longer.

Bukar asked me if the person we saw could have been Bob. I said no because I figured it was out of the question. López would never have asked him to do such heavy lifting at his age—and certainly not in the middle of the night.

Then I took a closer look. The box carrier's posture and heavy gait did closely resemble Bob's.

We walked toward the library and waved and called, »Hello Bob!« He didn't come out, and the delivery truck drove off. The job was apparently done. Then we saw through the library's windows that the lights inside had been turned off.

Bukar and I couldn't make heads or tails of it, but we weren't particularly concerned. How should we know who did what in the library at any particular hour of the day or night? It was none of our business.

But when we got to the front of the building, I stopped short when I saw a greeting card lying on the sidewalk. It was small—smaller than a standard envelope—and the delicate handwriting on it was wide, with irregular strokes, and reminded me of my grandmother's. I picked up the card and started reading.

MRS. H.H.A. BEACH
HILLSBORO, NEW HAMPSHIRE

The card was addressed to *My dear Mrs. Clement* and talked about banalities, like which train Mrs. Beach wanted to catch to Boston and where she could be reached—in the Copley Square Hotel. That was it. Amy Beach addressed Mrs. Clement, whom I knew to be a close relative on her mother's side, quite formally, but that was typical of her. Informality was not her thing. She even addressed one of her closest friends, Edward MacDowell's widow,[31] whom she regularly met at the MacDowell's Colony, as ›Mrs. MacDowell‹. I felt all the more flattered that she called me Petra—but, after all, more than a hundred years lie between me and Mrs. MacDowell.

Bukar said aloud what I had been thinking, that the letter must have fallen out of one of the boxes Bob had just loaded. Had Amy Beach's entire correspondence just been removed from the library? Why? And where was it being taken in the middle of the night?

Just before I arrived at the Ottendorfer the next morning, I decided not to ask Bob about what we'd seen. I didn't know anything about it and wasn't entitled to an explanation. At least not before talking with López about it.

Besides, pragmatically speaking, it wouldn't be clever to confront Bob with something that he could take as an accusation. Not when I needed his

---

31   The pianist Marian Griswold Nevins (1857–1956).

help. Remorsefully, I interrupted my own train of thought. Pragmatic like Tony in Boston?

* * *

In general, Bob never says much more than a few words at a time. He has to be in the right mood if he's going to share longer thoughts. The likelihood of that happening increases when the topic is close to his heart, like when he'd told us about racist police violence and his horrible experiences in psychiatric clinics.

Sitting with him on the second floor of the Ottendorfer, I started with a complicated question that I hoped wouldn't leave any room for short answers.

»Bob, when we were sitting with Amelie and Tony yesterday, he said you should tell us whether you see jazz more as Black music or as American music. And you said the question was too either/or.«

»That's right,« Bob said. »Stupid question.« He sipped his coffee and yawned. He obviously thought the interview would be a waste of time if I didn't come up with anything better.

»What would be a better question?« I asked.

I'd really challenged him. He thought about it, but the answer he gave was not really an answer.

»His question was stupid. Strange, wasn't it? He said a lot of smart things though.«

»Yeah, did he? Like what?« I asked.

Bob paused again to collect himself. »Sometimes I think he's a guy like me. Totally different, but also the same. He said he was a Bohemian with all the nationalistic junk that went along with that. He was also a musician, he said, which meant he had to leave the junk behind to become a universalist. And then he said that the financial pressure—you know, from his publisher—sometimes forced him to accept things he didn't really want to accept.«

»And all that reflects your own situation?«

»Man, Petra, what is that question supposed to mean?« asked Bob gruffly. »If you put a mirror in front of a white guy, you're not going to see a Black guy in it.«

I was taken aback by his reply. He didn't have to construct a cultural metaphor out of something so apparent. We couldn't have a normal conversation on those terms. Did Bob think I was culturally insensitive? Or was he just being grouchy?

»But I do see parallels,« he said, overcoming our standstill. »Origin, artistic expression, capitalism. That magical triangle that every artist faces.«

I let his words sink in, since I'd never heard these ideas expressed so succinctly before. »And how did you get along in the triangle?« I pried.

»Badly. I banged my head on everything.«

Bob grew quiet and I didn't ask which corner of the triangle he'd banged his head on. I didn't want to talk again about alcohol, drugs and schizophrenia. I simply waited.

»Petra, I know what you're thinking,« he finally said. »Drunks can't help but be offensive.«

I wanted to say that I didn't want to talk about that, but he rocked his head in an unsettling way and kept talking. »No, no. Sometimes, banging your head is a complicated thing to do. It took me years to make sense of all that.«

Bob took a deep breath, sat up straight and seemed to change the topic again. »You know, Petra, we're talking about identities. Nothing you can put in a tidy, academic box. And if you did, it might be a caterpillar, and what comes out of the box is a butterfly.« He exhaled loudly. »Is jazz Black music? Is jazz the most American kind of music? Yes or no? If only it were that easy! The question depends on undefined premises. What is jazz? What is America? Who is Black? What is Black music?«

»So tell me,« I said, seeing my chance to cut in. »What does it mean for you as a Black man to play music called jazz?«

»There we are, back at Dvořák,« said Bob. »He is a Bohemian and a musician. I'm a Black man and a musician. What does it mean that I'm Black? When my ancestors were dragged off to America as slaves, they didn't say to themselves, I'm Black. I'm African. They said, I'm from this or that clan in this or that village in this or that kingdom. I am a bit lighter or darker skinned or thinner or stockier or a better shepherd or hunter or blacksmith or musician than the neighbors. It was the slave trade that labeled my ancestors as Black, that shoved them into a group of creatures whose origin, religion, language, and music were completely diverse but who, in the eyes of the slave holders, had two things in common: the color of their skin and their low status among human beings. These things gave the slave holders their right to exploit us. And even though at first we all believed, spoke and sang differently, our fate as slaves bonded us together. We grew closer and closer until we became one big family of brothers and sisters and sooner or later we had a common language and music, born in American's melting pot. Not in the multicultural porcelain bowl that doesn't really exist, but in the raw, racist melting pot of slavery that reeked of burning skin. We were pressed into a big, catch-all group of Blacks. Our African origins are too diverse to trace today. But after racism had stirred us up in a Black soup, we made the best of it. We developed our pride, we believed in our advancement and we put our own stamp on this country. No one can deny that music in the US would be much different if we hadn't come here. Plantation songs, blues, ragtime, jazz…you know what I mean. So does that make jazz our Black music? Well, yes. And no. Yes, its very existence is uniquely tied to us Blacks. I'm not talking about formalities. Diatonic melodies, syncopations, the flatted fifth that's so essential to bebop. Formally speaking, jazz borrowed a lot of things from white people, like harmonies and instruments. No, I'm talking about something else, about the unique connection between jazz and the existence of us enslaved and disenfranchised Blacks.«

I wondered whether Bob should have been talking about African-Americans all along instead of Blacks. For Bukar, jazz didn't hold the same significance. But I understood what Bob meant.

»Do you know what I'm saying, Petra?« he asked, rubbing his hand over his head. He seemed to be begging me to understand him. »Jazz is more than a stew made in the multicolored melting pot. It's the music that expresses how we Black people experienced that melting pot, how it defined our existence with all of its contradictions and shortcomings—our existence in the past, the present and the future,« Bob said. »Glorified memories of a lost homeland. Slavery. And today, music can be a form of revolution, of our pride. Our vision of a better future.«

Bob spoke viscously, much more slowly and arduously than it looks when his words are written down. His pauses were excruciating. He would search for a thought, wince at the pain it caused when he found it, and then spit out a few words.

»Do you remember me and Amelie arguing about William Dawson? You'll find everything I just said in his *Negro Folk* Symphony.«[32]

»But the symphony has nothing to do with jazz,« I pointed out.

»Good point,« Bob said. »That brings me to my no. Let me explain. Music, I think, is not some DNA that someone gave you whether you wanted it or not. Music is an expression of life experience. We Blacks have had—and still have— experiences that are different from other people's experiences. But being different doesn't mean we can't share or talk about our experiences with others. Those who understand what we went through, or at least seriously try to, can express it musically, even if they are not Black themselves. We used to call them ‹white negroes‹; you heard me mention them before. I never had a problem with them.«

That's right. Bob had already told us how much he'd enjoyed playing with white musicians like Niels-Henning Ørsted Pedersen or Pierre Michelot.

»So why should I have a problem with Dawson, as a Black person, expressing himself in a language that is not his own, but a foreign language he's learned fluently? Again, I'm not talking about compositional technique. The building blocks of jazz are not purely Black, just like the building blocks of European music are not purely white. Over time, they have all merged together. I'm talking about the expression of experiences. As a Black man, I identified most with bebop. But if you can express your experiences just as authentically in another language, then do it!«

»Bob, what about your triangle,« I said. »You seem to be doing all right between the corners called ›origin‹ and ›artistic expression‹. I mean, without banging your head on them.«

»That's because I am replaying my life experiences on fast-forward. Day-to-day life was more complicated back then. Most of my opinions were controversial, even among colleagues, and among other Blacks.«

»For example?«

»For example, is bebop jazz? To put it differently: How much sophistication jazz can afford. When someone like me says that jazz reflects the African-American existence, that it gives us confidence in ourselves and in

---

32 The three movements of the symphony are: I. The Bond of Africa, II. Hope in the Night, and III. O Let Me Shine!

our abilities, then there are strings attached. First of all, it presents us with a duty to keep developing jazz and proving ourselves. You have no idea how important that was. When I was a kid, white people said that jazz was primitive dance music, that it belonged in shady clubs, that it wasn't sophisticated. Amelie believed that, too. Duke Ellington fought against that kind of ignorance. He composed African-American music that would win the respect of the experts in classical Western music ♦—although he did it by making huge concessions to the classical idiom. Other jazz musicians trained to be virtuosic and sophisticated and made fewer compromises than Duke did. Like Art Tatum. Bebop pushed this trend to the max. Technically, harmonically, rhythmically, it was extremely demanding stuff.«

»Do you mean that bebop was the culmination of jazz?« I asked.

»No, Petra, you're simplifying things again. There is no culmination in music, because everything always keeps developing. But bebop was a high point in jazz's quest to prove the musical equality of Black people.«

»So bebop is a very valuable form of jazz.«

»Yeah, that's what I say. And others, too. But there are those who say, my goodness, that is supposed to be Black music? Which Black person would listen to that?[33] Do you beboppers want to create a new musical elite? Don't you see what will happen if you strive to fulfill the expectations the white establishment has placed on art music? If you attribute more significance to one person's talent as a composer than to the improvisational talent of an ensemble—doesn't that undermine the very elements that had set jazz apart from classical music? You are betraying your beginnings, your Black foundation, and your effort to be socially subversive!«

Bob had worked himself up and needed a short break. He took a sip of water. His monologues were taking a toll on him.

»When a friend of mine told me that for the first time, you can imagine how frustrated I felt. With my music I wanted to achieve something for the Black community that I couldn't achieve with the white concert repertoire—Bach, Debussy, Chopin. I had pored over Hughes's poems and

---

33 According to a study published by the National Endowment for the Arts in 1982, jazz was primarily popular among young, white, urban individuals with above-average levels of education and income.

newspaper articles. For him, bebop was pure subversion.[34] And I wanted to be Mr. Subversive! Me and the others—we wanted to free our music from the stereotypes of the big bands and their feel-good Black music. Abstraction! That was the trend. Norman Lewis had started painting abstract works. He was tired of filling his canvases with African ornaments. Look, people! We Black artists are hip, we're not primitive! And then someone came along and said, hey, you're a traitor. That knocked me for a loop.«

Bob tensed his mouth to control the nervous twitch at the corner of his lip. He was brimming with emotion.

»And today?« I asked. »How do you see that criticism now? I mean, more young Black people listen to hip-hop these days than to jazz.«

»Yeah, unfortunately. I should have known that would happen. Dizzy Gillespie organized a tour with his band through the Southwest in 1945. A total flop. The people wanted blues, something they could dance to. But now, with a little distance, I don't see it as such a tragedy anymore. Nothing is forever. Young people always chase the latest fad. We beboppers overtook swing, free jazz came after bebop, then there was hip-hop. They all wanted the same thing we did. To play more than music—to play an attitude. I get that hip-hoppers are after that, too, and in that sense, I can relate to them. But their music…oh well. That too shall pass. Everything does. And that's how it was for us. In the end I think we did achieve something. Less for ourselves and more for the reputation of Black music and for the ability of Americans of all stripes to make music together. But personally, I really felt knocked on the head.«

»What do you mean?«

»The third corner of the triangle. Capitalism.«

»What was so bad about it?«

»We beboppers managed to hold up to the pressure for a while. The clubs and the recording industry wanted to twist and bend us so that we'd

---

34 An excerpt from James Langston Hughes's poem, *Montage of a Dream Deferred* (1948):

Listen to it closely:	(...)
Ain't you heard	Hey, pop!
something underneath	Re-bop!
like a– –	Mop!
What did I say?	Y-e-a-h!

go over well with the audiences at the finer clubs in Midtown. Indie labels published our live recordings and studio albums. Hermann Lubinsky, the head of Savoy Records, was a real genius. With hardly any money but a lot of idealism, Savoy Records managed to achieve a lot. They were really good. And they were good friends. But then, at the end of the 40s, our market value went up, and I fell into the grinder of the free market. In 1953, after one of my stays at Creedmoor, I was declared legally incompetent. Oscar Goodstein, the manager at Birdland, was named my legal guardian. I think I mentioned him when we were at Minton's. Lucky for Oscar! I was labeled crazy, but people still wanted to hear me play, so he could offer me contracts and sign them himself on my behalf. After he'd jacked up the price with an article in *Ebony* magazine, of course. The article said that clubs from San Francisco to Toronto were offering me a thousand dollars a week. So for a while Oscar made sure I didn't drink and always looked snazzy and then what did he do? He got Audrey Hill to seduce me. She'd been described as a buxom, music-loving white girl from Los Angeles. In August 1953, I married her without knowing who she really was: the babysitter Oscar had picked for me. When everything was going fine and I looked snazzy and didn't drink, she took off. Oscar was pulling all the strings. He took care of business and made sure I didn't overdo the booze but drank just enough to keep my motivation. Anything that was good for business. I didn't get squat out of it except that I ran myself into the ground in an *accelerando* tempo instead of *andante*, if you know what I mean. Alfred Lion, the founder of Blue Note Records, said I was an oversized talent trying to function in a materialistic society riddled with prejudice. He couldn't help me either. Alfred was a really nice guy. Maybe too nice. We'd go to the cinema sometimes. He stuck with me even after I tried to stab my cat right in front of him. Once I saw him cry. He'd found me lying in the dirt under a parked car. I'd hid there for no reason at all, apparently. He knew that I felt completely alone, and that my music was the only connection I had between my wounded feelings and the real world.«

I sat there speechless before this staggeringly helpless, sorrowful man, who had just unveiled his complicated psyche to me. After so many terrible experiences, he had learned with time to be wiser, more deliberative, more reasonable, even regarding his own mistakes. But had his wounds ever healed? If they had, why would he—out of anger or jealousy—have gotten rid of Amelie's correspondence?

»Thank you for being so open. What a story! A chapter of music history tattooed on your skin. Thank you for sharing it with me.«

Bob was stoic. I didn't know what else to say.

»Still in pain? Still angry?« I finally asked.

»Not like I used to be.«

»But enough to want to punish those who didn't have to suffer?«

»Yeah.«

That was all I needed to know.

* * *

Leaving the Ottendorfer after my interview with Bob, I was torn between two desires: justice and mercy. Should I tell López about what Bukar and I had seen in the night? That it had apparently been Bob who had taken Amelie's documents from the library?

I had felt very sorry for Bob during our interview. His closing words sounded a lot like a confession. López had a right to know what had happened to Amelie's stored correspondence, but I couldn't betray Bob. The truth could wait. Or couldn't it? I thought about what Bukar would say about letting the truth wait, then turned around and went back inside the Ottendorfer.

Bob looked at me inquiringly as I walked past him. I muttered that I wanted to say goodbye to López. When I got to her office, I gestured that we should keep our voices down because I had something confidential to say. Then I told her what Bukar and I had seen.

»I'll deal with it,« she replied quickly, without even stopping to think about what I'd told her. »Leave it to me to decide when I will speak with Bob and Amelie about it, okay? It doesn't concern you. You've seen how easily Bob is affected by trouble and stress. I've promised to make sure Bob survives. I'm committed to my promise.«

I had not expected such a clear, curt answer. »Even after he treated you so poorly at Minton's?« I challenged. So much generosity seemed a bit extreme, even for someone like López.

»Yes, of course,« she said, looking at me blankly. »A promise is a promise, isn't it? The impatience of an old, sick man or even the desire for revenge—why should anything stop me from keeping my promise?«

A promise is a promise. To whom did she promise to save Bob's life by protecting him from trouble and stress? To Fran, or to Charlotte Hubach? Or merely to herself?

Just a couple of minutes later, López escorted me down the stairs. The moment we reached the door, Bukar came up the steps looking very upset.

»I could strangle her!« he growled furiously.

López seemed confused. She didn't know what he'd been doing, but I did, and I suspected that June had spoiled Bukar's presentation at the German UN Mission.

»Let's go to the cafe across the street and you can tell me all about it,« I suggested.

Bukar was so agitated he couldn't think straight.

»It all started so wonderfully, until that woman…«

López interrupted him. »Okay, come on, let's go back inside.«

We walked up the stairs to López's office, where she started dishing out orders. She told Bob to take his lunch break early and sit in the doorman's office, and asked Gladys to go get us three Vesuvio pizzas from the pizzeria down the street. Bukar started talking as soon as we sat down.

»It started so wonderfully. Walter—you know, the German legal advisor, said a few introductory words that mainly focused on his article in the University of Michigan's *International Law Journal*. The International Criminal Court had the authority to try Boko Haram's crimes, even though acts of terror were not explicitly listed in the court's statute, he said. And it was of course also able to try any criminal activity by the army. With his brief introduction, Walter wasn't trying to show off his own academic achievements, he was paving the way for me to talk by rebutting a few concerns up front. Then a French woman from an NGO called Coalition for the International Criminal Court took the podium. Her statement was also very helpful. It is well known that the ICC has already conducted preliminary investigations into the events in Nigeria. What's important now, she said, is that the court didn't bail out at the half-way mark. It shouldn't get distracted by conflicts that were more prominent in the media, like Syria, for example. I was happy to see that Joshua was there. He's the Nigerian legal advisor, but he didn't say anything in this case. If he had, it would have been to sing the praises of the Nigerian justice system. But Joshua is a good guy; he wouldn't stoop to that. I met up with him a few days ago and told him what I was doing here. He told me not to expect him to agree with me in public. He couldn't afford to do that. But he wouldn't do anything to stop me either. Sometimes silence really is golden. Then it was my turn to present. I wasn't nervous at all, because I knew it was my big chance. My whole body and brain knew they had to do their job, and they did. My first slide showed the sites of Boko Haram massacres along with the number of victims at each site. I felt that some people in the room got a sense of the scale of the problem for the first time. On the second slide, I showed that Shekau openly confessed to committing war crimes and violating the Qur'an in the past, and that he plans to repeat his crimes. This had an impact on some of the legal advisors from Islamic countries. The third slide outlined how the Baga massacre unfolded. On the fourth slide, I gave a chronology of how the Boko Haram crimes and the insufficient reaction from the government have led to political disillusionment. As a result, politics have radicalized so much that the government is becoming more and more authoritarian. Then I made a brief plea that I'd memorized down to the very last word. I explained why the International Criminal Court was the best answer for Nigeria and why it needed to act now. By considering legal evidence, it could determine which crimes had taken place and provide an officially documented version of the truth. It could try not only Boko Haram for its crimes much better than the Nigerian judicial system could, but also the Nigerian army for its criminal acts of revenge. I know that's very important for many Nigerians. And the court can do something that no other tribunal can: It can give the victims an official status in the trial and offer them the possibility of monetary compensation.«

Bukar paused to take a sip of water.

»Well, that all sounds really good,« I said as he waved his arm in the air and continued.

»Yeah, the beginning was good. But then, during the discussion, June was one of the first to raise her hand.«

»June?« asked López.

Bukar explained who she was and what ideas she and her NGO represented, then mimicked her comment, putting on an arrogant tone: » ›With all due respect for your efforts,‹ June said, ›it's been sufficiently proven that retributive justice is pointless. So that makes me wonder why you're still talking about it.‹«

»What is retributive justice?« asked López.

»In a nutshell, retributive justice punishes perpetrators, while restorative justice heals them,« explained Bukar.

»But if healing is the alternative, wouldn't that make it the better choice?« countered López.

»Yes,« said Bukar, »if it's the alternative. But in reality, it's not the alternative. I warned the audience not to pit retributive and restorative justice against each other. They're not opposites. In real life, they go hand in hand. Perpetrators are not locked up or fined just to punish them. They are punished as a warning that breaking the rules can have serious consequences. If the warning works, the result is the 'restorative' hope that the perpetrator will stop committing crimes. Then June claimed I'd spent too much time at Western universities, and asked why I, as an African, didn't know that the wish of the African victims was not to punish the perpetrators but to receive material or non-material reparations. African victims were generous people, she said, willing to let the perpetrators go unpunished or even to forgive them. At this point, the discussion got really toxic. I tried to steer June's comments in the right direction. The few African advisors in the room were nodding their heads with her, as if June had given them the opportunity to celebrate an idealized African identity.«

»So it's not true that forgiveness is more important than punishment? Isn't grace a core value of Christianity and, correct me if I'm wrong, but also of Islam?« asked López.

»I'm glad you asked,« Bukar said. »That's a topic that can be confusing. An individual can forgive. Your religion and mine, and probably many others, ask us to do so. But what does that mean? Nothing more than setting aside our hate and desire for revenge. But in the judicial system, it's not about an individual coming to terms with something that has happened, rather about a community reaffirming its views of right and wrong and taking action to prevent future infringements. As an individual, the common interest is not at your disposal, neither through your forgiveness nor through your unwillingness to forgive or your eternally burning hate. In other words, justice is not a private matter.«

»I see what you're saying. But what about June's other assertion that African victims expect reparations and are willing to forgo a punishment?« asked López.

»I want to be totally honest,« Bukar said. »There is no clear answer to that. My impression is that the Boko Haram victims do expect the perpetrators to be punished. But they also expect material restitution from them. That is particularly true for people whose houses were destroyed or plundered, or whose livestock was killed or stolen. But for many of the Boko Haram crimes, restitution is illusory. Money cannot bring back the lives of the murdered, whether they are mainstream Muslims or Christians. Or think of a woman who is abducted, then forced to marry one or several different Boko Haram fighters, gets pregnant, and has a baby. When she returns to her village, she is disgraced. Money cannot remove her stigma. The only way to restore her honor is to ensure that the rape that led to an innocent child is denounced as a crime. June said that the 'horrible and extremely regrettable' problems in Nigerian society could only be overcome if every affected Nigerian looked within themselves, grew spiritually, and accepted and forgave their neighbors. Thank you, June, I thought, in the name of all the women who've been raped, that you blame our problems on spiritual underdevelopment. After she repeated a few of her arguments, she pulled out her best conversation-stopper. She said it didn't make sense to discuss a Boko Haram trial until a poll had been conducted among the victims to find out how they wanted the Boko Haram crimes to be dealt with. Did they even want a tribunal? ›Can you deliver?‹ she asked me provocatively. ›If not, forget it!‹ That put me on the defensive. Of course it's not a bad idea to ask the victims what they want and how they would like justice to be served. But there, too, the devil is in the details. Here's a simple example. Who should participate in the poll? Anyone on both sides of the conflict who has ever experienced injustice? And then, should the poll differentiate between victims who experienced the murder of their relatives, or the destruction of their house, or impressment or rape? Or would it be sufficient to survey a representative group of people? If so, then how do you identify that group? Here's another example. How do you poll people who were both perpetrators and victims? People usually want other people to atone for their wrongdoings, but how many of them are willing to do it themselves? Take an average soldier. He could be a perpetrator. But he could also be a victim of a Boko Haram bombing, or a victim of his superiors who sent him to fight without the right equipment because they sold his weapons, his ammunition or his radio and pocketed the cash. I mentioned one point that June avoided, although she was certainly aware of it. Surveys like the ones she was talking about have already been conducted in a few towns in Nigeria. The results, it seemed, were very ambiguous. In Bama in 2014, Boko Haram murdered in cold blood civilians lying on the ground and then burned down the town. A large majority of the people surveyed there said that compensation was important, but that it was more important to punish those responsible for the crimes. But, in the interest of peace, the people were willing to forgo punishment and grant amnesty. That's pretty confusing, isn't it? My interpretation is that the survey participants differentiated between their short-term and long-term expectations. In the short term, everyone obviously wants the violence to stop. But in the long term, they felt it was important to punish the perpetrators. Some of those surveyed even explained why. Punishment is a deterrent, they said, so without it there was no guarantee that the violence wouldn't flare up again.«

López was spellbound. She found the new subject interesting and seemed to admire Bukar's idealism. I remembered that, on our way back from Minton's a few days earlier, she'd been particularly empathetic when Bukar had expressed his frustration.

»Bukar, this all makes sense to me,« she said. »It's fascinating how you explain all the ifs, ands, and buts. You're very professional and convincing, at least for me. June wasn't convinced, but what about the other participants? What did they say?«

»A few people made comments to support me. Most of them were legal advisors or NGO representatives who admire and support the International Criminal Court. But, honestly, there were also a lot of cowards who didn't say anything or didn't take a clear position at all. One legal advisor, I think from Morocco, told me and June that we should work out our differences between the two of us. Even Walter tried to be diplomatic. He said he agreed with my arguments, but that the point of the meeting wasn't to pick one side or the other. The ICC would decide for itself what it was going to do, he said. The meeting was a place to exchange ideas.«

»Do you think you achieved anything for your cause?« asked López.

»Honestly, no,« Bukar said, lowering his eyes.

»Okay. Then we have to do something about it,« said López energetically.

»What can we do?« asked Bukar.

»Man, Bukar, do I have to spell it out for you? You're the journalist,« she replied. »Use the power of the press!«

»But how?«

»Let's meet this afternoon here in my office. In the meantime, you'll need to think of a few stories that you can remember really well. Boko Haram victims pouring their hearts out, sharing their hopes. Try to remember exact quotes.«

»But I can write a heart-wrenching story on my own,« said Bukar.

»Of course you can. But let's work together anyway. It'll go faster. You tell me the stories or write down passages if you have time. I'll make sure they fit the house style of the *New York Daily*. During my time as a ghostwriter, I was well connected with some of the long-time editors there. If I send them something, they won't turn it down. I'm sure of it.«

»Really?« Bukar's eyes glistened. He could hardly believe his luck.

»Sure. Think about it from a practical standpoint. You can't sit at your computer all week. You have to go back to the UN and lobby for your cause. If you disappear now, you can forget the whole thing.«

Bukar shook his head in disbelief and gratitude for the old lady's panache.

»So we have a deal?« asked López.

»It's a deal.«

»Good. Then I'll see you this afternoon. Come well prepared.«

* * *

Amelie and I had agreed to meet at Pete's Tavern that afternoon so we wouldn't bother López and Bukar at the Ottendorfer. I was more eager than ever to get a few secrets out of Amelie, not only as a researcher but also as a woman.

When the bar opened at four o'clock, I was the first customer. As usual, Anglo-Saxon folk music was playing softly in the background. I sat down at the table where I'd first met López. My office in a bar. I could hardly wait for Amelie to show up. She'd promised to bring me something special.

At half past four, Amelie still hadn't arrived. I started to get worried. Was she not there because she could only appear with López, who was meeting with Bukar? That couldn't be, my ghost instincts told me. López knew that Amelie and I were supposed to meet here. She would have come up with a magic solution if our arrangement wasn't in compliance with her rules of witchcraft.

I couldn't call Amelie. She had a cell phone, but she never charged it because she hated the thing. Maybe Gladys or Bob would be able to help me. When I called, Bob was even less talkative than usual. He basically said that Amelie had dug around in the safe and then left, but in fewer words. I interpreted that to mean that López had not yet spoken to her about the disappearance of her documents, but neither had she spoken with Bob.

A few moments later, Amelie came. Through a window in the bar, I watched her get out of a cab at the corner and cross the street. Her plump figure quavered as she strode quickly but strenuously. Her braided purse, which always seemed so old-fashioned to me, bobbed arrhythmically at her side.

I noticed right away that Amelie was discombobulated. She greeted me with a wave of her hand and ordered a Baileys at the bar while walking toward me. She unbuttoned her light grey blazer as she sat down.

»The letters I wanted to bring,« Amelie wheezed, still out of breath, »they're gone!«

I pretended I didn't know what she was talking about, just as López had asked me to. »Your correspondence with Farwell?«

»That and everything else. It's all gone! All of it!«

»What else?«

»The letters from Arthur Farwell, from Béla Bartók…and…oh, yes, Marian MacDowell and Ethel Hier from the Society of American Women Composers. And there were many drafts of my letters to friends and acquaintances. They're all gone!«

I did my best to calm her down. »Are you sure the letters were in the safe? When did you last see them?«

She thought for a moment. »More than twenty years ago, I'd say. It must have been in 2001, after the renovation of the library. You're probably thinking what a long time ago that was. So much could have happened since then. But could it have? The safe behind the bookshelf is inaccessible.

López or the doorman would have noticed if someone had tried to open it.«

Just as I was going to ask Amelie what she was going to do about it, like call López or the police, she changed the topic.

»But I brought you something nevertheless, from home, not from the safe,« she said, digging around in her purse. She pulled out a folded sheet of staff paper, flattened it out and handed it to me. I could see that it looked like a piece for piano. »My very last composition!«

I took the page with both reverence and uncertainty. What I saw did not look anything like a work by Amy Beach. There was no identifiable key, the notes on the page were scarce, it was only twelve bars long, and the title was in a language I did not understand. I thanked Amelie profusely, wanting to know more about the unusual composition.

»I see you're surprised. Indeed, the piece has a special story that I want to tell you. You'll learn a lot about me.«

My curiosity grew.

»Béla Bartók was perhaps the most difficult, most sensitive, but also the most honest and authentic person I've ever met. Unfortunately, I knew him just for a short time.«

»You mentioned that before. When and where did the two of you meet?« I asked.

»It was the spring of 1927, in March, I believe. I met him in New York in the studio of my friend Ethel Hier. She was also a very good composer, by the way. Bartók and his friend, the renowned violinist Joseph Szigeti, were touring the United States. They played in Ethel's studio for quite a discerning audience. Ethel had a good nose for new music, and she was particularly interested in avant-garde. We listened to Bartók's Second Violin Sonata, then the *Hungarian Folk Songs* ♦,[35] and finally his *Peasant Songs*. I spoke with Béla after the concert. His violin sonata was horrible, but back then I thought everything modern was horrible. However, I liked the other two pieces, since I appreciated folk music so much. Frankly, Béla's approach to folk music was—how shall I put it?—a lot more

---

35 Béla Bartók: Five pieces from his piano cycle *For Children*, arranged for violin and piano by Joseph (József) Szigeti (1926). Historical recording with Béla Bartók and Joseph Szigeti.

refined, unspectacular, selfless than mine. But I didn't realize that until we started corresponding in 1927.«

If those letters were truly lost, I thought, then it was all the more important for her to tell me about them so that I could write about what she said in my dissertation.

»What did you correspond about?« I asked.

»I can't really say exactly any more. That is, I cannot distinguish between what he wrote me and what he said during his lectures at Harvard in 1942 and 1943.«

»You met him again at Harvard?«

»Yes and no,« Amelie said. »I went to a number of his lectures and was very impressed. But at the same time, I avoided direct contact with him. It had only been three years since my heart attack, and I was in poor health. Maybe you don't know about that. Today, I'm still rather stocky, but back then I suffered from being quite overweight. I dragged myself to the lecture hall against my doctor's orders. That was hard enough. The stress of a conversation would have been too much.«

»But why were you so interested in Bartók's lectures?« I asked.

»As I said, he was an impressive person in his own way. So uncompromising about everything—not just artistically, but also politically. Everything flowed together for him. He emigrated to the United States from fascist Hungary, even though he didn't have to. But he was convinced that, as a humanist, he needed to make a statement through emigrating. He called art the spearhead of humanity, saying that was why he had to be political. He was humble and shy, though, and admitted that he never really wanted to be vocal about politics. Bartók as the spearhead of humanity. Picture him coming as a refugee to New York in 1940, a country where he was only famous in certain circles and where his style was considered even more modern than it was in Europe. He passed up concert invitations, composition commissions, help from his few local admirers, and why? Because he had more important things in mind. He wanted to complete his life's work. The systematization of several thousand Serbo-Croatian and Turkish folk songs. He said he owed it to the common people who permitted him to record their songs. He owed it to the body of research conducted on the origin of music. He did not compromise!«

»And that's what he talked about in his lectures?« I asked.

»He was much too humble to celebrate his own achievements like that. But neither did he talk much about his political views. We wrote about those later. In his lectures he talked about many other things that directly impacted my creative process, like the relationship between musical tradition and modernity. Once a musical revolutionary, Bartók now considered a revolution impossible. He said it in such a sad way. Perhaps because he had wanted to be a revolutionary outsider in his younger years, or because he was simply always sad, or maybe he only sounded sad because he had such a weary, shy voice. Or maybe he was already very, very ill at that point,« said Amelie.

»But there were musical revolutionaries,« I pointed out. »Arnold Schoenberg, for example.«

»I'm glad you brought up Schoenberg,« she said. »Béla mentioned him in his lectures as an example for the impossibility of a real revolution. Even Schoenberg didn't manage to write music without relying on the musical foundations that had been laid before his time. If artistic revolution means doing away with everything that came before, then there cannot be one, said Bartók. Humans are not capable of perceiving something new without some connection to what preceded it, he said. In one lecture, he explained it like this: Just as our eyes are not capable of perceiving two completely different images at the same time, neither are our ears able to hear two tones without constructing a tonal relationship between them, thus creating a tonal system.«

»So you can't negate the past, even if you reject it?« I asked.

»No. Béla says that, at least.« She paused, then added, »And so do I.«

I wondered whether this insight could be valid beyond musicology, but kept my musings to myself.

»As you know,« continued Amelie, »Béla wrote music that went beyond conventional tonality. But in his lectures, he maintained that his music was neither atonal nor polytonal. He called it polymodal.«

I admitted that, even as a musicologist, I found it difficult to differentiate between these terms. Amelie laughed sympathetically.

»That's how I felt, too,« she said. »What Bartók meant is this: His music does not use just one tonality, nor does it use two tonalities simultaneously; then it would be polytonal. Instead, it combines various musical styles with their respective tonal patterns, including the folk music that is so elementary for him and different strands of post-classical modern. Béla's music is not ethnographic or Classical or avant-garde, it is all of them at the same time, and that is what makes it typically Bartók.«

My head whirred with a thousand thoughts. I dwelled on my dissertation and wondered whether it would be easier if my advisor had given me Bartók and not Bartók and Beach as the harbingers of the contemporary debate on identity politics. I quickly cast the thought aside. The intellectually stimulating crisscross of European, Black and Indigenous American music would have been lost. On the other hand, I was fascinated by how Bartók's music, teachings, and biography had outlined great truths decades before the current identity debate. Identities are hybrids. My contemplations went a step further. Are identities not always hybrids?

»This all led to Béla challenging me quite directly in one of his letters,« continued Amelie. »He wrote, ›Take the next step. I know and admire your *Five Improvisations* for Piano ♦ which must be the most modern works you've ever written. But keep going. Connect everything you've learned musically, and don't overdo your romantic tendencies. Write a piece that is only one minute long.‹ I was amazed and, frankly, a bit annoyed. I found that I had already come a long way on the musical reduction path and didn't need any admonishing. But I also thought, why not? So I followed his suggestion. The piece is exactly one minute long. The melody and the accompanying chords are based on the repetition of a very simple pattern: half-steps, sevenths, plus the interval between them, that is, the perfect fourth. The result is constant dissonance to which the listener quickly becomes accustomed, and which is not in the least obtrusive. You could say it's a pleasant dissonance. I had never composed anything like it before, but I nevertheless identify with this little piece that is not at all shocking—on the contrary, it is almost poetic. The Hungarian title contains Bartók's parameters and my impish comments. *Túl rövid (Egy perc)*. That means, *Too Short (One Minute)*. Here's the piece—for you.«

I thanked her and promised to practice it as soon as I could. »Has it ever been published?« I asked.

»No, unfortunately not. It disappeared in Bartók's estate. I'd forgotten about it myself, actually, until it turned up just a few years ago,« she said.

»Would you say that your relationship with Bartók impacted you as an artist?« I asked, curious to learn more about him.

Túlrövid (Egy Perc)

Amelie wavered. She made eye contact with the waiter, pointed to her empty glass, and ordered another Baileys. There was an awkward silence until her drink arrived. While she collected her thoughts, she twirled the glass between her palms. My question seemed to have struck a nerve. Yet again, it seemed that Amelie didn't like talking about her feelings. Finally, she spoke, carefully.

»My first impulse is to say no. We met too late in my career for a real change to occur. Besides, although I respected his work very much, it was stylistically too different from mine. But the correct answer is yes. Perhaps a different yes than you'd expected. Let me try to explain. A lot of what Bartók composed and thought bears similarities to what other composers composed and thought. But the big difference between him and the others was that everything that came out of him was absolutely authentic. It was as if his music, his life and his way of thinking were an intrinsic part of himself. Not an attribute, a mood, a detail, not an opportune gesture. No, everything was an inseparable part of him. Here's an example. I'm sure you're familiar with Bartók's music and his many pieces that imitate the nocturnal sounds of nature. Bartók's night music, as we call it. Crickets, birds, insects can all be heard in his five *Out of Doors* pieces for piano, and in the flickering intermezzi in the slow movements of his First and Third Piano Concertos. He wrote me that the bird calls in the slow movement of the Third Concerto were meant to imitate the wood thrush and the tufted titmouse he had heard in North Carolina.«

»You were also inspired by bird calls,[36] just like Bartók,« I recalled.

»Yes. That's why I immediately appreciated his love of nature, and his attempts to express it in his music. I felt a connection with him, until I came to realize that our respective bird calls originated in very different spheres,« Amelie said.

»What do you mean by that?«

»My bird call pieces can be compared to lovingly painted watercolors. Images whose colors I perceived in sound. Maybe my synesthesia was at the

---

36 Two of Amy Beach's best-known works for piano include the melody of a hermit thrush which she had heard at the MacDowell Colony in 1921: *A Hermit Thrush at Eve* and *A Hermit Thrush at Dawn*, Op. 92, No. 1 and 2. In other compositions she imitated hummingbirds, fireflies, and more.

root of my love of nature.[37] For my songs, I liked to choose poems in which birds, flowers and trees were not only described, but had allegorical significance, such as heavenly and earthly love, the coming and going of seasons, life and death. I worked hard on these pieces, but—let's be honest—there's no shame in admitting that they were small and tasteful, but not particularly profound vignettes of my personal, idyllic moments of happiness and contemplation. Bartók was completely different. His bird songs and cricket chirps were musical manifestos. Although personal, they went beyond him as a person. ›Do you hear the voice of nature?‹ his birds sing and his cicadas chirp. They declare, not timidly, but penetratingly, ›Our songs are the origin of music!‹ Yes, that's what Bartók believed. Don't ask me why. It was simply one of his fundamental dogmata. Music comes from nature, from simplicity, from the huts. His night music was not about his personal happiness, but about the act of creation in its most elementary form—not sophisticated ornateness like in Mahler's works. Bartók wasn't capable of being sentimental. He unpacked his nature sounds where other composers would have written romantic slow movements. That was his form of romance, and he made no compromises. He was very honest, and quite a role model!«

»And you wrote about all of that in your letters,« I asked, still processing everything Amelie had just said.

»Yes. It's really too bad.« She drank half of her Baileys in one gulp. »I hope not all is lost. The correspondence with Bartók was the best. There were maybe five or six letters.«

»Not more?«

»No. Perhaps even fewer. But each letter contains so much.« She gave me a sideways look as if to see whether I could read her private thoughts.

»And the correspondence with Farwell?« I asked before the moment of silence became embarrassing.

---

37 Amy Beach had perfect pitch and was a synesthete. That means that she was able to perceive the stimulation of two senses at once. For her, a sound could have a color and vice versa. The following key applied to her perception:
C = white / E = yellow / G = red /A = green / A-flat = blue /D-flat = purple / E-flat = pink.
Amy Beach's synesthesia played a role in many of her compositions. The downside was that she considered the transposition of her songs to another key to be a musical distortion.

»I exchanged more letters with him than with Béla.« Amelie impulsively took a small white handkerchief out of her purse and dabbed her nose. »My goodness, what a tremendous loss it would be if they were gone! Arthur really enjoyed writing, and he did it well. He was good at reminiscing and mulling over new ideas.« She paused for a moment, then added in a chilled tone. »But he could also be terribly brusque.«

»Can you give me an example?« I asked.

»The first one that occurs to me was his reaction to my Four Commandments.«

I had no idea what she was talking about.

»Let me go back a bit,« she said. »In 1903, Arthur published his so-called *Articles of Faith* with his Wa-Wan Press. These were a list of principles for dealing with Indigenous American music. He wrote things that would make your hair stand on end. Things like: To the extent to which ›Indian‹ music is a fertile part of modern music, it has to be permanently absorbed by it. He also wrote that, for American composers, ›Indian‹ music was as important as a stick is for a hiker to reach the top of a mountain. I couldn't help but contradict him. Indigenous American music was not a means to an end. Besides, there was no point in only discussing Indigenous music when we should have been talking about guidelines for dealing with any kind of foreign music. His *Articles of Faith* fell short. I suggested that he publish a text in his magazine about general principles for dealing with music from other cultures.«

My ears pricked up. In the current debate about cultural appropriation, there is a lot of discussion about what we can and cannot do. This or that is no longer allowed, people say, rather than offering positive, proactive suggestions. Instead of coming up with interdictions, wouldn't it be more helpful to say that cultural contact is good in principle, but that it should follow certain precepts?

»You wanted precepts. What did you have in mind?« I asked Amelie.

First Commandment: Ask the party concerned what they think of your composition plan.

Second Commandment: Respect the cultural context and ceremonial function of the music you're dealing with.

Third Commandment: Make it clear that your adaptation is an adaptation. It's neither the original nor a copy.

Fourth Commandment: Avoid clichés instead of perpetuating them.

»My Four Commandments. You might also call them guidelines. The First Commandment is, ask the party concerned what they think of your composition plan. I say ›party concerned‹ because I can't think of a better word. If you were talking about copyright, you would say, ask the owner, but folk music has no owners. They're more like treasure keepers. Ask them.

»My Second Commandment is, respect the cultural context and ceremonial function of the music you're dealing with. Make it clear what the piece should convey. You can use a funeral song to write another funeral song, but not a revue number.

»The Third Commandment is, make it clear that your adaptation is an adaptation. It's neither the original nor a copy. In my opinion, there is nothing wrong with enjoying a piece of music from another culture and expressing that in your own musical language. Isn't that part of the essence of art? Monet, van Gogh and Mary Cassatt were influenced by Japanese art, but remained themselves in their own work. Goethe was inspired to write his West-Eastern Divan by translations of the works of the Persian poet Hafez. I admire the honesty of these great artists. They said their aim was not to be an authentic Japanese or Persian artist, but to be an authentic Monet, van Gogh, Cassatt, or Goethe and to understand as much of another culture as they could. When I finally understood that, I was ready to make another, more earnest attempt at completing my Indianist compositions. The first example was *Blackbird Hills* ♦. It incorporated original melodies with an accompaniment in a very different style all my own, verging on atonal. That was the solution. A short time later, I tried the same approach in my String Quartet in One Movement. A couple of years later, I heard Béla's *Hungarian Peasant Songs* at Ethel Hier's. They were composed according to the same principle, confirming that I was on the right track. Excuse me, I've gotten off topic. But purely artistically speaking, the Third Commandment is the most difficult, which is why I had to explain it.

»And finally, the Fourth Commandment: Make an effort as a composer to avoid clichés instead of perpetuating them. It's not always easy to determine what that means. Of course, distinctive cultural features like a particular scale or certain instruments have to be emphasized so that they can be recognized. But what I was getting at with this commandment is certain taboos. There should be no abbreviations, no parodies, no caricatures. Nothing offensive.«

»Fantastic,« I said. »And how did Farwell react to your Four Commandments?«

»With a single, insulting sentence. ›Don't try to reign in my artistic freedom!‹ he said.« Amelie looked at me lividly, as if she had just revealed a scandal that required redress.

She had written Farwell a letter or two explaining her position and asking him to publish her Four Commandments with Wa-Wan Press, as a discussion point at the very least. He could even write a statement disagreeing with them, if he felt that was necessary, she'd suggested.

»Farwell didn't bite. That was the end of the story,« said Amelie.

Too bad, I thought. Her Four Commandments would still be relevant today. And now…that was it? Because Farwell was too stubborn and Amelie not stubborn enough?

»It was Béla who opened my eyes to Arthur,« said Amelie with a bitter undertone.

»What do you mean?« I asked.

»When we first met, I thought that Bartók and Farwell had a lot in common. On the surface, they both had these unbelievably intense, probing eyes. And they shared a love of nature. Even their artistic careers began in similar ways.«

I knew nearly nothing about Farwell's biography and looked at Amelie questioningly.

»Shortly after the turn of the century,« she explained, »Arthur dedicated himself to Indigenous American music—as a composer, theorist and publisher. I already mentioned Wa-Wan Press which he founded to support indigenous music without any interest in turning a profit. Around the same time, Béla Bartók turned his back on the artistic establishment in Budapest, which he felt had misjudged him, and began researching folk music among minority groups in Hungary, Romania and other countries. Arthur and Béla were tired of civilization, both of them sought spiritual fulfillment in simplicity, both found new artistic meaning in the documentation of folk music. But then they each went their own way. After I met Béla, I started to see he was an authentic humanist, while Arthur was a self-indulging charlatan.«

»Farwell a self-indulging charlatan? Isn't that kind of harsh?« I asked.

»Absolutely not! Well, maybe you're right. I admit to having been overly apodictic. But, you know, it's not easy to talk about Arthur. He was so full of contradictions. An emotional person who wrote really long letters to his friends to give them good advice in difficult situations. He had a good and selfless heart. And yet he was a narcissist. For example, his conviction that he could single-handedly change the musical world in the United States from the bottom up—with the defiant apodosis that, if he didn't manage to do so, he would no longer call it his country. And, Petra, seriously, someone who travels around like a missionary to give lectures on the true music of America, someone who founds music associations everywhere with the intention of personally directing them from afar, someone who sees it as his calling to take on the role of a prophet in his own pageants—would you not call such a person a narcissist? But you're right. I have to be more precise about the differences between Béla and Arthur. Both men believed that music could connect people and that the uniting element in music was simplicity—that is, folk music. Based on this idea, Béla created a system that shaped his compositions and his immensely studious ethnomusicological research trips. With Arthur, on the other hand, I often had the impression that everything was all mixed up in his head and that his aims stood in the way of each other. When he realized that Wa-Wan Press wasn't able to live up to its two contradictory goals—to publish every single piece of folk music, Indigenous or else, and only to publish the pieces of highest quality—what did he do? He gave the publishing house away—and that was the end of it. Béla was working on something that was clearly definable—folk music from deeply rooted cultures. Arthur, on the other hand, labored for something that he could not define, namely American music, and that, as Tony said the other day, nobody can define. But Arthur was not deterred. He was convinced that humans needed restless activity and intuition rather than logic or rationality in order to create. He even wrote a book about it. That is, he started writing a book. Typical Arthur. As I said, his unsorted thoughts constantly pushed him off his path and into a field of contradictions. Here's another example. Arthur was obsessed like no other in his generation with creating *American* music ♦. He saw himself as the foremost enforcer of Dvořák's testament. Sometimes he was aggressive in demanding a break from the German music tradition. But he himself was not willing to distance himself from his own musical idol,

Richard Wagner. He even set up his own outdoor version of Bayreuth in the California mountains.[38] There he performed his own pageants, complete with thunderous Wagneresque sound and light effects, claiming that he was not honoring Wagner as a German composer, but as a folk musician.«

»Wagner—a folk musician?« I wondered.

»I suppose he meant the folk of the Nibelung,« said Amelie, fully aware how absurd that sounded.

»But that's a sham!« I argued.

»Well,« said Amelie with feigned nonchalance, »don't we all juggle with the souls in our breast from time to time? But all jokes aside, you're right. It was nonsense, but I wouldn't call it a sham. It was self-deception. Or rather, an attempt to straighten out his self-deception as best he could. That's why I called Arthur a charlatan earlier and not a hoaxer. But just you wait, there's more to say about the charlatan. Arthur was deeply spiritual. Art was not a craft for him, but the language of the universal spirit uniting all people. That is what drove his interest in the spirituality of the Indigenous Americans. But there, too, his goals landed him on a collision course. The music of the future was supposed to be American in his mind, but also incorporate all of humanity, meaning that Indigenous American music could only constitute one ingredient—with Americans leading the way to the future. Not the softies from the East Coast, but the *real* Americans—the pioneers and their direct descendants whom Farwell met in California. In one of the pageants he composed in California, *The March of Man*, he blurred the boundary between the ›Indian‹ spirit of nature and the white ›soul of the world‹. This soul, multiethnic but well versed in ›Indian‹ spirituality, was aided by the predominantly white society of California to victory over the European Occident. Arthur's favorite historian had predicted the decline of the West—Oswald Spengler, whose work he had gotten to know while studying in Munich. And who directs the revolution in the pageant? He himself, the Seer.«

»That's crazy!« I said.

»Yes, really crazy. Arthur got way off track sometimes when he was singing the praises of the Californians. He often wrote about a ›new age‹ and ›new men‹. In one newspaper article, he attributed the superiority of the

---

38 The *Theatre of the Stars* in the San Bernardino Mountains.

Californians to the fact that they didn't have to deal with ›hordes of more or less unassimilable aliens‹. It probably doesn't surprise you that my contact with Arthur dwindled during this time, around the early 1920s. I occasionally heard about the radicalization of his ideas but didn't take it seriously. Just a fad, I thought, that's how Californians are. I thought I knew what I was talking about, since I had lived in California for several years as a young woman.«

I was shocked by Farwell's terminology. »Unassimilable alien hordes.« I was about to put Farwell in a box labeled *Ethno-Nationalist Jerks* and never take him out again. But then I thought, what a strange man he was, and took a moment to try to understand him. He wanted to unite the world through music. Farwell, the universalist. But he needed a leader for this global unification. Farwell, the nationalist, was caught up in the thinking of his time. This Farwell said leaders can only be nations. People who define themselves as a new, idealized nation that sets itself apart from others. True Americans, not alien hordes. That may sound like blood-and-soil nonsense, but it's miles away from genocidal hate speech.

I outlined my thoughts to Amelie and she responded intelligently and thoughtfully, as always.

»I've thought about that before as well,« she said. »Take Tony. He's a composer of world music and a nationalist all in one. He recently told us how he reconciles these two divergent spheres. Arthur didn't manage that balancing act. He was, to put it bluntly, a folkish internationalist.«

»Or a nationalist who romanticized about global reconciliation.«

»And first and foremost, he was highly irrational. A living contradiction. His spiritual heart cried, 'Be embraced!' He believed in the middle of World War I that collective singing would bring peace and international democracy. But he also had a very typical American heart. The heart of an American pioneer with a sense of mission, not uncommon in those days. Arthur, the unwitting herald of manifest destiny.«

»Would you say he was more of a dreamer than anything else?« I asked.

»Yes, indeed. A dreaming prisoner of his time. It's rather tragic. You can love him or hate him.«

After a brief pause, Amelie added, »But it's fairer to love him.« She leaned forward and glanced quietly at her folded hands.

»Did you ever speak with him about these contradictions?« I asked.

»No, that was impossible. Conceptualizing was not his strength, although he was constantly coming up with concepts. There was only one constant in his intellectual chaos: himself, the priest of a new age.«

Amelie emptied her glass of Baileys. »I can't deny that Arthur's interest in Indigenous Americans was authentic and full of empathy at its core. Neither can I deny that Arthur created something great with Wa-Wan Press, something that he kept alive for ten years thanks to his tireless efforts. And it's also undeniable that Arthur's struggle between his musical gift and his programmatic confusion resulted in a number of lovely and daring piano pieces ♦. The intuition that Arthur loved to talk about in his endless, scatterbrained speeches is indeed useful in music. But in politics?«

»And that's the difference between Farwell and Bartók?«

»Yes, one of the differences. While Arthur thought only of one person—himself—, Béla thought only of one thing—music—which he approached academically, not as a shaman. Béla's weariness with the system led him to humanism, to the defense of minority groups, to pacifism, and to the rejection of authoritarianism. Whereas Arthur—I guess today you would call him a populist.«

Amelie put her elbows on the table and rested her chin on the backs of her folded hands. She pondered for a moment, looking into the past. »Béla was a good guy,« she said finally. Memories seemed to be passing through her mind. »As a young woman, can you imagine that I fell for someone whom I'd only seen once up close and just a couple of times from a distance and otherwise only knew from letters? No flirt, no kiss, no lovemaking.«

Her question surprised me, especially that she had said *lovemaking*. In the back of my mind, I kept thinking about the label that had been slapped on Amy Beach: *Passionate Victorian*, with the emphasis on *Victorian*, as in the subtitle of Adrienne Fried Block's biography. A label reinforced by Amelie's plump, old-fashioned appearance and her deliberate avoidance of feminine accessories.

»Did you love him?« I was confident she wouldn't mind such a direct question, not after everything she'd already shared.

»Whom?«

»Him. Béla Bartók.«

»Oh. I thought you meant Arthur.«

»Or Arthur. Did you love him? Or both of them?«

Amelie looked absently at the wooden beams in the ceiling, then over to the bar. She signaled to the young man behind the counter that she wanted to order something. When he used hand gestures to ask whether she wanted another Baileys, she declined and pointed to a bottle of sparkling water at the table next to us.

»That's a difficult question, Petra. It's never been easy for me to sort through my feelings. Love is... Let me put it this way. When Henry died in 1910, I was forty-three. I believed that my time as an attractive young woman and potential mother had passed. I wasn't really looking for a new husband after Henry's death, but I did think about whom it might be worth sharing everyday life with. I thought the longest about Arthur Hyde, the organist. I had the feeling that it was one-sided, which made me want to prevail all the more. But then he died in 1920.

»In the final phase of my useless wooing of Arthur Hyde, I discovered that I was falling for the other Arthur. Thank goodness that was only a short phase. Two Arthurs at once? I didn't want to act inappropriately. I was sad, but also relieved when Arthur Farwell permanently moved to California a short time later. In the weeks before his move, I had imagined that a relationship with him could be exciting. What appealed to me more than our shared interest in music and nature were the things we didn't have in common. His wildness, the apodictic weight of his thoughts, the way he navigated between heaven and earth, his huge enthusiasm for following really crazy goals. He was the opposite of a Brahmin, if you know what I mean. The Brahmin daughter in me was drawn to him. If he had abducted me, I think I would have let him. Was that love? I don't know. What attracted me back then was my desire to achieve together with him the goals that my status made unattainable for me. Perhaps I gave in to my infatuation so wholeheartedly because I knew that he had just gotten engaged to a beautiful actress and was unavailable. In retrospect, I'm glad he didn't abduct me. His gaffes in California clearly showed what he was most concerned with: himself. He likely would not have had the extra time and energy he would have needed to show me the appreciation I wanted.

»With Béla it was completely different. I was more mature. I had learned that it wasn't about finding in him as much as possible of myself and my hidden desires. On the contrary, apart from music and his love for nature, he seemed to be a rather poor candidate for discovering a reflection of myself. He seemed sickly and introverted. And he had quirks that others found strange. Apart from the incredibly hard work he brought to his folk songs, there was merely a deep, dark depression. Only his clairvoyance remained fascinating, as did the beauty of the thoughts he used to defy his own dejection. He held an unwavering belief that Death, which regularly appeared to him in his New York apartment, became more tolerable when he approached it as a noble, inwardly pure person. I found this perspective so amazing that I wanted to be a part of it. But was it love? Or a motherly protective instinct? Or the wishful thinking of an old woman struggling with heart problems and arthritis who undeniably belonged to the old guard? Again, I don't know. The best thing I can say is that, if I was fooling myself, it was more forgivable with Béla than with Arthur.«

It was incredible how Amelie was suddenly opening up. I hadn't thought she would. And indeed, she seemed to be feeling overwhelmed by it herself. Abruptly, she started hectically rummaging around in her purse. She wasn't really looking for anything particular, it appeared, but just wanted to end the personal conversation. She raised her finger and changed the topic.

»Do you hear that?« She pointed to a jukebox over by the restrooms. The sound coming from the speakers on the ceiling was so muted that was nearly inaudible. I'd been so caught up in our conversation that I hadn't paid attention to the music.

»*Goirtin Ornadh*...«

I didn't understand what Amelie meant, but the melody was unmistakably the one used in the second movement of her *Gaelic* Symphony.

»*Goirtin Ornadh*,« repeated Amelie. »My Gaelic song of a dream ... in a little barley field.« Then she suddenly became livid and pointed out the window.

In front of Pete's Tavern, a group of young people were leaning against the fender of an old Toyota Corolla, with their backs to the bar. I got a brief glimpse of two of their faces, one Latino, the other white. I couldn't make out the ethnicity of the others, but guessed they were a melting pot, based on the different degrees of nimbleness they demonstrated while moving their upper bodies to the rap music that gushed out of the half-open front passenger door of the Corolla and slammed into us. The two-tone loop that repeated itself endlessly in the background and the rattle of the overworked speakers annoyed not only Amelie but also me and some of the bar's other guests.

»What is that ridiculous racket? I can't hear my own music anymore!« Amelie huffed.

I tried to explain. *Who Gon Stop Me* by Kanye West and Jay-Z. A song that equates discrimination against Blacks in the United States with the Holocaust. I told Amelie a bit about the music, saying that she could probably imagine the polemic that such comparisons can unleash. Especially considering who was singing it. Kanye West, a Black guy said to be a friend of Donald Trump and a supporter of his white supremacist stance, who had scorned the Black Lives Matter movement, and who regularly made racist and anti-Semitic comments.

Amelie jumped up and ran out. Through the window I saw her talking to the young people. Her spunk impressed me. I was ready to jump in and help her. In the end, I decided to stay in the bar. Her chat with the kids appeared to be going just fine.

* * *

Ten minutes later, Amelie came back into the bar. To my surprise, she ordered a third Baileys. She seemed to believe she deserved it. Her pink face shone like rhubarb pudding. She asked the barkeeper to play the barley field song again. A good customer always gets what she wants.

»You really showed them!« I praised Amelie as she sat down at our table. »How did you manage it? They look like saints out there right now.«

»What do you mean?«

Amelie's question confused me. »I mean, you were outside to show those wayward kids the straight and narrow, right? Did you talk about the absurdity of People of Color for Trump, about the dangers of relativizing the Holocaust?«

Amelie stared at me in disbelief.

»Politics? With them? Goodness no! I asked them very politely to turn down the volume on their infernal machine because it was keeping me from following an interesting discussion I was having with a nice young lady. I said I hoped they understood that older people sometimes have difficulty hearing. They didn't argue with me. The matter was resolved, and we were free to talk about other things. You wouldn't believe how nice the kids were. Not nearly as bad as I'd expected. Yes, and then I told them that I found their music rather primitive, but that the flexible speech rhythms interested me quite a bit as a composer. When I said that I was a composer, they pricked up their ears, stood up straight and told me all about the art of rap, and about loops and beats, in a colorful mix of words.«

Your music is primitive, let's not talk about politics, but I'm interested in the rhythm. Wasn't that exactly what Amelie thought back in 1893 on the Midway Plaisance? Was Amelie, in her conversation with the kids, once again hiding behind her musical interests to avoid taking a clear political stance?

Suddenly, there was a crack in my idol, Amelie. Just a little one. She was still an admirable authority and, I hadn't forgotten, the subject of my doctoral thesis. But the crack could not be undone. It was big enough for me to start viewing Amelie more critically, and to listen more carefully. I felt all the more obliged to explore the potentially precarious terrain of politics with her.

»Can we go back to Bartók? You said he opened your eyes, regarding Farwell. Did that eye-opening also apply in general to your political standpoint?« I asked.

Amelie thought for a moment. »Bartók didn't change my stance, but confirmed the change that was already taking place. Do you understand what I mean?«

»I think I do.« Amelie's reply was calculated, as it so often was. A bit of yes, a bit of no.

»I was a Republican my whole life. Not just in the passive sense of putting my X in the right box on the ballot every four years. No, I made appearances at Women's Republican Club meetings and in late 1926 I even postponed my second European tour so that I could vote in the primaries.«

Amelie changed the subject for a moment. »Petra, as a European, you may not be so familiar with American history. You may think, Amelie is a Republican, so that makes her a supporter of Nixon, Reagan, Bush, and Trump. But you would be gravely mistaken. In my time, the Republicans were different. They were respectable back then. Most importantly, they were the party of Abraham Lincoln. The Democrats, on the other hand, were considered proponents of a bloated government where the pockets of corrupt fat cats were lined with graft. The Republicans were well-meaning conservatives, and that's what I wanted to be, too.«

»But with a penchant for authoritarianism?« I asked provocatively. »When you were in Germany just before World War I, you spoke highly of Kaiser Wilhelm I, and when you went to Rome in 1929, you and your friends there revered Mussolini. You even offered to play for the Duce.«

»Yes, that's true. But try to understand me. I have never been a politician. Maybe I was naive in that regard. Caring for others is a supreme virtue, in my opinion. That was always my maxim. My most important work was helping other female musicians. Also, in a broader sense, I believe that people need to understand and help each other. So, in 1914, I felt it was at least worth lending an ear to the Germans' inferiority complex and the Emperor as its most prominent mouthpiece. Likewise, Mussolini's appeals to the people left an impression on me, as did Hitler's call for a strong and united Germany. I thought he expressed himself in a most vulgar way, but—from what I knew at the time, and I didn't know the ugly part—his statements didn't seem wrong in principle. After visiting Germany, I liked the Germans. My concerts in Munich, Berlin, Dresden, Leipzig, and Breslau were marvelous. When, in a speech broadcast on the radio, British Prime Minister Neville Chamberlain justified backing down after the Germans occupied Czechoslovakia in November 1938—it was later called *appeasement*—I fully supported him. I thought like Chamberlain did: Hitler, the uncouth loudmouth, has to be placated until the next, better leader takes his place. I had met enough good Germans to be sure that this was true. At the time, I hadn't heard anything about the racial laws, the concentration camps, or the pogroms. But when I found out in greater detail about the repression that was taking place, I was upset and felt the urge to do something. In January 1939, I was the first to sign the petition of the Musicians' Committee to Aid Spanish Democracy and call on our government to lift the arms embargo against Republican Spain, indirectly supporting the fight against Franco's fascism.«

»But what does that have to do with Bartók? All that happened long before you saw him again at Harvard,« I pointed out.

»True, but in the only letter that Bartók wrote me in 1938, at Christmas, he asked me whether I had heard of the Committee. He said I just had to support it. That was a political wakeup call. My interest in everyday politics grew in general. At New York University, I attended a lecture series on foreign policy. I began keeping a diary of political events; I wrote, for example, about my disappointment over Norway's capitulation in June 1940 and my elation in April 1944 that Rome was in the hands of the Allies. In October 1944, I dragged myself to a festive gathering at the Town Hall Club, although I had great difficulty walking. But the occasion was important to me—the liberation of the Netherlands, Belgium and Luxembourg. I wanted to be there. I remember it so well because at the same time, tides turned in the Balkans, too. The Red Army advanced in Bulgaria and Romania and liberated Belgrade, together with the Yugoslavian partisans, on the day of the party in the Town Hall Club. I wrote to Bartók that I hoped I would soon be able to toast the liberation of Hungary as well. His reply was very pessimistic. Typical Bartók, I thought at first; calamity was unavoidable in his mind. But in 1956, I realized that he was right. ›There is no end in sight,‹ he wrote. ›The destroying of Europe (people and work of art) continues without respite and mercy. The destiny of poor Hungary, with the Russian danger in its back—the prospects of the future are rather dark.‹«

Amelie's insights into her artistic and political interactions with Bartók were unexpected. I felt like I was uncovering a hidden treasure and hoped that the midnight heist was only a dream and that Amelie's correspondence was not really lost, so that I would have a chance to document the discovery of the treasure.

The bad feelings that had arisen ten minutes earlier over Amelie's political unprincipledness had dissipated. It was the right time to bring up another topic. I remembered that Bob, when we were in Minton's Playhouse, had accused Amelie with unbridled agitation of always underestimating African-American music and instead developing a preference for Indigenous American music.

First, I asked Amelie whether I could order her anything else. I hoped she wouldn't ask for another Baileys. Her flushed cheeks told me she'd had enough to drink, although her precise way of expressing herself and the agility of her thoughts still seemed quite sober. But Amelie turned down my offer. She appeared concentrated and unimpressed by the intensifying jostle of the crowd at the bar; the whirr of voices overpowered the background music. Amelie reached more and more frequently for the handkerchief in her purse to dab her face yet again.

»In the United States, talking about politics necessarily means talking about race relations,« I said, introducing my next topic.

»Yes, I know,« began Amelie. »Such a difficult topic. Excuse me for being so direct, but the subject makes me feel rather unwell.«

Amelie got right to the point. »Bob's accusations are wrong,« she said. »I'm sorry he feels that way. I would like to explain to him that he's wrong. But that's my problem. I feel like I'm on the defensive and don't know how to get out of it. He says something about me, namely, to put it bluntly, that I'm a racist, and I can't disprove it. Logically, it's easy to prove that you *are* something—say, a pianist. But try proving that you *aren't* something. Sometimes it seems difficult to have an identity, but it's even more difficult trying to get rid of an identity you've been labeled with.«

»But the explanation you recently gave sounded quite convincing to me,« I said. »Whether African-American music was a foundation of American music constituted a systemic question, you said, and your doubts had nothing to do with your judgment of Black music and certainly not of Black people. You told us that you were very interested in the musical performances in the Dahomey Village at the Chicago World's Fair and that you weren't aware of the degrading representation of ›savage‹ settlements.«

»Yes. I could add further examples, like the Black female musicians and composers I recommended, sometimes successfully, for orchestra positions or concert series. I also remember one situation with Harry Burleigh. As you may know, I was always very hopeful that radio programs would become a means of disseminating sophisticated music. I urged Harry Burleigh not only to sing in a radio music program, but also to talk about himself, his music and his tradition. I thought it was important since I considered him to be a significant voice among Black composers. He was hard to convince, since he was very shy. But he ultimately agreed and, afterward, he wrote me a moving thank-you letter. It must be in the box with my other letters. If I kept thinking, I'm sure a few more incidences would occur to me. But I won't fool myself, the facts speak against me. In the circles in which I grew up, there were hardly any Black people, apart from domestic workers. I didn't choose those circumstances, they simply were. I only supported a handful of Black female artists because there were so few of them in general.«

My ears pricked up and a red flag waved inside of me. »But couldn't you have made up for what you missed doing back then?« I asked.

»Made up for it? How should I have done that?«

»Well, with Gladys?«

»Gladys? Who is that?«

The red flag flapped harder. It was difficult to believe that Amelie went in and out of the Ottendorder all the time and didn't know who Gladys was.

»Gladys, the intern. You must know she's a musician,« I said.

»She's a musician? How should I know that?«

Quite simply, I thought. By talking with her. What had become of Amelie's legendary approachability and care for others?

»In the Ottendorfer, I only ever have contact with López and Bob, and with Tony of course. You know, I have my reasons…«

All clear. I'd judged too hastily. I nodded to show I understood what her reasons were, although the more often I met with Amelie and Tony, the more I forgot about them.

»Gladys is a flutist,« I told Amelie. »I've chatted with her two or three times in the past few days. She told me how much she admires you—apparently without knowing how close she's come to you. She won first or second place in several competitions, and in Chicago she performed your *Variations for Flute and String Quartet* ♦. But in the spring, her probationary period at the orchestra was brought to an end in a way that really shocked her.«

»Poor thing! I understand her so well. Terminations always seem unfair.«

»She didn't call it unfair, but ›shocking‹. She's positive that her contract was not extended because she's Black.«

»Oh. That would be shocking indeed. But—purely hypothetically, of course, and not to make any hasty judgements—perhaps she was rejected simply because she wasn't good enough? I mean, there are so many very good musicians who have no opportunity…«

»No, no. She overheard other members of the orchestra talking about her skin color and scheming against her.« I filled in the details.

»What should I say? I am not familiar with the case. Ultimately, it would be one person's word against another's.« After a brief hesitation, Amelie added, »But I've heard from credible sources about similar cases. Actually, not much has changed since my time. Or, let's say, things have changed. You're not hit over the head with racism, it happens behind your back.«

»That's what Gladys said, too.«

»And the worst thing that can happen to you as a musician is that you're there to fill a quota. The quota woman, the quota Black person. As a quota filler you have two functions. Firstly, you're great for marketing purposes, a curiosity to put on show. And secondly, you're a pill to quiet the conscience of those in charge. But there is no room to further your career. In 1977, there was an event that ruffled feathers for a short time. Fifteen years after he had become the first Black musician to get a permanent contract with the New York Philharmonic, Sanford Allen said frustratedly, 'I'm simply tired of being a symbol.' That was big news back then. Today, it's different. We have Black Music Month, concert programs fill the Black composer quotas—and Asian and trans and who-knows-what quotas. Recently, I heard about a conductor who directs an orchestra somewhere in Belgium. People say that she got the job because she's a Black lesbian. How nice, two quotas filled at once! But the poor woman—in the long run, her career is hopeless, no matter how good she is. And that is typical for the quota fillers. After one or two fireworks, it's over. The next contract or the next composition commission will go to the established musicians who are all white just like the audience.«

Again, Amelie challenged me to rethink my opinion of her. She seemed well aware of problems and was discerning. But the question remained: What would she make of it?

»Amelie, if you see these circumstances so clearly, then do something. Please! For Gladys. You could be anonymous. Gladys deserves it and it would really make her happy. Bob, too, would appreciate your support and change his opinion of you. I'm sure he would!«

»Very well then, I promise,« said Amelie with a spontaneity I hadn't expected. »The way you describe Gladys, and you know what you're talking about, she most certainly deserves it. I just don't know exactly what I can do. I'm not a magician.«

Yes, you are, I thought. What Amy never managed, Amelie could do if only she tried!

»We'll see,« said Amelie, as if she'd read my thoughts. »But I'm skeptical about Bob. I don't think his resentment toward me has anything to do with Gladys. It runs much deeper.«

»What are you thinking?«

»My attitude toward jazz. Bob knows my opinion and holds it against me. I didn't think much of jazz back then. Good dance music, okay. But it was constructed too simply to be suitable material in the study of serious music. That was a judgment I made in the early 1920s, admittedly from a very academic perspective. I didn't know back then that Duke Ellington shared my view, he just expressed it inversely. Jazz must develop in such a way that it becomes an interesting subject of study for musicologists, he said. Ellington, Bob and a few others proved this was possible. I've told him that, but he doesn't listen. Instead, he holds it against me that in 1924, after hearing Gershwin's *Rhapsody in Blue*, I thought the piece was vulgar and had a bad influence on the development of musical taste.«

»Wait a second. He accused you of calling *Rhapsody in Blue* vulgar?« I asked, surprised. »He was the one who called it a 'perversion of Black music.'«

»He accused me of thinking it's vulgar because it's so Black, while he thinks it's vulgar because it's so un-Black. Do you see how complicated that is?« Amelie looked at me as if she were pleading for help. »We can disagree on my taste back then, but does that make me a racist?«

I could see how hurt Amelie was by the accusations, which she apparently viewed as deeply unfair. I looked at her commiseratively. At the same time, I thought about how wide the gap can be between how we see ourselves and how others see us. This wasn't a topic I wanted to discuss with Amelie. »Have you spoken with Bob about it?« I asked.

»As I said, I told him that my opinion about jazz had changed over the decades. I hoped to share some thoughts with him about the educational role of jazz. But he didn't want to talk about that. He doesn't seem to see me as competent enough to exchange ideas with. And otherwise…«

»I think he feels horribly disadvantaged and wants to dump the guilt on someone else,« I said.

»Yes, I think that's true,« said Amelie. »Even though he doesn't have to do that. He doesn't have to dump it on me, in any case. I don't have any bad will toward him.«

I wanted to jump to our next topic: Amelie and feminism. I paused for a moment to give Amelie's feelings some space and not seem so businesslike. Then I overheard two words from the table behind us that raised another red flag.

I leaned toward Amelie and said quietly, »Please do me a favor. Talk about the Society of American Women Composers or something like that. I won't be listening to you. I'm sorry, but I have to listen to something else back there. I just have to find out what they're talking about. Would you do me that favor please? It's important. It's about Bukar.«

She looked at me with motherly concern. »Well, okay then,« she said, and started blabbing away while I leaned back in my chair.

* * *

I got home before the rainstorm started. Bukar wasn't there yet. The window was closed, but I heard the tsk-ing of hundreds of car tires as they sucked up the rain and spit it out behind them. Sometimes I heard the sound as a diffuse background loop, then it became clearer, then mixed together with all kinds of other sounds. The longer I listened, the more intrusive it became. I tried to imagine the Third Avenue water music written down as a score. A *tutti* with slight *diminuendos* and *crescendos*. A few fast-driving soloists stood out among the *con sordino* flow. Their water waltz sounded higher, a bit louder, pompous. Sometimes there was a horn, an aggressively trumpeting ambulance, a nasally buzzing firetruck. Who was driving where? It was undecipherable, unimportant, *ad libitum*. Part of the workday traffic murmuring down there in the street.

Later that afternoon, as I peered through the windowpane mottled with raindrops and reluctantly allowed myself to be magnetized once again by the water music, I wondered whether the comings and goings in the street reflected my inner feelings in the past few days. A wide, self-propelling river. A *flow*. A flow? No, that sounded too positive. Not a flow in the sense of unimaginable sources of energy catapulting you to unthinkable psychedelic heights. My flow was more like a sluggish stream of lava. I saw myself in the middle of it on a lost island. A signal would arise now and then from the searing mass and then disappear again into the glowing liquid rock. Horns, ambulances, fire trucks. Alerts. Impending danger all around. Incomprehensible things had happened throughout the last few days. Tense conversations, out of the blue, about the depths of the human condition. The nighttime relocation of a box of books. The crack in Amelie's heroic image. Bukar's strategic shift—an experiment with unforeseeable consequences despite López's literary talent. The conversation I'd overheard in Pete's Tavern.

I was nervous, full of anxieties. But Bukar rescued me from my island. When he came home, he was drenched, but upbeat and very pleased. He hung his dripping raincoat on the coatrack and brought me to the sofa. »I'll tell you everything,« he said, »but first a cup of tea.« I was grateful for his momentum. Not the least because if he started, I wouldn't have to talk right away about the strange things I'd heard from the other table in the restaurant.

»López is a real pro,« he said. »She understands the format she's after and asks very precise questions. We quickly agreed on the framework. I'll be publishing four feature reports under my name. More wouldn't be possible with the *New York Daily*, she said. Political background, direct quotes from eyewitnesses, my commentary on them, information about a trial at the International Criminal Court. It all has to flow together. The facts and quotes have to be watertight. As many direct comments as possible from ordinary people, all asking for justice in different ways, lots of hard-hitting reality. No sentimentality. The emotion has to come from the sheer facts, not be pasted in. When a mother says her child was killed, the impact is not in her tears, but in the fact that she doesn't cry.«

Bukar's plan was understandable, but it also seemed cold and disturbingly hard-nosed. How far did he and López have to go to suppress their true feelings in order to pander to the paper? I kept my thoughts to myself.

»The working title is *The Quest for Justice in Hell*,« continued Bukar. »We also considered *Justice Haram?*, but we weren't sure which associations the word *haram* had for the average reader. Is it clear that we're referring to Boko Haram? Or could it suggest that the series offers general, flat criticism of justice in Islam? We didn't want to take any risks, so we dropped it. Then López and I talked about the content of the articles. López asked whether we could peg the series to a current event. I told her yes and explained why Boko Haram violence had recently flared up again and would likely continue to do so. Boko Haram and the Islamic State's

West Africa Province—ISWAP is an offshoot of Boko Haram—have been bitter rivals for years. Abubakar Shekau—you remember who that is? Boko Haram's leader. He was killed in May, supposedly in a battle between Boko Haram and ISWAP. Abu Musab al-Barnawi, ISWAP's leader, is also said to be dead, killed just a few days ago by either Boko Haram or the army. No one knows for sure. The two organizations are going to fight each other even more intensely than before to work out which one is dominant. A ton of money is at stake. And each group will try to be more violent than the other to show that, even without their leaders, they are more capable than ever.«

It was tedious trying to understand the twists and turns of the jihadists' squabbles. »A turf war between Boko Haram and ISWAP—between Satan and the Devil? They killed each other's leaders? While both were fighting the army?«

»I'll explain it another time. It's a long story. In a nutshell, ISWAP, who are no saints themselves, accuse Boko Haram of committing acts of excessive brutality. In other words, brutality in the name of a just cause is okay, as long as it doesn't go overboard. One example would be the massacres of worshippers in mosques. Theological subtleties in action. ISWAP thinks most moderate Muslims are misguided and therefore enemies, but still Muslims. Boko Haram, on the other hand, denies that they're Muslims—and that's a license to kill.«

»Crazy,« I said. »It's unbelievable what religious zeal is capable of. Shouldn't the Chief Prosecutor of the International Criminal Court subpoena an ISWAP representative to testify that Boko Haram's brutality is excessive?«

Bukar didn't find my suggestion funny. »Come on, Petra,« he said. »The conflict with the jihadists has cost four hundred thousand people their lives. Nice try with your satire. But as a Nigerian, I can't make jokes about it.«

I started to apologize, but Bukar went on to tell me about his meeting with López.

»López said the political context was confusing and that I should write up that part, since she didn't have the background knowledge. She wanted to start writing the features and asked whether I'd brought any material. I gave her my collection of earlier reports. She read the headlines, scanned the texts for no more than thirty seconds a piece, and put the papers away.

Then she laid her phone on the table and said, ›Tell me about your father‹. And, ›Tell me about the fishermen in Doron Baga‹. And, ›What did the woman say who'd been kidnapped and forced into marriage when she returned to her home village?‹ I was surprised. She could have read it all in my reports. If she had wanted to, she could have just copied it. But she said, in order to write authentically, she needed not only the facts, but also, as she put it, the *spirit*. That was something she couldn't read; she had to see and hear it. I knew she was right. So I started to talk. It didn't take long for me to open up. The stories spilled out of me. López asked me helpful questions along the way to keep me going and ordered me at least three cups of coffee. When Bob brought them, he would stay a while and listen. He seemed to be interested in my stories. It was really sweet that he put the sugar in my coffee and stirred it for me, as if he was worried that I'd stop talking if I had to move my arm. And every time before he left, he would listen to the end of the story I was telling and grumble some comment like, ›That's right!‹ or ›Man, those guys are assholes!‹ I didn't even notice the time until López said it was enough for today and I should go home before the rain got worse. But she wanted to talk again tomorrow. When I looked at my watch, I saw that it was almost seven o'clock. Dang, I thought, and walked home. On the way, I thought about what I want to tell López tomorrow.«

»I'm glad that you seem to be working so well together,« I said. »You sound really hopeful that something will come of it.«

»Yeah, I think so.«

Then Bukar asked the question I'd been dreading the whole time. »And what about you?«

»Well...,« I said hesitantly. »The interview with Amelie was excellent. She talked about Bartók, whom she knew, which was very interesting.«

I swallowed. »But then something really bizarre happened. We have to talk about it.«

Bukar looked at me in surprise.

I told him how, in the middle of my meeting with Amelie, I had overheard the words *Boko Haram*, spoken twice by a man's voice with an African-sounding accent, at the table behind us. That had piqued my curiosity. The man was talking with a woman who also had a slight accent, sounding a bit like German. The man promised the woman that his government would lease to her organization a small unoccupied army base for a symbolic sum. She could use the facility as she liked for training programs. When they stopped using the word *organization* and started calling it JUICE, I felt like I'd been struck by lightning. I hadn't seen the man and the woman, but suddenly I knew who was sitting behind us. June. Who was she with? I wanted to find out, so I leaned over to Amelie and told her I was going to stand up and take a picture and she should stay seated and smile. Just when I was about to stand up, the man said something terrible. ›But you have to make sure that stupid justice freak bangs his head against a brick wall,‹ he said. June answered, ›I'm making progress. His reasoning is totally off. He doesn't stand a chance.‹ I stood up and took a picture of Amelie, but flipped the camera so the people at the other table were in the photo, although I only got the lady from the back. While I was doing that, the man said something like, ›We can't allow a wedge to be driven between the people and their protectors.‹

Bukar was flustered. »You have a photo? Show me. If it's Joshua and he's going behind my back, I'll kill him.«

»Joshua?«

»The Nigerian legal advisor. He always said he was on my side.«

»That's right. You mentioned him.«

I found the picture on my phone and showed it to Bukar. He zoomed in so he could see the man's head more clearly. Bukar was certain, even though the photo was blurry.

»No, it's not Joshua,« he said, sounding relieved despite everything. »I didn't really think he'd do that.«

Bukar took another look. »I don't know the man. Who could he be?«

He thought for a moment. »He made June an offer in the name of the Nigerian government. So he must be an official, presumably from the Nigerian UN Mission. Maybe from the political department or the secret service. Or…he offered her a building that belongs to the army. So he could be a member of the military advisor's staff.«

»Why would the military be interested in supporting esoteric seminars?«

Bukar was becoming more and more sure of his hypothesis. »It's clear. Esoteric justice is the exact opposite of the International Criminal Court which would also investigate the army. Who doesn't want that to happen? The army, of course! So it tries to whitewash itself with a few painless self-discovery courses in June's juice factory.«

It was all just a theory, but it made sense. Typical Bukar. And he was even able to squeeze in an off-color pun with the name of June's organization.

»Juice factory? Not bad,« I praised. »Anyone who gives an NGO a name like that has pre-programmed the jokes. Do you even know what JUICE is supposed to mean? Does it have some deeper significance? The abbreviation can't just be a coincidence.«

»No, June explained it to me when we first met. It's a play on a poem by some guru in California. Justice is the juice of life and the juice flourishes best inside yourself, or something like that. It fits, don't you think?«

»Definitely. I can just picture June at the military base she's getting, taking the participants' pulses, putting her thumb to one side or the other just to listen to the magic juice bubbling inside of them,« I said, laughing.

»And them begging the divine June to gently extract their juices, like a credit card machine quietly emptying a bank account…«

»…which June gladly does, in order to make esoteric jello from the juice…«

»…and sell it as a miracle cure in the gift shop of her seminars.«

We chuckled, but actually we weren't in the mood for wisecracks.

»What are you going to do now?« I asked Bukar.

»I'm going to get to the bottom of it. Can you send me the photo?«

* * *

I held Karl Kerényi's book *The Gods of The Greeks* in my hands. Bukar was in awe when I read aloud the story of the goddess Mnemosyne, or Memory, the daughter of Gaia and Uranus. Through her daughters, the Muses, fathered by Zeus, Mnemosyne made humans another gift: Lesmosyne, or Lethe—the ability to forget their suffering and end their worries. In a Boeotian landscape, two fresh water sources, Mnemosyne and Lethe, represent the dialectic between remembering and forgetting.

We were lying next to each other on the bed, still dressed but for our shoes, although it was late. My head was resting on Bukar's arm. He had called me that afternoon during a break between his meeting with López and their take-out pizza.

»I have to know more about Calliope,« he had said quickly on the phone.

»Who? López?« I'd asked.

»About Calliope,« he'd repeated.

»Why?«

»I'll tell you later,« he'd said, leaving me hanging in the air.

I was about to tell him to go to the Ottendorfer and check out Kerényi's book on Greek mythology, a classic that every good library was bound to have. But then it occurred to me that López might wonder why Bukar was suddenly interested in Greek mythology. So I went to Barnes & Noble on the north side of Union Square and bought the book myself.

»Remembering, forgetting, healing. All in one family. Those Hellenes were pretty cool!« exclaimed Bukar. »And I always thought it was only transitional justice that made us aware, two decades ago, of the connection between those three things.«

Bukar's knowledge of Greek mythology was limited, but, I had to admit, probably better than my knowledge of Nigerian mythology. Last fall, we had flown to Athens for a long weekend and visited the Acropolis Museum. I think all the nude and mutilated gods and goddesses confused Bukar more than anything else.

»That's what I thought, too,« I told him.

In the foreword of the book, I read aloud that for Kerény and his friend, Swiss psychoanalyst Carl Gustav Jung, Greek myths were more than a collection of frivolous stories. They interpreted the legends as a divinely inspired window to the human experience—as a handbook for psychology and anthropology.

Bukar returned to the story of Mnemosyne and Lethe. It had struck a nerve in the topic closest to his heart. »Have you heard of the right to truth before?« he asked me.

Yes, I had. Two years ago, during my internship with the South Tyrolean Member of the European Parliament. But I knew so little about it that ›no‹ was the better answer.

»It's a human right,« Bukar explained. »It's not in the Universal Declaration of Human Rights, but it's still important. One of the most important for my work. Here's an example. We recently talked about the girls that Boko Haram abducted and forced into marriage. For their parents and siblings, it's tormenting not knowing whether their daughter, their sister is still alive, where she lives, how she lives. Not knowing will eat you up. One of my—López's—articles deals with this terrible feeling. That's how the right to truth started—with the right of victims' relatives to know. Over the years, it became the right to truth. A right that has to do not only with the clarification of disappearances, but of all kinds of violence and atrocities. For that reason, it's a right that not only belongs to the relatives of those who've disappeared, but to the whole community. Going one step further, some human rights activists have argued that the individual's right to know should be complemented by the state's obligation to make the truth more accessible. An obligation to remember human rights violations, also in order to prevent their recurrence.«

»It sounds like they viewed truth as the key to overcoming conflicts,« I said.

»Yeah, you could say that. As a therapy for post-conflict societies. And that's how the therapy works. Uncertainties are resolved, a story is completed, truth crystallizes, perhaps a very bitter truth, but an irrefutable one. This lets you mourn and accept what happened. Without knowing the truth, you cannot mourn, you cannot begin again. You know that from your own experience. Think of your grandfather. The circumstances of his death were horrible. But knowing them, working through them, makes mourning possible and allows you to move on.«

»That's right. I remember well how I used to sit with your mother and we managed to find meaning in Grandfather's death. That was really helpful.«

»Yes. But conversely, it means that uncertainty about his death would have made it impossible to grieve. It would have led to melancholy and paralysis.«

I became absorbed in my thoughts about my grandfather and Fatima until Bukar brought me back to reality.

»So it's all about truth. But what is truth, actually?«

»Good question, especially these days,« I replied. »Ever since Trump as President of a democratic state made lies socially acceptable, trust in governments as the protectors of truth has drastically declined.«

»Exactly. That makes me all the more convinced that the judicial system is the best answer to the call for truth. I don't mean to say that justice is always right or that it always produces the whole truth. But what judges do— weighing the evidence and filtering out the truth—can't be done better by anyone else. After carefully and fairly evaluating all the pros and cons, judges say, these are the perpetrators and those are the victims. That's the kind of truth the victims expect. And, with all due respect, that's a truth that June, with all her methods, won't be able to offer the victims,« said Bukar.

»But let me play devil's advocate,« I said. »Why can't she? Truth is not an absolute, it's only an optimum. Why should one truth that you find within yourself, with or without June's help, not also be an optimal truth? A way to wipe the slate clean of the past and of your suffering?«

I was sure that Bukar wasn't hearing my argument for the first time, but he thought about it for a moment anyway.

»Historical truth is not a personal matter. It's not about *you, your* truth, *your* clean slate, *your* new beginning, but most of all about a collectively accepted truth and a new beginning for the community. To use the image of truth as therapy again, it's about group sessions, not individual ones. For sure, the truth that you work out for yourself is important. It is the first and most crucial step toward personal forgiveness. But the collectively achieved truth is a prerequisite for collective reconciliation. This collective truth— sorry, it's getting complicated here—can take two very different forms. It can mean that both sides accept certain historical facts, or it can mean that both sides accept that each side has its own version of the truth. They can agree to disagree, as the diplomats would say. Now here's my most important point. Politically speaking, there is a hierarchy between personal forgiveness and collective reconciliation. Don't misunderstand—I'm talking about a *political* hierarchy, not an ethical one. Ethically speaking, forgiving and reconciling are equally large accomplishments. But to reinstitute peace and follow up a negative past with a better future, a mutually agreed truth and a collective new beginning based on truth are a far greater achievement than your honorable efforts to come to grips with your feelings, while blindness and hatred continue to wreak havoc all around you.«

Bukar would make a good teacher, I thought.

»And now back to your question,« he continued. »At the very most, June can help you come to terms with your personal feelings—for a small fee, of course.« He chuckled sarcastically. »But she cannot influence political circumstances for the better.«

Bukar sighed. »That's the annoying thing about these esoteric people. They live in their narcissistic egotistical world and don't understand politics.«

I went over again in my head how Bukar described the dynamic between establishing truth, grief, acceptance, and new beginnings, moving ahead confidently, further and further into an uncharted future. I admit that it is only now, as I write this chapter, that I fully understand how right Bukar was when he suggested the title of this book, *Goin' Home and Far Away.* Every homecoming holds the chance of a bold new departure.

Bukar stood up and closed the half-open window. It was getting windy outside; lightening slashed the sky in the distance. He stretched out his legs on the bed.

»Enough of that,« Bukar said. »Didn't you want to read me something about Calliope?«

»Yeah. Where were we?«

»At the part about the goddess of memory.«

»Mnemosyne.«

»And Lethe and the end of worry and the Muses who were responsible for that.«

»Good job, Bukar, you were paying attention. Now we're getting to the part about Mnemosyne and Zeus's wedding. Listen.«

I read about Zeus and Mnemosyne lying together, according to Kerényi, for nine nights in their holy camp. After one year, Mnemosyne gave birth to nine daughters, the Muses. Their names were Clio, Euterpe, Thalia, Melpomene, Terpsichore, Erato, Polyhymnia, Urania, and Calliope, the one with the beautiful voice. She was the most eloquent of all the Muses, otherwise she wouldn't have been associated with heroic poetry, the most eloquent form of literature. Speech and song flowed sweetly from the mouth of whom she loved.

Bukar looked at me meaningfully. »I understand,« he said thoughtfully.

»What do you understand?«

»It's really quite simple,« he snorted as his demeanor suddenly changed. His loud, bright laughter confused me. »Nine nights together, and bam!«

»Stop it! Come on, just be serious. What do you understand?«

»Ok, I'll be serious.« He folded his hands together against his chest and looked, fully engrossed, toward the ceiling.

»Calliope loves me. That's why the words flow so sweetly from my mouth. And after that she'll write everything down. She's so sweet!«

Bukar was such an unpredictable jokester. Then he became earnest and put both of his hands on my shoulders.

»Calliope is the key.« He looked at me as if he'd just given me the final answer to an unanswerable question. »Again from the beginning. The daughters of the goddess of memory, the Muses, give people the ability to forget their suffering and to stop worrying. But which Muse? Calliope, the most eloquent! And how does she do that? With her heroic poems. What is a heroic poem? It's not a chat with yourself. It's not a sermon about your own experience, squeezed out with a juicer at a military base in Nigeria. It's a public statement! It's poetry! Music! Bob's performances where he sat at the piano, lamented his fate, and found a way to escape it for one whole evening. It's him finding healing in playing the piano. It's documentation of the atrocities Nigerians have suffered from. That is heroic poetry!« Bukar's enthusiasm spilled out of him and his eyes glistened.

»So Calliope is the…the medium that brings healing to the suffering?« I asked.

»Yeah, exactly,« Bukar replied. »That's what I'm saying.«

I hesitated, unsure whether I wanted to agree with his logic, and came back to the impetus for the whole conversation. »When you were in the Ottendorfer with López this afternoon, what made you curious to know more about Calliope?«

Bukar thought back to their meeting. »Actually, it was pretty simple. I was sitting there with López. We were exchanging information, discussing formal and stylistic details, weighing the implications of each argument. López was really calm. Once, when I wasn't sure how to continue, she said, ›Relax and leave it to Calliope‹. I didn't even notice she was using her real name and not her nickname. But when she did it a second, then a third time, I was intrigued. Calliope must have special significance for her. The name must express a certain aggregate state of López.«

»A certain aggregate state?« That was a strange word to use to describe a person, I thought. »Don't try to tell me again that López isn't really López, but a medium or a Greek Muse.«

»Come on, Petra,« said Bukar, dispelling my concerns. »López is López. She's a remarkable woman, but she's a woman, not a goddess. She probably wanted to say that she knows a lot about the mythological Calliope and she wanted to play around with her namesake's name.«

»That's possible,« I said, grateful that he wasn't still nurturing any ethereal theories. But then the little devil in me, which always wants to challenge my own rationale, took over. »What if López really were a muse? Just think about it. First, she comes and clears the way for an unbearable truth with her heroic poems about truth. Then she clears the way so that this unbearable truth can be mercifully overcome. And while she's in the process of clearing things, she also clears the way for the people who are needed to find the truth. I'm talking about Amelie and Tony who then disappear again after the work is done.«

»Man, you have a pretty wild imagination for a rationalist,« said Bukar. »So you mean that with López's help we run into people like Tony and Amelie, people who've been gone for a long time, because they're essential to the quest for truth?«

»Maybe?«

»You mean because they are essential to *your* quest for truth? To *your* dissertation?«

I knew what Bukar was getting at.

»No disrespect for your thesis, but don't you think that if López had these powers, she would use them to resurrect dead people that were more useful to the general good?« asked Bukar.

Why did Bukar have to be so damn smart, I thought, realizing that we had just traded our roles as the rationalist and the dreamer.

»I think that Calliope's power is based on something else,« he said. »You just read, ›Whom she loved, from his mouth flowed speech and song so sweetly.‹«

»That's it! The kiss of the Muse!« I exclaimed.

»Is that what it's called? The kiss of the Muse? Well, then, Tony and Amelie were kissed, and that's how they became immortal.«

Now it was my turn to split hairs. »Good news. You also feel like you've been kissed. I mean by the Muse. You just said that. Does that make you immortal, too?«

Bukar laughed and puffed up his chest. »Yeah, I told you!«

»But what about all the artists who've been unfairly forgotten about? Is it because the Muse skipped over them and didn't kiss them?«

»Good point,« said Bukar, now back in the world of mortals.

»No matter how you look at it, the divine selection mechanisms seem to work pretty badly. They're unjust.«

Bukar exhaled heavily. »Let's try thinking about human traits. Maybe López just has a really strong aura about her.«

»A supernatural aura?« I joked.

Bukar didn't get off track. »Strong enough to suggest all the stories we've just composed in our heads. Everything we *wanted* to compose in our heads.«

»Yeah, we *want* them to be real. We compose people with skin and hair and identities...«

»...Amelie, Tony...«

»...because we want them to be real, even though they're not anymore...«

»...or never were?«

»What do you mean? Tony and Amelie were real.«

Bukar looked at me questioningly. »Abraham?« he asked. »Or the mythical grandmother we're all descended from, according to my clan?«

»She didn't really exist?« I asked.

»I don't know, I guess not. But everyone believes so strongly that she did, that she was a real being. Some people know exactly what color her eyes were, how she dressed, what she liked to eat. What's allowed, what's not. She is reality—a suggested reality.«

Bukar tilted his head and said, »López definitely has a very, very strong suggestive power.«

I sat there ambivalently in the grey area between reality and fantasy. »Because she's a muse?«

Bukar turned toward me, stroked my forehead and put his arms around me. The weather was getting worse outside. The flashes of lightening, still far but coming closer, revealed the outlines of our bodies against the comforter. It sounds like a cheesy movie, but that's how it was. We undressed quickly.

»Hello, muse,« said Bukar as we lay together. Did he realize what a strange compliment that was?

»What does it mean to be your muse?« I asked.

»You're a*mus*ing,« he said, then added, »Forget it. That was a stupid joke. You are who you are.«

»Or who you want to see.«

Bukar laughed. »You're real. That's the most important thing.«

We kept bantering for a while until Bukar stood up, locked the window, and closed the blinds. The storm was intensifying.

After a longer, wordless, but hungry intermezzo, I asked, »Are you looking for something?«

He breathed in my ear: »A cave that feels like home.«

* * *

When we woke up and looked out the window, the sky was milky gray. The weather had done a one-eighty overnight. It was raining; broken branches littered the sidewalk. New York's incessant refrain sounded again and again: firetrucks and ambulances with their fateful melodies. No garbage trucks because it was Sunday.

Bukar was making his morning coffee when his phone rang. López. He ended the conversation with »Okay, I promise,« then told me what it was about.

After the unconfirmed but allegedly documented killing of Musab al-Barnawi, the leader of the Islamic State's West Africa Province, the *New York Daily* wanted to publish an analysis of Nigeria's prospects for democracy, the future of ISWAP and Boko Haram, and ties between Nigeria and the United States. Suddenly, Bukar's series of eyewitness accounts and his introductory policy overview had become very urgent. López had promised to deliver the overview by that night and the first personal report by the next evening.

»Now I'm really going to have to hustle,« Bukar groaned. A night owl by nature, he'd just been condemned to early morning work. But when he walked into the kitchen to get his coffee, nodding his head and whistling through his teeth, I knew he was enjoying the new challenge.

After finishing his first cup of coffee, Bukar went to the kitchen table, opened his laptop and delved into his work. Then he drank two more cups as his fingers flew across the keyboard.

He paused only once. Standing up, mug in one hand and the phone in the other, he crisscrossed the apartment, pacing nervously, almost excitedly. He said something like, »Can you help me, brother? I have to meet your military advisor. He should be informed of my plans. It's good form, you know.«

Joshua seemed to respond. Their conversation was fairly short. Before he hung up, Bukar said, »Ok, see you tomorrow at one-thirty in Angeletto's.« That was one of Bukar's favorite restaurants near the United Nations, just three blocks from the Nigerian UN Mission.

At noon, Bukar went to the Ottendorfer and returned an hour later. He wanted to talk to López discreetly about Bob, he told me, but nothing came of it. She had refused to say anything, instead offering the plausible excuse that she was too busy writing her first article.

The interesting thing about his short visit was this: When he got to the Ottendorfer, Bob greeted him, grumpy as always, and said, ›You just came? I thought you were already here. A young woman asked about you fifteen minutes ago.‹ When Bukar questioned him, he said it had been ›a young goose with red hair and a tattoo on her calf.‹

June. Bukar asked what she wanted.

»To talk to you,« Bob said. »But I told her no. I thought you'd already been here for a while and were sitting up there with López. So I told her that you're busy with López, writing those horror stories from Nigeria again.

»When she heard that, June looked puzzled. ›What?‹ she asked, ›the two of them are writing something together?‹ I told her that I thought that this is exactly what you're doing.

»Of course I was horrified by the information Bob had given out, but I can't blame him, he didn't know the context. Then I asked Bob whether the ›goose‹ had left a message,« Bukar said. »But Bob said no, she'd left in a hurry.«

Bukar looked uncertain. I could see the wheels turning in his head.

»It all seems really strange to me. Why did June go to the trouble of visiting me? What did she want? And why did she call it off so abruptly?« he asked.

I think Bukar and I had the same suspicion. But we didn't dare say anything.

It was my turn to go to the Ottendorfer at around four o'clock. On the way there, I wasn't able to sort my thoughts and go through my interview questions as well as I usually did. Instead, the same nasty question kept popping into my head: Why in the world did June show up at the Ottendorfer?

When I finally sat down with Amelie in the children's library, I felt ill-prepared. But what bothered me even more than my lack of professionalism was an uncontrollable feeling of listlessness. Where did it come from? I had a hard time understanding myself back then. Was it all the poking around in a glorified past? Had all the remarkable conversations I had had recently become too quotidian?

Now I know what was going on. Back then, I was overcome by a paralyzing sense of certainty—that I would not be able to write my dissertation. Too many human entanglements that didn't belong in a thesis, no matter how fascinating they were. Too much unscientific magic.

This feeling overcame me at the worst possible time—at the very moment when a particularly revealing chapter about Amelie's life was on the agenda: Amelia and feminism. I had resolved to pick up where we had left off the day before in Pete's Tavern.

* * *

Amelie was wearing the same light-gray flannel suit she'd had on the previous day. Indeed, it occurred to me, she'd worn the same thing every time we'd met. The same cream-colored blouse with the embroidered lace at the collar, both sides of which were loosely held together by the same dark blue silver-rimmed brooch. I had the blasphemous but humorous thought that, in her ›condition‹, she no longer needed to worry about mixing up her wardrobe.

Amelie didn't need any prompting to start talking with enthusiasm.

»You know, when I was a girl, there was a debate raging in the better newspapers as to whether women were even suited to composition. In *Women in Music*, quite a respected book at the time, George Upton wrote that music was the language of feelings, but putting notes on the page required a man's intellect and capacity for abstraction. Women, he wrote, weren't capable of that. This notion upset me deeply. I knew from my own experience that it was nonsense, and I was glad that some female musicians spoke out against it. If women were given the same opportunity to receive a solid music education, they would not have any trouble keeping up with men, or even surpassing them.«

Amelie sounded competent and combative. She kept fiddling with the small, old-fashioned purse that had caught my attention before. Feminists would avoid accessories like that, but I shouldn't get caught up in such details, I told myself.

I asked Amelie what the lack of training for female musicians had meant for her personally. Her first music teacher, her parents and her husband had advised her not to receive formal music training, she said, so—with a great deal of hard work—she taught herself. Was she disadvantaged as a result?

»No,« she said. One single, simple word, and it sounded like, *I didn't need any of that.*

There it was again, that confounded crack down the middle of the picture of Amelie my mind had painted. It could not be overlooked; the crack was becoming a crevice.

Did Amelie consider herself brilliant? So brilliant that she thought she could do without the extra boost of women's promotion? Did her self-confidence make her less of a feminist trailblazer than I had taken her for?

The crevice deepened as she continued to speak.

»Women have to band together in order to get more attention in the concert world, more performance invitations and better pay. I lobbied for that in the National League of American Pen Women and, within that organization, I founded a Composers Unit,« said Amelie.

In my head, I filled in what Amelie had left out. The organization was needed so that *other* women became part of the repertoire, but her own professional success was not a women's issue, but the natural consequence of the quality of her work. When the Unit's musical level became too mediocre for her taste, she founded the Society of American Women Composers, following the same line of thinking: Let her colleagues seek their fortune in the union of the mediocre, while she hovered in higher spheres.

Was that a fair criticism? No, I told myself, stop thinking like that. This couldn't be. What was my view based on anyway? Certainly not on academic sources. None of the people who had known her personally described her as arrogant. On the contrary, her acquaintances considered her to be good-natured, approachable, modest if somewhat stuffy—and anything but flamboyant.

So what was her problem? My second attempt at an explanation was not any friendlier. A pattern was beginning to form, one I'd hardly noticed over the past few days, but that was crystalizing more and more clearly: Amelie had a habit of beating around the bush. She presented herself as a spokeswoman for women composers, like when she spoke up for female musical talent in the face of Dvořák's disparaging remarks and by being a board member of organizations set up to support women musicians. But at the same time, she turned a blind eye to questions that would have really shaken up the system: the structural discrimination against women because of their gender or color.

She distanced herself from her friend Helen Hopekirk who advocated for women's suffrage, and her many appearances in conservative organizations like the Women's Republican Club and the Daughters of the American Revolution gave the impression that she was managing just fine in the patriarchal system.

Amelie was enough of an artist to develop her musical skill and become interested in music from other cultures. At first, she disagreed with Dvořák's open-mindedness towards African-American music and told him that he should stick to his Bohemian roots. Later, her convictions evolved, but she saw it as superfluous to explain her shift in opinion in a self-critical manner.

In discussing race, she argued—quite credibly, in my view—that she held no prejudices. At the same time, whenever the topic at hand was delicate, like her impressions of the Chicago World's Fair or the promotion of Black music, she would claim ignorance, naïveté or pragmatism. Her chat with Kanye West fans outside the bar was the icing on the cake.

She saw herself as a pioneer, at the very least a *prima inter pares*, but did not publicly share her own personal development. Letting a broader audience in on the evolution of her own consciousness could have made her a person of greater consequence, a role model.

Why did she hold back? Did Amy Beach's upper-middle-class background and the cultural climate in Boston, where people were constantly patting themselves on the back in self-affirmation, make her too complacent? Was she lacking the existential challenge she needed to fully develop her genius? What if, like Claude Debussy, she had grown up in an educated but rather modestly endowed family? What if she had been obliged to struggle? On the other hand, would it have been considered unseemly in her circles for a woman to take a public and, consequentially, a political stand? Once again, was Amy a victim of her circumstances?

Or was I being too strict? After all, I had read in her biography about her attempts to break free from excessive domesticity. There was her piano concerto[39] in which she expressed the tension between her own compliancy, her dominant husband and an imaginary liberated version of herself. And there was the bohemian Arthur Farwell, an acquaintance for whom she may very well have had stronger feelings. How did this fit together?

At some point I interrupted Amelie's monologue, which I had stopped following in detail anyway, and said, »Amelie, there's something I don't understand. You take a conservative stance, but rave about Arthur Farwell, the outsider who, for that very reason, was an inspiration to you. Did you ever go against the flow? Did you ever fight for anything?«

Amelie seemed surprised by my question. She thought for a long time before offering a clever but vague reply, as if she could read my thoughts and wanted to confirm them.

»Petra, your question is really quite problematic. You are expecting me to confirm one of two clichés: either that I was a conformist my whole life and didn't fight, or that I swam against the tide but wasn't successful and gave up. You and I don't see eye to eye. You imply that rebellion must be public, but my battle was fought in private. Thunder and lightning can also strike behind closed doors, without making a big deal of everything. In private, we can communicate with each other more humanely, don't you think?«

That may be, I thought. But, politically speaking, public bursts of thunder and lightning are much more effective. »Ok, then I'll ask a different question,« I said. »When you had the brilliant idea for the Four Commandments and Arthur didn't want to publish them, why did you give up so quickly?«

»It's simple. I didn't want to pick a public fight with Arthur.«

In one sentence, she had confirmed my suspicion. Amelie didn't want a scandal. Even her dissonances should sound nice, she had said the day before.

---

39 Amy Beach: Piano Concerto in C-Sharp Minor, Op. 45 (1898-99)

»Why should I fight with him over my Four Commandments after he had given me so much?« she continued. »Without his passionate efforts to connect me with Native American music, I would never have left my Gaelic ghetto.[40] I would never have written my 'Eskimo' piano pieces ♦. I was indebted to him. In May 1907 at the spring concert of his American Music Society's in Boston, I had the opportunity to present my *Variations on Balkan Themes* ♦.[41] Should I have butted heads with him because of my Four Commandments?«

Her excuse reminded me of Tony's speech on why he didn't confront Hale in Boston. »Think about how critical it was for my career to make a name for myself in Boston,« Tony had said.

»Besides,« said Amelie, »how could I have impressed upon Arthur the importance of propagating Commandments that I didn't uphold myself in my early Indianist pieces? I'd never asked an Inuit what they thought of my pieces. Three of the four pieces had titles that had nothing to do with the original melodies.[42] The harmonization is largely Late Romantic. The one commandment that I did uphold was respect. Believe me, Petra, I always had respect, even though I wasn't sure at first how to express it. To learn how to do that, and to live up to the other three Commandments, I first had to outgrow myself. As awful as it sounds, I had to wait for Henry to die.«

Hm. So many carefully chosen words, all of them reasonable, but I still couldn't see a firm position. Once again, Amelie had done everything right. She had shown respect, which suited her—and found respectable excuses for her mistakes. Excuses for deficits that she easily confessed to me in private, but not in public. That wasn't necessary, she believed. She didn't owe

---

40 Amy is referring to her *Gaelic* Symphony.

41 Amy Beach: *Variations on Balkan Themes*, Op. 60 (1906).

42 Amy Beach: *Eskimos*—Four Characteristic Pieces for Pianoforte, Op. 64. The titles of the pieces are: *Arctic Night, The Returning Hunters, Exiles,* and *With Dog Teams.* Amy Beach wrote in the foreword to the first edition: »These songs are sung by the Eskimos in their own language, and upon various occasions. Some of them are dance tunes, some associated with games, and some are descriptive of events in their past or recent history... The titles of the piano pieces are the composer's own with the exception of *The Returning Hunters* which is the genuine name given by the Eskimos.« This is not quite correct. According to Beach, *The Returning Hunters* is a children's song, while Franz Boas states that it is »sung by the women who stand looking out for the returning hunters.«

the public anything. Her public was the handpicked circle of MacDowell's widow Marian, including artists like Marion and Emilie Bauer, Helen Dyckmann and Ethel Hier. In the 1920s, Amelie had spent summers at the MacDowell Colony with them; they predominantly exchanged praise, not criticism.

Amelie differed from Tony. He was by no means the epitome of straightforwardness. The zigzagging between his Bohemian heart and his German audience. His ability, demonstrated during and after his time in the United States, to get excited about new ideas only to drop them shortly thereafter like hot potatoes, including his American opera project *Hiawatha*. His genteel reticence in response to Philip Hale's racist remarks during his inaugural visit to Boston and the accusation that Amelie was a coward. He was what a South Tyrolean would call *schlutzig*—a smooth talker.

But when it came down to it, Tony tread without wavering. He held fast to his appreciation for African-American and Indigenous music even when high society turned their noses up at it. And he admitted his extravagancies (that is, his obsession with card-playing and his childish interest in trains) to wealthy patrons even though he knew these were considered inappropriate for an aspiring artist like himself.

At least, I consoled myself, Amelie wanted to stick up for Gladys.

I was running out of steam and felt I needed to end the interview quickly, yet politely, so I feigned a technical problem with my recording device and we parted ways.

On my way home, I was annoyed with myself. Why were women always so critical of other women? Were they more critical than with men? Is this a feeling that is instilled from a young age to compensate for the subtle sense of inferiority that they are raised with? Is it the residual age-old attitude that it is not enough for a woman to be as skilled or virtuous as a man? Tony was also being very self-contradictory. Why was I not equally strict with him, let alone with Bob, who I could more and more vividly imagine in his younger years to be a contradiction in the flesh: namely, a heartbreakingly sentimental brute.

* * *

I was still plagued by my paralysis, but Bukar was in top form. The journalistic hound dog in him had been awakened.

Later that afternoon, he returned from his lunch with the Nigerian military advisor. The whole thing sounded like a comedy show, the way he recounted it. As soon as he'd walked into Angeletto's, he'd spotted Joshua, sitting with two other men at a quiet table under a huge rack of bottles. They were on a small gallery separated from the restaurant bustle by a railing.

Bukar's cheeks puffed out theatrically, his belly protruded, he exaggerated a grim expression as he told me about the men.

»One of them was as thin as a grasshopper. He sat there absent-mindedly, with his shoulders hunched and his face buried in the menu. The other one was a real bull. His bulk came from both muscle and fat. He was wearing a white shirt that was a couple sizes too small for his broad shoulders. When I got closer and he stood up, I saw how big his belly was. It was so huge that he'd hardly managed to tuck his shirt into his dark green pants. The guy was wearing his beret at a slant and had on dark blue sunglasses. They were obviously a status symbol, like the gold chain and pendant that got squished beneath his greasy chin. He'd opened the top two buttons on his shirt to show them off.«

I played along with the farce. »Nigeria's next military dictator?«

Bukar paused to consider my joke. »Interesting. So you see him as a military dictator? Fat guy in a uniform, sunglasses, gold chain. You must be thinking of Idi Amin. But in Nigeria, fat guys with sunglasses and gold chains evoke spoiled rich kids. They get good jobs in the army without even having to fight. Their paychecks come from the government and they get an official car and an assistant.«

I wondered why my association was so different. Was it the media, the action movies?

Bukar watched me think. »One person, two presumed identities.«

»I guess so. You and I have different filters.«

»Yeah, but let's talk about that another time. I want to tell you what happened at the meeting. So I was standing across from the huge guy and thought, okay, the good thing about him is that he doesn't look at all like the man in the photo, which was a relief.«

Bukar started acting out the scene again. He stuck out his belly and rubbed it, then he pulled an imaginary pair of sunglasses down to the tip of his nose.

»So he's not the guy from the photo« I said. »That's good.«

»Just wait,« said Bukar, slinking into his chair. »I was about to shake the big guy's hand when I noticed the grasshopper man. He was really skinny and his face was pockmarked. He sat up and reached out his hand to me and it struck me that his suit was really ugly. Light-brown trousers, dark-blue tie. He cleared his throat quietly but in a way that was so ice cold that it was obvious he was the boss. I'd say he had an air of authority—his fear-mongering aura and his evil eye overpowered his cheap appearance.

»›Pleased to meet you. I'm the military advisor.‹« Bukar quoted the grasshopper boss with feigned boredom, falling back into his chair. »Joshua started to fill out his resume a bit more—›Brigadier General So-and-So‹—but the military advisor interrupted him before Joshua could even say his name. He said to me in a soft but venomous voice, ›So you are the seeker of justice.‹ And then he mocked me: ›Bravo! We need justice.‹ I thought, ›you're right, you barf bag, and we'll get it—in spite of you.‹«

Bukar smiled, satisfied like a hunter gripping his victim, and opened the photo app on his phone. I knew what he was going to say next.

»He was the man in the picture, no doubt about it.«

Bukar told me about his short but mistrustful conversation with the military advisor. The two had circled each other like cat and mouse while Joshua sat there in amazement and was the only one who managed to eat more than half of his Caesar salad.

»First, the military advisor wanted to put me in my place because of the article I'd written for the *New York Daily*. By the way, have you read it yet?«

Yes, I had seen the print version, but not until the late morning. Too late to talk with Bukar about it and congratulate him. It was on page 24, but had taken up an eighth of the page and been framed in an eye-catching black box. *ICC to Grasp Golden Opportunity for Justice Between Two Waves of Violence in Nigeria*, read the headline. Three more articles featuring the author's interviews with those directly affected would follow over the next few days, the *New York Daily* wrote in italics beneath Bukar's article.

»It's no surprise that he didn't like the article,« I said.

»Not at all. At the beginning of our conversation, he mentioned the word ›traitor‹. He said it indirectly, like he wasn't talking about me, but he still meant it as a warning. He made some general remarks about how easy it is to be blacklisted and what the consequences are. Then he asked me whom I wanted justice for—for all those who found themselves in the line of fire because they've cooperated with Boko Haram or ISWAP? What a sly piece of rhetoric, I thought. Victims are to be blamed if they find themselves in the line of fire. ›Or,‹ he asked, ›do you want justice for the brave soldiers who sacrifice their lives fighting the blindly raging hordes of fanatics? For the sake of our people's security?‹

»›Justice for all,‹ I told him. ›It's not a question of either, or.‹ To reassure him, I quoted what the chief prosecutor of the International Criminal Court had found in December 2020 at the conclusion of the preliminary investigation, which is that the vast majority of the crimes were the responsibility of Boko Haram and its splinter groups. But he didn't let up. ›For everyone. Of course,‹ he said, ›but you mean that while nobly pursuing justice for all‹«—Bukar wrinkled his mouth contemptuously like the military advisor had at these three words—»›our highly deserving military leaders should risk having to explain to a bunch of ignorant civilians in The Hague—‹

»›You mean the judges,‹ I interrupted him.

»›—which unfortunate measures must occasionally be taken in the fight against barbarians?‹

»Unfortunate measures?« continued Bukar. »War crimes, he meant. Unfortunate measures that nobody wants, but are, alas, inevitable in the fight against those barbarians. I wasn't shedding any tears of sympathy. Instead, I told him that the highly deserving military leaders don't necessarily have to talk to the international judges in The Hague. They could just explain the necessity of their unfortunate measures to a military court in Nigeria. The Hague only steps in when the Nigerian judiciary is either unable or unwilling to conduct trials for possible war crimes itself. I added in my sweetest voice, ›You didn't mean to suggest that the Nigerian military justice system is unable or unwilling, did you? Should I tell you how many Nigerian prosecutors and judges attend training courses at the Nuremberg Academy[43] every year?‹ The military advisor knew all of that of course,« Bukar explained. »He also knew that my insinuation that he thought the Nigerian military jurisdiction was unable or unwilling wasn't very nice, which it wasn't. And he knew he had to return the blow, which he did, although I wasn't sure what to make of it. It seemed pretty harmless for what should have been a merciless quid pro quo. He squinted and whispered, ›Today's article and the three others to come—did you write them all yourself?‹ I immediately thought of Bob's word to June, indicating that I wasn't available because I was writing articles about Nigeria with López. Could June have leaked that information to the military advisor? I realized in a millisecond that he had just confirmed what I had already suspected. Of course, I couldn't give him a direct answer, so I jokingly asked him if he wanted to contribute as well? If so, he could write a letter to the editor, I suggested. That was basically the end of our conversation. Joshua politely tried to change the topic and ended up with soccer, of all things. We listed our favorite teams and players, as if they mattered. Joshua mentioned women's soccer and my father's story. You know—his execution. The military advisor took a sip of his drink and looked bored. ›Just for being a coach?‹ he asked, then kept telling the story of how his favorite player had to fill in as goalie once and even blocked a penalty shot and was an all-around great guy. I was convinced that the military advisor was a zombie. Someone whose capacity for empathy had died. But I was grateful not to get a hypocritical *I'm sorry for your loss* from him. We both left out the jibes when we said goodbye, turned around and walked away.«

Bukar wasn't nearly as energetic as he'd seemed at the beginning of his report.

»And?« I asked. »Was it worth it? Did you achieve anything?«

»In some ways,« he said. »I now know that he's against me. And I have reason to believe that he's in cahoots with June. I suspect they want to defame my articles based on López's involvement.«

---

43 The International Nuremberg Principles Academy in Nuremberg, Germany, is an institution dedicated to the advancement of international criminal law. In particular, it aims to educate individuals who take part in bringing to justice the perpetrators of genocide, war crimes, crimes against humanity and the crime of aggression.

»Okay, so you learned something. But didn't you also move further away from your goal?« I suggested. »If I understand correctly, the army must cooperate in the criminal case against Boko Haram. Through witnesses, through military expertise, through whatever. You didn't get closer to winning their support. Instead, it seems like the positions have become even more entrenched.«

»Yes, you're right. But firstly, the military advisor is just one voice in a much larger organization. I have to trust that there are more enlightened people in the army. Like those who send members of the military judiciary to the training courses at the Nuremberg Academy and, of course, those who've participated in the courses themselves. And secondly, you don't expect me to kiss up to the military advisor and naively assume that my irresistible charm will change his mind, do you? No. If there has to be a conflict here in New York, then so be it. I'll just have to deal with it.«

You roar, my lion, I told him, feeling proud of my own personal hero.

The gray sky hung lower than before. We didn't know what to expect over the next few days, but a sense of foreboding settled over us. Otherwise, we wouldn't have been so eager to celebrate our own heroism.

* * *

Was I awake or having a nightmare? I still don't know, so I'm writing it down as it was ingrained in my memory.

Bukar was lying next to me. The window was partially open. The lightning wasn't flashing into the room as it had the previous two nights. The cooler air and the gusty wind indicated that the cozy part of fall was giving way to the stormy part. And those sirens. Always the sirens. Did New York only consist of heart attacks, bike accidents, broken pipes, and stove fires?

Bukar was also restless, either awake or half dreaming. At times, I reached for his arm. When I found him, I felt safer. But sometimes he was far away.

He was sitting in his pajamas on a bookshelf in the Ottendorfer, looking down to Bob at the reception desk. Bob, sitting behind a sheet of plexiglas, was sliding back and forth on the wheels of his office chair and complaining, »I was so naive!« His words dripped like slime from his contorted mouth.

Hit by a gust of wind, the sashes of one of the high bull's-eye windows at the front of the building suddenly opened, slammed against the wall, and bounced back. A puff of snow blew into the entryway. Bob didn't pay attention. He kept drooling. »I was so naive! Everything down the drain, all stolen!«

Tony was suddenly there, too. His head filled up a picture frame that was hanging on the wall above Bob, right next to Valentin Ottendorfer. Tony took his pipe out of his mouth and moved his lips. A talking picture like in a Harry Potter film.

»Bob, stop yammering!« said Tony.

»Yeah, stop whining,« echoed Bukar from up on the shelf. »Why are you whining like a whiner?«

Bob was still drooling. »Was in Minton's, playing my gigs with the white negroes. The classy asses! While we were playing, bam, they stole it all.«

»What did they steal?« asked Tony from inside his picture, stroking his beard.

»Benny Goodman stole swing. Elvis stole rock and roll.« Bob gasped for air and went on. »Eric Clapton stole the blues. And his eminence, Mr. Eminem, stole hip-hop.«

»Fiiiiinally!« cheered Tony. »Atrocious music! Away with it!«

»Yes, away with it!« called Amelie. She had appeared next to Tony in the picture frame and was squeezing a pimple on her oily nose. Suddenly, Bukar was sitting next to Bob at the reception.

»Stop yammering,« he said empathetically and put his arm round Bob's shoulder. »What did you tell the Nigerian on the subway? Stop yammering. Stop feeling like a victim all the time, you told him.«

Then suddenly we were all sitting in the subway. I wanted to go over to Bukar and stood up, but the train shook so violently that I plopped back down onto my seat. Tony was standing in front of me and I found myself awkwardly staring at his abdomen. Finally, Tony turned toward Bob.

»Goodness gracious!« he said. »Everything stolen? Bad, bad boys. Someone out for revenge because you stole the white piano?«

Bob was indignant, but before he could say anything, Tony kept talking.

»And the saxophone? And the bass—yeah, that too! Maybe you stole that from us Bohemians?«

»We didn't steal first!« Bob was defensive.

»Oh yes you did!« nagged Amelie from inside an ad for a pregnancy help center.

»No, we didn't! You don't know anything!«

»Yes, I do!« griped Amelie.

Then we were all back in the Ottendorfer. Bob dragged himself to the window and closed the shutter to keep it from flapping to and fro. While he was coming back, his upper body quivered again in a strange way and made little jerking movements like a broken wind-up doll.

»It's not about the piano, sax or bass. It's about the whole thing!« he croaked despairingly.

Then Bob looked very, very small. I was standing next to him, as tiny as he was, and heard Tony's and Amelie's sneering and cackling as a distant echo. We were so close to each other that I could see the pearls of sweat on his forehead in microscopic clarity and smell his stale breath. He looked at me, muddled, begging for help, with such sad, teary eyes that I fell into a leaden numbness.

»Petra, you get me,« Bob said. »Everything original in American music can be attributed to us Blacks. It's true, isn't it? Ragtime, jazz, bebop, and so on. And white people? They claim it all. Especially the profits. We're only allowed to keep the suffering our music was born from, and I look like an idiot. Shit!«

I looked to my right. Someone was suddenly standing there. I didn't recognize him—or did I? A tall, slender, conspicuously good-looking, lighter-skinned Black man. He had prominent, bright eyes and a thin, meticulously trimmed mustache above his upper lip. A middle part had been combed into his short hair and he smelled of hair tonic. His light grey suit was a size or two too big, perhaps intentionally to make him look cooler.

Bob croaked a greeting to the new guy: »Beautiful Bill! By God!«

William Grant Still,[44] I told my dreaming self. The other day you noticed him on the cover of a CD, I reminded myself, because you hardly knew anything about him. The booklet said that he had long been considered the doyen of Black composers, an icon of the Harlem Renaissance. He composed an *African-American* Symphony, the cantata *And They Lynched Him*

---

44 William Grant Still (1895–1978) was an American composer and arranger. In 1955, he became the first Black conductor of a major orchestra (in New Orleans).

on a Tree, and the anti-racist opera *Troubled Water* based on a libretto by James Langston Hughes.

I said hi to Beautiful Bill, but he ignored me and turned to Bob, who immediately picked a fight.

»Bill, are you still trying to rescue us niggers?« asked Bob, pronouncing the N-word with unmistakable cynicism. »Still trying to shove us up a rung on the ladder of civilization? Make white Blacks out of black Blacks? Racial uplift? You still believe in that?«

Beautiful Bill didn't let himself get riled up. He replied calmly and self-composedly. »A guy like you would ask that? What are you playing? Jazz for elites? Isn't that the same? Uplift? Why are you doing this?«

»So you won't say that jazz and blues are primitive,« snarled Bob.

»Oh, I won't say that. Quite the contrary. But what I will say is that we Blacks have to play in the major league.«

»I'm saying that, too,« interrupted Bob.

»With major league, I'm talking about the classical scene.«

»Nonsense,« said Bob gruffly. »The major league can be everything. The most important thing is that you stay Black.«

»Am I not Black?« asked Still, his tone souring. He gave Bob a stern look. »You think I'm not? And you're the one who decides whether I'm Black or not?«

The scene suddenly changed. My professor in Innsbruck was standing in front of a blackboard. The chalk screeched as he wrote *Uplift* on the board with two arrows pointing out from it. The arrow on the left pointed to the words *Classical Music*, and he'd written *Bebop* on the right.

After that, Bob and Still intensified their little quarrel.

»Do you know, Bill, what your friend Hughes wrote? ›This is the mountain standing in the way of any true Negro art in America—this urge within the race toward whiteness, the desire to pour racial individuality into the mold of American standardization, and to be as little Negro and as much American as possible.‹«

»He also said…«

Tony appeared in front of me, Bob and Still: He interrupted the two of them. His cardigan smelled of pipe tobacco, his unkempt mustache stuck out in all directions. He put his meaty hands on Bob's and Bill's shoulders.

»I'm telling you as the old man that I am, as a Bohemian, and not least as your forerunner: The powerful people, the Habsburgs, the Establishment, they all want the same thing. To be the be-all-and-end-all. Everything lumped together. That's the policy of the mighty ones.«

Bob wrenched himself out of Tony's shoulder grip and yelled at Still. »Did you hear what Tony said? Lumping everything together is what the mighty people do. Lumping it together into a standardized *white* pile.«

Tony's warm voice wasn't deterred by Bob's interjections. »When the powerful demand uniformity, how should I reply as a Bohemian? Or you as Black people? It's simple. Long live diversity! It's our weapon. Thanks to diversity, I've been a Bohemian, a Slovak, a Burleigh.«

»And Hiawatha,« added Amelie.

»And always a vagabond, jolly and bright,« I exclaimed to my own surprise.

Everyone stared at me. Embarrassed, I held my tongue and tried to climb out of my dream. Then my professor in Innsbruck turned up again.

»American music,« he said, his voice echoing as he lectured from a podium, »is always at its most original when it does away with European role models and their penchant for big, monolithic forms, and brings together the many smaller, colorful fragments that make up America.«

»Right,« said Tony, continuing the thought. »Many colorful fragments! *Hiawatha*, that sure would have been something! My American opera. ›Indian‹ libretto, Burleigh's plantation music, and all of it in Bohemian B Minor.«

»Exactly,« I called loudly as I grabbed Tony's jacket sleeve and shook him. »Diversity! Blend everything together, without regard for place, time, taste, convention, or deference. Noodles with spinach and teriyaki sauce, tortillas with caviar. That's possible only in the United States. That *is* the United States.«

I felt Bob's and Bill's dumbfounded stares and once again looked for the emergency exit out of my dream. Bukar rescued me by walking into the middle of it all. With his arms outstretched like a messiah, he said, »Stop it! This is ridiculous! Can't you put two and two together?« He sounded really upset, which was unusual for him, but not for a savior. We all kept quiet.

»Tony is right,« said Bukar. »Diversity is wonderful and important. It's our weapon against the cultural purity that the mighty ones invoke to impose their will and their standards on us. But, people, then there shouldn't be something like cultural purity among Blacks. Diversity must also flourish in Black culture, whether it's high-brow, low-brow, American, Caribbean, Nigerian, or anything else.«

Bob grunted in agreement.

»Then it's not ok to pit one form of diversity against another,« continued Bukar. He avoided looking at Bob, although it was clear whom he meant: Bob and his resentment of Indigenous Americans. Did Bob understand what Bukar was trying to say?

He was listening, but didn't say anything. Or, if he had said something, we couldn't hear it among the buzz of word fragments that spun around us as everyone started talking at once. More and more new and absurd phrases flowed together, forming a dogmatic, frenetic, and frightening vortex. Floundering in the middle of it, I saw myself as a bug being washed down the drain, powerless to swim against the spiraling water. I was pulled into the center, certain that I was about to be swallowed up by the deep, dark, unknown depths.

Then Bob's voice emerged from the gurgling whirlpool. He harped again on his current obsession: theft. »Tony, don't let yourself off the hook so fast. You prophesied that we Blacks would become *good* and *important*. But not that our achievements would constantly be stolen.«

Still eagerly took his cue. »Steal?« he exclaimed, suppressing his surprise. »*You* are talking about stealing? With *me*, who was robbed of everything? Whose melodies were stolen by Gershwin in his big hit, *I Got Rhythm*? Whose conducting position was stolen, yours or mine? You know what I said. If Gershwin is going to steal, then so will I! When he wrote his *Rhapsody in Blue*, a pseudo-Black jazz symphony, I thought, okay, well done, not bad, but I can do it better. So I wrote my Second Symphony, *A New Race*.« ♦

»*A New Race*?« Bob interrupted him, shaking with rage and skeptical that the damn race issue could be resolved with *A New Race*.

»Yeah, *A New Race*. That is the future. A patchwork of all Americans. Overcoming opposites. Stealing will be unnecessary.« He rubbed his hand across his gelled hair with a sweet-sour coolness that covered up how much he was torn between his constant desire to catch up with the establishment

and his bitter experience with violence and rejection. »But since we're not quite there yet, I'm going to take back what Gershwin stole. Not because it belongs to me—music belongs to everyone—but because it doesn't belong to him.«

»You're taking it back? Wouldn't that be nice!« snorted Bob. He was so exasperated by Bill's naïveté that he started limping around in circles. Still kept talking.

»And when the white establishment smacked me in the balls, then, okay, Harry Pace and I went and founded our very own record label. Black Swan Records. And I conducted our own orchestra.[45] It went really well.«

»I could laugh my head off!« sneered Bob. »It went really well? For how long? Three years! And what did Black Swan take back from the fat cats? After three years, Paramount got *you* back!«

»But in those three years, we brought art music to hundreds of thousands of Black people,« argued Still, who was starting to get annoyed.

»And who did that help?«

»Well…you, for example! Or do you think that an average Black person would have wanted to listen to your bebop out of the blue?«

To my right, a children's choir was swaying rhythmically and causing a disturbance. An evening sun was setting solemnly on a screen; in front of it, Bukar was conducting the choir as it sang ecstatically, »Take it back! Take it back!«

Bob kept stomping stiffly in circles. His mood had worsened since the beginning of the dream.

Meanwhile, Tony explained the Central European view on taking back something that had been stolen. »A Wiener schnitzel is a Wiener schnitzel. When the Milanese steal it and call it *scaloppa milanese*, then I say, it's still a Wiener schnitzel. And then I say, enjoy your meal!«

Amelie laughed at Tony. She had toured Europe three times, she said, and knew very well that a Wiener schnitzel and a *scaloppa milanese* were not the same thing. Tony's tone soured as he asked whether three European tours meant she really knew better than a local?

»Oh yes,« retorted Amelie. »Being a local doesn't mean you know more. It only means you're more biased.«

---

45 The Black Swan Symphony Orchestra (1921-1923)

Tony didn't reply. *Bitchy witch*, said the look on his face.

Bob was still quarreling with Still. His belief in *uplift*, he said, had quite literally been beaten out of his head and expelled in therapy.

Amelie interjected that she didn't want to hear about *new race* because it reminded her too much of Arthur.

Still was mumbling to himself about how difficult it was trying to talk to Bob about higher standards. No wonder, considering he'd swapped classical music for bar tunes. Then Still made another plea for *uplift*. Duke Ellington's *Black, Brown and Beige* ♦. Just the kind of Black art music he was thinking of. Jazz, but with classical training. Good jazz.

Black, Brown and Beige. A color spectrum that stands for generations of rape. And for the pride and solidarity that the Black community—unified in its diversity—has always depended on.

Gershwin couldn't compose something like that.

Amelie still had Bukar's messianic speech in her ear, but had misunderstood its meaning. Cultural purity wasn't a bad thing, she nagged. Where would we be without purity, there was already so much filth in the world, she had just heard an avant-garde piece, and that Kanye West, absolutely not…

And just as I wanted to tell Amelie that Bukar was not talking about cleanliness or propriety, but about forced uniformity, just as I was about to say that, Bukar screamed in the middle of his dream. »Stop!«

He was so loud that I was instantly sure my dream was over.

I felt Bukar's strong grip on my forearm as he screamed. Then he screamed again, still beside himself. »Stop! Stop fighting! You all want the same thing—justice!«

Then Bukar also woke up. He sat up straight in bed and whispered to me as his dream came back to him. »Justice?«

The streetlights that shone faintly into the bedroom spookily exaggerated the uneasiness in his eyes. The folds on his face, accentuated by the dimness, were straight out of a horror film. He got up and went to the window. Before he closed it, I thought I saw a few snowflakes blow into the room and melt as they landed on the computer.

Bukar came back to bed. We slept restlessly until we were roused by the alarm clock.

* * *

»What did you dream about?« I asked Bukar after turning off the alarm clock. In particular, I mentioned his scream (»Justice!«) that had made him jump in the middle of the night.

»I can't remember,« he answered sparingly, but I had my own theories about his dream.

»And you?« he asked.

I told him and he listened carefully to all the details. His surprisingly simple reaction only strengthened my doubts about whether it really was a dream.

»We really have to talk with Bob,« he said.

It had been two days since we'd watched Amelie's correspondence being removed from the library. López had made it clear that she would protect Bob from any accusations. Nevertheless, it was easy to imagine that the pressure on Bob was growing—pressure that López wanted to keep away from him. He had to pretend to us and Amelie that he didn't know anything about the incident. In my dream, he had made himself out to be the victim of theft, but was unable to defend himself when Tony accused him of having committed one. It was all just a mazy dream, but it was rooted in reality. Perhaps it was an indication of what was going on inside of Bob. In any case, things could not continue as they were.

»Let's go over there together today. Somehow we have to get Bob to talk without breaking through López's blockade.«

Bob was sitting at the doorman's desk when we got there. He greeted us with his usual mix of grumpiness and taciturnity. In a couple of words mumbled under his breath, he mentioned that the red-haired chick had come to the library right after it opened.

»Did she ask for me again?« wondered Bukar.

Bob thought for a moment, then said, »No. That's strange. She just wanted to know whether you were writing stories upstairs with López again. I told her no, but maybe you would later. That was enough information for her. She didn't leave a message and left the library with a weird grin on her face.«

For Bukar, everything was crystal clear. »Bob, if she comes back, don't say anything to her. Nothing at all. She's spying on me. She wants to hurt me.«

»Hurt you?« asked Bob, bewildered. »I thought she admired you!«

»Not at all. She wants to hurt me. And employ you as her useful idiot.«

»Me? I'm the idiot again?«

»No, not an idiot. A *useful* idiot. Her unwitting helper. That's what I meant.«

With trembling fingers, Bob took another one of his little pink pills. The wrinkles on his face were bulging. It was pitiful, inexpressibly sad to see how crumpled up Bob looked. He stood up and took a few steps away from the front desk. Then he stood next to Bukar and put his hand on his arm.

»Brother, can you forgive me?« he asked abruptly, letting his head fall forward toward Bukar's chest.

Bukar was surprised. Or maybe he wasn't, but he acted like he was. »Forgive you? For what?«

»I've fucked up again.«

Bukar smiled kindly at Bob.

»I've screwed you over. And your nice girlfriend, too. Man, Bukar, take care of her. She's a gem.«

I looked away, as if I hadn't heard what Bob had said.

»Your Petra, she wanted to look through Amelie's letters. Right? I'm sorry. There are no more letters. I got rid of them.«

Bukar and I were not surprised. We'd suspected him. But I thought about Bukar's right to truth. Bob had dared to step out from under the protection that López offered him and tell the naked, bitter truth. Simply because he believed it would make him feel better. Courageous, very courageous. And wise.

At the same time, Bob's confession upset me for selfish reasons. Irreplaceable letters and notes, a piece of music history—gone.

I was also miffed at myself. When I was speaking with Bob three days ago, I had dug deep into his motives, perhaps deeper than anyone else had. I didn't approve of Bob's act of destruction, but I could understand why he did it. Three days ago, I had decided that I would forgive him when his guilt was proven, which was only a matter of time. But I hadn't forgiven him just yet.

Before I could express my feelings, Bukar put his hand on Bob's shoulders and said quietly, »Yes. We thought so, but weren't sure. That's why we came here this morning.« Bukar reached for Bob's hand and gave it a squeeze. »But no need for an interrogation now. You took care of it yourself.«

»And no electroshocks?«

»No electroshocks.«

The tension had dissipated. After another squeeze that turned into a brief hug, Bukar said, »Thank you. Thank you for your honesty. I'm sure that wasn't easy.«

Bob also spoke. Just one word, as big and deep as an ocean: »Thanks.«

The two embraced again. Then Bukar asked, »Where are the documents now? Can you get them back?«

Bob was uneasy. »Yeah, sure, I'll have to try.« He shuffled back to his desk, picked up the phone and dialed a number. The call didn't go through, so he dialed another with a show of frenzied effort to make it clear to us that he would keep trying. Bukar and I sat down at a nearby table at the front of the reading room. Ten minutes later, Bob came over to us.

»Shit. Nothing. But I'll keep trying.«

Bukar couldn't help but give Bob a lecture. »Do you know why the letters are so important? They're one-of-a-kind, and they have historical value. Especially for Petra, you're right about that. But there's more to it. There is nothing worse than not knowing the truth because of a lack of evidence. In my real job, furthering justice, we aim not just to assume evil, but to prove it. With documents, because they're a hundred times more reliable than witnesses. Your opinion of Amelie and your actions show that you see her as an enemy. But now that we can't study her correspondence, you'll never find out what Amelie really thought about Black people and their music. My impression is that she is not as anti-Black and pro-›Indian‹ as you take her to be. She's too empathetic for that. In her own quirky, conservative way, she's much too philanthropic. But that's just my feeling. I can't prove it. And you can't prove your feeling either. And if Amelie's letters are gone, then we'll have to spend the rest of our lives in doubt.«

»My life won't last much longer anyway,« interjected Bob sarcastically.

»Yeah, yeah,« said Bukar, suddenly becoming very snide. »I see it the other way around. The less life you have left, the more you should be afraid of leaving this world with unresolved doubts.«

Bob hadn't expected Bukar to say that. He chewed his own mouth, his lower jaw quivering.

»And think about this,« continued Bukar. »I still have a long life ahead of me, and so does Petra. We're sufferers of doubt just like you. Don't dodge the issue. We'd all be better off if we knew where the letters were.«

Bob shook his head. »Dammit! You're right again,« he groaned. »I've got to apologize to Amelie and López.«

»Try calling again,« Bukar urged him, then indicated that we were leaving the library.

We found a restaurant that served breakfast and read the *New York Daily* over blueberry pancakes. We spotted the first full-length article in the series on justice in Nigeria. There was a story about the children that perilously escaped a Boko Haram re-education camp in the Sambisa Forest and had been placed in a home to deal with their nightmares. Bukar was familiar with the details. His sister Rehinat, a medical nurse, had told him about it. Bukar admitted that López had worked wonders with his (and Rehinat's) material. She understood the *New York Daily*'s recipe for success: monumental, enlightening and witty sentences that give way to the next equally monumental sentence.

Bob called as we were finishing our breakfast. He had reached the guy with the van. No luck. Everything had landed in the shredder that same night.

»Hmm,« sighed Bukar. »How frustrating! Have you confessed to Amelie and López yet?«

I could hear Bob's reply through the phone.

»Yes.«

»And?«

»López tried to comfort me. She was encouraging and said everything would be okay.«

»And Amelie?« asked Bukar.

»Strange bird.«

»Why is that?«

»Instead of getting upset, she just said, ›Good for me, you old donkey. Now you just have to believe what I say. Even if I can't prove it.‹ She's right, that bitch.«

For the rest of the day, Bukar sat at his computer and wrote, made calls to NGOs, and read up on the latest news from Nigeria.

Under the surface, I felt deeply frustrated. Not least because the destruction of the letters had been confirmed. I suddenly felt the urge to take a break, to go far away. I lay in bed for half an hour and felt sorry for myself in the most common way, effortlessly squeezing out two or three tears. The stress, the nightmares, the frenetic dealing with things that had happened decades ago or in faraway countries, the human disappointments, the failure of my dissertation.

Was all that worth ignoring the opportunities New York had to offer? I was young, I liked music, I liked going out, experiencing cool atmospheres, discovering the cultural scene. Did I have to restrict myself because of all the old stuff I was surrounded by? Minton's Playhouse was okay, I didn't mind it. But what else was going on?

Usually, I could count on Bukar to pull me up when I was feeling down, but this time he was all about his project. Had I finally become a real New Yorker—restless, full of big ideas, but too drained to follow through on them and enjoy life?

* * *

Things were happening quickly. The next morning over breakfast, we read the second article in the Nigeria series. This time it was about the abducted schoolgirl who had been forced into marriage and was released after the government paid a ransom. Disgraced and rejected back home, she moved to the city where she was ostracized for being alone. Nevertheless, she carried on and joined an NGO in order to find justice.

Joshua called while we were reading the article. Bukar was furious. He told me what Joshua had said. An article on the third page of the *New York Examiner* was propagating a wild conspiracy theory. It talked about a campaign that was using questionable arguments to pressure the International Criminal Court into initiating a trial against Nigerian military leaders, even though experts agreed that doing so would only worsen the crisis in Nigeria.

»The *New York Examiner*?« I asked. I'd seen the sensationalist paper on display at the kiosks and occasionally in the hands of subway travelers. »I never thought they would write an article about the International Criminal Court.«

»That's the point,« commented Bukar and explained indignantly why the article was such a dirty trick. »A paper like that doesn't write about the ICC, and it most certainly wouldn't get worried about the court. It writes *against* the ICC, in line with its authoritarian tradition. It calls the court a rabid agent of destabilization in Nigeria which, thanks to its army, is such a stable country. The court, it says, it a compliant instrument of obscure circles, left-wing opponents of law and order. *That* is the message. Stay away from the ICC! I was surprised that they didn't suggest that a global left-wing conspiracy was behind it all, or maybe it was the Democrats, which is practically the same thing to them. And do you know what the most deceitful thing of all is?«

»No, what?«

»The obscure, left-wing circle with their ethically questionable campaign—they're talking about me and López! The *New York Examiner* always informs its readers very precisely. At the heart of the destabilization campaign is a series of articles in the *New York Daily*, written by a ghostwriter who thinks she can speak for Nigerians although she isn't one herself. She should be ashamed of herself, the paper wrote. As should the Nigerian who offered his name to cover up her duplicitousness.«

I found the whole thing grotesque and, not knowing what else to say, turned to sarcasm. »How scandalous! Somebody should cut off that Nigerian's head!« Then we didn't feel like making more macabre jokes.

Bukar called Walter, who was totally surprised at first. Understandable, considering that he probably didn't read the *New York Examiner*. He immediately understood Bukar's warning that a campaign against the International Criminal Court with potential for mass impact was taking shape. Walter promised to organize another meeting right away.

I asked Bukar for June's business card and spontaneously decided to dial her number. I wanted to call her out and hopefully find evidence that JUICE was working together with the Nigerian army and the *New York Ex-*

aminer. If I could collect enough proof, then I could shut her down for all to see and rescue Bukar. I was about to become a real fiend. My plan B—if I was able to talk with June—was to pressure her into standing down and not destroying Bukar's big dream. Maybe his and her views on justice could flourish in parallel worlds.

My attempt failed. When I reached June on the phone, I felt butterflies in my stomach. To be put through to her in the first place, I said I was a researcher and was very interested in the article in the *New York Examiner*. Since she was so knowledgeable about the issues surrounding justice, I asked whether she might be able to comment on the article. Or, even better, whether we could meet in person that very day.

She hesitated only briefly and answered sweetly but curtly, »No, I'm sorry. I'd like to help you, but I don't know what you're talking about.«

Of course she wasn't the innocent lamb she was making herself out to be. My conclusion was that she was more cunning that I'd thought. Was she suspicious because I spoke English with an Austrian accent and she already knew from Bukar that I'm from South Tyrol?

* * *

»I hope we're not making a mistake.«

Walter welcomed us at the entrance to the German House with these rather discouraging words. His hellos and how-do-you-dos sounded friendly, but the rings under his eyes revealed his exhaustion. He waved to the German security officers as we went into the foyer. They let me and Bukar pass through the metal detector without inspection. We only had an hour until the event started.

The big conference room was on the second floor of the German House. As we climbed the stairs, Walter's words echoed in our ears: *I hope we're not making a mistake.* Entering the room, I was surprised by how plain it was. It stretched from the front to the back of the building and had windows on three sides. At the front, where an elevated stage had been set up, heavy black rubberized curtains covered the windows. A Steinway grand piano had been pushed to the back of the stage. In the middle, there were three steel-gray, cube-shaped armchairs and a coffee table with chrome-plated legs. The table held accessories typical for a panel discussion: four cordless microphones, water glasses, two pitchers of water (one sparkling, one still). A bouquet of flowers would have been nice, I thought, but apparently the organizers didn't have time to pop down to the closest flower shop two streets over.

Walter pointed to the three chairs. »Bukar, I'll be sitting in the middle and you'll be to my left.«

»And on the other side?« I asked Walter. I feared the worst. June? He wouldn't be so draft, would he?

»Gregory,« Walter said. »Honestly, I hardly know him at all. It came together just last night. He is a journalist with the *New York Daily*, and he really wanted to be here. I though, okay, it can only be in our best interest. I'm sure the *New York Daily* will defend its own series.«

Bukar tilted his head and looked at Walter questioningly. »Are you really so sure about that?«

Walter was confused. Why the uncertainty?

»Well,« Bukar began carefully, »the discussion might also touch on ethical standards. Who I am speaking for, who is López speaking for. That's where they want to find a weak spot. You know all about the trouble June and her helpers have gotten us into. Of course, the *New York Daily* wants to prove that no one can outdo them in terms of ethical standards and that I am a good and legitimate author. The *New York Daily* and we will be on the same page up to that point. But what if something goes wrong? Then Gregory will do an about-face and find a scapegoat to save his employer's reputation.«

Judging by the wrinkles on Walter's face, he could hardly be more frustrated. What I had to say didn't help much.

»Bukar has a point, unfortunately,« I said. »This morning I read the reader comments under his article. Almost all of them referred to the who-can-say-what question. Apparently, the moral wellbeing of *Daily* readers is more important than the fate of the fishermen in Doron Baga. They all went on like a broken record. Was Bukar allowed to get help with the article? Why did he need to do that since he's a journalist himself? What was the ghostwriter allowed to contribute? What motivated the *New York Examiner* to publish their story? Why is the *New York Daily* not being as clearcut with their work ethic in this case, as they had been a few months ago when they fired a staff member for using the N-word at an internal meeting—

while quoting someone else. And so on and so forth. Of course, there were a few people who actually commented on the content. But, honestly, they were not in the majority.«

Walter asked, »Could it be that the people who are interested in the content simply write fewer comments than those who need to bang a drum of indignation to prove their own greatness?«

»Absolutely,« replied Bukar. »I assume it's just as you say. But who can guarantee that this afternoon the friends of indignation won't be wordier than the friends of objectivity?«

Guests started arriving at the entrance.

»Two colleagues from the NGO Coalition for the ICC,« Walter said. »I have to speak with them. They can help keep the focus of the discussion on Nigeria and not on this or that person.«

A short time later, López, Bob and Gladys arrived amidst a small group of other visitors. We said hello and looked for seats in the fourth and fifth rows, close to the wall. It seemed like the best place to follow the discussion.

López's disconcertment was written all over her face. She knew, of course, that her contribution to Bukar's article could become an important and potentially toxic part of the debate. She looked anxiously to the right, then to the left, and chewed a piece of gum with small, quick motions. I'd never seen her do that before. López and gum simply didn't go together. Between them lay worlds of fine deportment, the boundaries of which were now collapsing under the influence of insecurity. Gladys, too, seemed to have noticed the gum. She took López's arm and gave her a bright smile as a quiet encouragement that López would manage just fine.

I followed one of López's glances to the back, turned around, and saw that Amelie and Tony had also arrived. They were sitting behind us. We greeted each other with a pat on the shoulder and no more than the necessary words. Then we fell silent. I thought it was a nice gesture that they both came to support Bukar and López, even though they probably didn't care very much about the events in Nigeria.

Amelie whispered something to me and tipped her head toward Gladys. »Is that her?« When I nodded, she muttered, »Good.«

Just before the beginning of the discussion, June walked in accompanied by two young women and a young man. They looked like a promotion team for a cell phone company. A politically correct mix of Africa and the Caribbean, East Asia and Europe, man bun and pixie cut, clean-cut and bohemian.

Walter welcomed them just as politely as everyone else. He didn't need to offer them a seat. They went straight to the second row and claimed the chairs on either side of the center aisle, draping a jacket or scarf over the backs before walking off to socialize. June was wearing a shabby, calf-length wool dress again, this time in turquoise, and black sandals.

When Walter walked by me, I asked whether he knew June's body-guards.

»Never seen them before,« he answered without stopping.

I couldn't help but watch June. Everyone seemed to know her. In any case, she was holding court among the fifty-odd guests that had assembled in the meantime. She greeted some people with a kiss on the cheek—despite the coronavirus—, tossed around words and phrases, and was as giddy as a victorious gladiator. She made a point of flirting with all the men who were more or less in her age range, or slightly older, like she must have done with Bukar when they first met.

Why was she like that, I wondered. She was definitely pretty. Her finely chiseled features did not reveal any past trials and tribulations. It didn't look like she had ever had to fight for education, status, or success. But these observations were superficial. I could not look inside her.

What had gone wrong in her life and when and why? Was she searching for respect, or for the love she was denied as a child? Was she young enough to change her ways and become a responsible grown-up at some point? Could I help her do that? Or was she a hopeless narcissist, smitten by the uniqueness of her unusual theories? I had no idea.

I was just about to give her the benefit of the doubt and assume she'd lost her way and deserved my sympathy. But then I stopped short and told myself not to let my protector instinct mollycoddle the woman. If not for myself, then I needed the reminder for Bukar's sake.

The discussion was about to begin. Walter walked onto the stage with a practiced, relaxed gait, greeted the audience and introduced the topic of the panel discussion. A criminal case against the perpetrators in Nigeria was a very real possibility, he said, but was teetering on a knife's edge. A well-known New York tabloid—Walter didn't say its name—was trying to discredit the ICC's proceedings. He said he believed the judges would not be impressed, but it was a fact that the ICC was reliant on the United States to conduct the trial. The Americans brought intelligence and the ability to track down individuals when international arrest warrants are issued. Therefore, it should be taken seriously when an influential newspaper, regardless of its quality (everyone knew that Walter meant *poor*), talked down a Nigeria trial. All the better that the guests had the opportunity today to hear from Bukar, an investigative journalist from Nigeria, and Gregory, a journalist from the *New York Daily*, about the series of articles that had been making waves this week, which the audience was surely familiar with. The series of features gave an emotional voice to the Nigerians' desire for justice.

»Who wrote the articles?« shouted June from the second row.

Walter was prepared for the interjection and stayed calm. »Thank you for your question. The authorship was noted in the invitation to today's panel. If you still have questions about it, we will come back to that later,« he said in a businesslike manner. »First I would like to finish my introduction and ask all participants to wait to be called on if you have a question during the discussion period, which I look forward to as much as you do.«

June wasn't so easily deterred. »Can my question be answered now? It doesn't make any sense to talk about a series of articles when we don't know who wrote them and what their context is.«

Walter was about to shoot down June's comment when one of the French women from the NGO Coalition cut in. »With all due respect for dear June,« she said, »let's agree to focus on the issue and not on the author.«

»But the one can't be separated from the other,« countered June.

From the podium, Bukar spoke into the microphone. »Walter,« he said sweetly, »you know my time is limited today. Gregory told me he also has other commitments. So if it's okay, I'd suggest we check off June's question and hope everyone else plays by the rules from now on.«

A faint murmur of approval rippled through the room. Walter gave Bukar the floor with a quick nod.

»So, about the question of authorship,« said Bukar. »I'm Bukar from Nigeria. Everything you read and will read in the *New York Daily* is based on *my* research, *my* interviews with victims, and of course on *my* evaluations. I would like to add that I'm grateful to my dear and wonderful friend López, who used her unparalleled feel for words and her profound understanding of justice issues to help me translate my Nigerian babbling into clean American English.«

Bukar said the last bit with a funny exaggerated Nigerian dialect and everyone laughed. Good job, I thought. 1-0 for Bukar. June backed down for the time being.

Walter completed his introduction, staying true to his habit of sorting his arguments into *first* and *second*. He introduced Bukar and Gregory very briefly. Bukar: an investigative journalist from Nigeria with a focus on justice, known in Nigeria for his reports on the massacres at Lake Chad and in Maiduguri. His father was murdered by Boko Haram. Gregory: an international affairs reporter for the *New York Daily* for four years. Prior to that, a West Africa correspondent for another respected publication.

Walter then summarized the current situation of the Nigeria trial at the International Criminal Court. He emphasized the reasons why the court had been particularly cautious thus far. First, respect for the Nigerian judicial system which could conduct a trial of its own if it wanted to. Second, the fact that a disproportionate number of trials involving crimes in African states were already pending. As the audience knew, this had brought about claims that the court was biased, although the disproportionate number of pending African trials was easy to explain: The African states in question had called on the ICC themselves. But, Walter continued, the whole discussion about the court's alleged bias showed two things. First, how easy it was to erect political hurdles on a flimsy or even false foundation. And second, how sensitively the court believed it had to be in dealing with the situation. For this reason, Walter said, it was important to confront the ridiculous accusations in the *New York Examiner* against Bukar's articles. We, as supporters of the International Criminal Court, would certainly benefit from Bukar's and Gregory's input, Walter said, and closed his remarks by saying that he wanted to turn the discussion over to them without further ado.

Before he could do so, June interrupted. She just stood up and started talking loudly, casting indignant glances both at Walter and the audience as she turned toward the back of the room and ran her fingers through her hair in feigned exasperation. Employing dramatic body language, she asked the guests to join her in her outrage as if it were the only obvious reaction and any other was terribly ignorant.

»Walter, excuse me, but I have to comment on that and I'm sure many of the guests here today feel the same way. Personally, I don't think much of the *New York Examiner*, but to write off their concerns as ridiculous before we've had a chance to discuss them with Bukar and Gregory and before we've clarified the role of Bukar's mysterious ghostwriter in writing the articles—that's going too far. Besides, everyone knows, especially my colleagues from Africa, that the International Criminal Court's serious acceptance problem has to do not only with its selection of cases, but especially with its totally misguided approach to justice, which, unlike JUICE…«

Walter interrupted her. While June was fulminating, his face clearly showed what he was not capable of. He was good at elegantly presenting rhetorically refined ideas, which, along with his calming manner of speaking, had garnered him approval at first. But conflict put him in a quandary. The corners of his mouth quivered and the prominent wrinkles on his forehead bulged so much that it was easy to see how uncomfortable he felt.

»Excuse me, June, but we haven't started the discussion yet. I would appreciate it if we could listen to what Bukar and Gregory have to say first,« said Walter.

June was still standing. Then she stepped up onto her chair and looked around the room, as if she'd just scaled a barricade and had to organize the opposition in the room against the conspiring representatives of stupidity and dishonesty on the podium. »Do you have something to hide? Why are you avoiding the question that everyone here is asking?«

It was an old trick that always worked. Present yourself as the leader of an unverifiable majority that does not accept minorities. I was curious how Walter and Bukar would respond.

»No, of course we don't have anything to hide. What would we?« A big mistake, I thought. Now he had entered into June's narrative.

»It's obvious! You're not disclosing who the ghostwriter is and what her interests are!« screamed June. »Who is controlling this person from afar? What is Bukar scheming with her? What does Bukar have to gain from working with this person?«

I was appalled. She was asking a bunch of tendentious and vile questions. All of them suggested that an egregious conspiracy was going on that any right-thinking person would want to unravel.

One of the French representatives of the NGO Coalition spoke loudly so that everyone could hear: »*C'est absurde!*« But she wasn't contradicting June.

In retrospect, I realized that López had known that things would unfold in this way. She had sensed that the matter would come to a head, and she had accepted, with her typical inner balance, that she would have to make a sacrifice.

She stood up and said, »I am López, the person who helped Bukar write the articles. Hello and good afternoon! Let's stay on topic. The accusations against Bukar, which I've just heard, are completely off base. Ask me, if you like.«

López's appearance surprised the audience. I saw respect and goodwill in their faces.

Walter also noticed the wave of affirmation, but proceeded to make his next big mistake. He invited López onto the podium. That made her a pinboard for everyone who wanted to post their agreement or disapproval.

López acted coyly for just a moment. She knew her fate was sealed. Calmly and collectedly, she got up and walked without haste to the stage. Walter quickly took an extra chair from the room and put it to the right of Gregory, but sat down on it himself and offered López his chair in the middle of the podium. Walter's third mistake. López was now the main protagonist. The original choreography of the event had been turned on its head.

Walter tried to keep things under control.

»Hello López,« he said. »Thank you for joining us here on the podium. How should I introduce you? As a writer? A journalist?«

»I'm first and foremost a librarian,« said López. She sat up straight, ran her palms over her thighs, and looked around the room with those warm, noble eyes that had left such an impression on me when she walked down the stairs at our first meeting in the Ottendorfer.

June, committed to her role as wrecking ball, interrupted yet again. After casting a brief glance at López, she turned to the audience, as if she expected to be rewarded for her biting irony. »And you're a born and bred Nigerian? May I ask where you're from?«

López remained calm.

»From Los Lagos.«

June wasn't listening closely. »From Lagos? You? You can tell my grandmother that, but I can see that's not true.«

»What do you see?« shot back López with a suddenly stern, fiery glare.

»That you're not from Nigeria!«

»Because I'm not Black?« López sat back in her chair, relaxed. She gave June a critical, challenging look. With her objective, level-headed manner, she clearly dominated the atmosphere. One point for López.

López asked, quite smugly, »My dear June, you're Swiss. Would you also tell Breel Embolo, the forward on your national soccer team, that you can see from his skin color that he's not Swiss?«

Laughs sounded here and there among the audience. Neither they nor I expected López to have such detailed knowledge of the Swiss national soccer team.

»That's...that's totally different,« stuttered June.

»No, it's not. Don't talk yourself out of it. As a Nigerian, I should be deeply offended by your comment. And I am. Even as a non-Nigerian.«

Laughter again from the audience. June was growing uncertain and didn't say anything. López kept the punches coming.

»Miss June, perhaps you should work on being woke even when it goes against your own interests.«

June was boiling with anger and looked like she wanted to eat López alive.

»But didn't you say you were from Lagos?« asked June.

»No, June, I did not say that. I'm from *Los* Lagos. That's a golf club in Fort Mohave in the state of Arizona. The club is on a reservation, the Fort Mohave Reservation, which is why it's allowed to have a casino. Good business for the owners, bad for the natives. My father, who was Greek, was a gardener at the club, which is why I grew up there. My mother was not Mohave, she was a Diné. But that didn't make her a stranger, since the Diné and the Mohave share the reservation.«

»Diné?« asked June.

»Yes, Diné. In the language of the conquerors, perhaps also in your own, we are better known as Navajo, but we call ourselves Diné.«

June muttered something like, »Sorry, I didn't mean to offend you,« and seemed relieved when a lanky young man drew the crowd's attention to himself. He was one of June's bodyguards and spoke with a Caribbean accent. He wore a dark-blond braided ponytail and a Palestinian scarf as a badge of his irreproachability.

»So you're a non-Nigerian, Indigenous American ghostwriter who wants to express the sentiments of Nigerians.« He paused. »Hmm.« He paused again for effect and then his tone suddenly became pointed. »Do you think that's okay?«

López continued to remain calm. »Your question contains an inaccuracy. You certainly meant no harm, but I would still like to correct it. The Nigerian sentiments that you read about in Bukar's articles are not Bukar's and certainly not my own. Rather they are the sentiments of the affected Nigerians. You surely don't want to suggest with your question that Nigerians cannot articulate themselves. My role is limited to translating the information at hand into literary terms.«

Another point for López.

»And you can also translate something that originated from a set of emotions that are not your own?«

It was great to see how professional and even-tempered López was in her rebuttal.

»Thank you for asking such interesting questions. They deserve thorough replies. But that might go beyond the scope of this event. Right now, I'll just give you two short answers. First, yes, as a ghostwriter you do need to be able to fully immerse yourself in the thoughts that you are putting into words,« she said, using the word *ghostwriter* for the first time. »That is the most enjoyable part of my job because it allows me to expand my horizons. Second, geographic distance does not necessarily imply emotional distance. Such a perspective would only repeat the ostracism with which colonialists drew strict boundaries between their own emotional world and that of the people they conquered. As a Diné, I believe that I can speak with authority on this matter. I'm sure you'll agree that we've learned a few things since the colonial era. Some feelings are universal. They are phenomenally powerful because they are universal. I would bet that the majority of the NGO representatives sitting here today view universal feelings as the premise of their work—pain, empathy, the pursuit of justice.«

The ponytailed bodyguard didn't seem to understand what López meant. »Africans' feelings don't differ from, let's say, Europeans' feelings?«

»As I said, if we're talking about universal feelings, then the answer is no.«

Another member of June's entourage entered the ring. Her voice quavered with emotion. »Don't you think it's pretty disrespectful to deny that people have their differences?«

»Am I doing that?« retorted López. »Or have I expressed myself poorly? I'm happy to explain it again. I'm deeply convinced that there are characteristics and feelings that differ from person to person. In addition, there are also characteristics and feelings that are universal. I was talking about the latter. Do you understand now?«

López sounded more irritated than she had before. Her patience with June and her team of hair-splitters was cracking.

»You just confirmed my worst fear,« groaned the ponytailed guy with a theatrical sigh of disappointment.

I wondered whether June and her bodyguards had planned to take turns drilling López. The shifting roles was an impressive demonstration of the distribution of power. It was not a duel; they were a lurking pack of wolves waiting to pounce on a lone sacrificial lamb. With declamatory arm gestures, the ponytail guy accused López of trying to lump everything into a pile called *Universal* and denying individuality.

»You get a kick out of writing about one topic, then another,« he said harshly. »You don't care about anything else. Be honest, you don't really care about the Nigerians at all, do you, because secretly you have other interests.«

To my surprise, Gladys suddenly leapt to her feet. I had gotten to know her as a dreamy artist and was impressed by how dynamically she made her point both with words and body language.

»I don't believe it. Has the world been turned upside down?« called Gladys with a strong voice. She looked around her and put her hands on her hips.

»Would you mind introducing yourself?« interrupted Walter.

»I'm Gladys. I'm a musician with a flute degree, but I'm currently unemployed. No, not really. I'm an intern because I'm unemployed. And that's my point. I lost my job as a musician because I was cataloged as a Black woman. And you want to take away something from López—her right to advocate for a good cause—because she cannot be cataloged as Black? Did

I miss something here? Music and justice—are they not universal? Can we just stop cataloging people? Who the hell should care about my or López's DNA when universal issues are at stake?« Gladys looked around agitatedly. »People, I'm telling you! If you want to play that game, you're not only playing against López, you also have to deal with me!«

I heard Amelie whisper from the row behind me, »Right on! Give it to them, strong lady!«

Ponytail guy had waited out Gladys's intervention with a cold countenance. He seemed to have figured out that since she had been sitting next to López, they must know each other.

»Where are you doing your internship?« he asked.

»In the Ottendorfer Library. Does it matter?«

»Yeah, it does. So López is your boss.«

Ponytail guy grinned arrogantly and went on without waiting for Gladys's reaction. »What a goody-goody you are to stand up so passionately for your boss. Maybe now you'll be offered a permanent contract.«

Gladys interrupted him. »Man! Stop being so smug! I'm a musician and I want to work as a musician. Don't think I'm going to bend over backward just to become a secretary in a library. To become a musician, I need colorblind access to everything that unites us. Music, justice, dignity. And you? Do you want to reverse what's universal? To corral people into ghettos like they did in Europe in the Middle Ages?«

Ponytail guy tried hard to keep his composure. »Congratulations, Gladys. You have a talent for rhetoric. But the fact is that you're López's employee and that makes you noncredible for me.«

Someone called from the background, »Hey, man, keep it fair. You work for a boss too, don't you?« There was laughter, punctuated by a few shouts of support for Gladys.

June was aware that the mood was turning against her. »Walter, can you help get us back on track? These emotional outbreaks aren't very helpful.«

The slugfest was becoming more and more uncomfortable. Was this still about Boko Haram or were we in the middle of a López tribunal? The attempts to foist career motives on Gladys and to corner López with sophistic questions suggesting a conspiracy were despicable. *López and her secret motives.* Why didn't Walter intervene? Or anyone else? Walter and the two French women from the NGO Coalition stayed quiet. Cowards.

Without thinking about whether I was being tactical or not, I stood up and asked Walter for permission to speak by making eye contact with him. He gave it to me as he slumped down in his armchair in frustration. He must have been grateful that he didn't have to throw himself into the conflict himself.

I introduced myself as Bukar's girlfriend and challenged June. »Your colleague just accused Gladys of putting her career before the truth. He also accused López of having ›other interests‹. Of course he gave no indication of what kind of obscure interests might be, just a bit of venom, hoping it would do some damage, or, at the very least, plant a seed of doubt. May I ask what your secret interests are?«

June pretended to be indignant. »What kind of question is that? I'm the president of JUICE. Everyone knows my NGO's ideals, everyone knows me, and everyone knows that I am passionate about fighting for the true path to justice. If you don't know that, then ask anyone in the room.« June was feeling powerful.

»And three days ago, you met with someone from the Nigerian Mission. What was that about?« I asked in the gentlest voice I could manage.

June hesitated for a moment to construct her defense strategy. »What meeting? Are you hallucinating?«

»No,« I replied coolly. »I'm in my right mind. In the meeting with the Nigerian officials, you discussed how you could thwart Bukar's efforts for a trial at the International Criminal Court and what you and JUICE could gain from it.«

I noticed that dozens of eyes were staring at me in surprise. The audience didn't know me and couldn't judge whether I had uncovered a real scandal, whether I was pushing my luck, or whether I was, in fact, hallucinating.

»What…what do you think you're doing?« yelled June. »Are you crazy? Do you have any proof of your outrageous accusations?«

Just as I was about to say yes, June shouted, »Joshua!« She hoped he would be her lifesaver. »Can you confirm that you or anyone else from your delegation had a meeting with me, as this woman is claiming?«

June was really taking a gamble, but it worked. Joshua's uncompromising, but pedantic honesty was no match for June's meanness. »I did not meet with you. But I cannot be completely certain whether or not another one of our delegates did. Even if...«

Before Joshua could disclose what he knew from Bukar about the meeting between June and the military advisor, June celebrated her victory.

»Ah-ha! Have you all heard that? Joshua denies the meeting that woman is talking about ever happened.« She looked at me like a hungry tiger. »How broken and desperate does someone have to be to make up a lie like that?«

I stayed cool. »June, I'm not lying. You know that. Joshua merely said that he was not at your meeting with the Nigerian military advisor and that was why he could not confirm that it happened. But he did not deny that it happened. I, on the other hand, can confirm it. Do you want to see the photo?«

Anyone who thinks that I'd pulled out the winning joker and everything worked out fine, is wrong—unfortunately. In retrospect, two things were most disappointing for me. First, that the good people didn't have the guts to stand up to the bad people. Second, that perpetrators have the best chances when they present themselves as victims. June knew how to play it; it doesn't matter whether she was doing it consciously or unconsciously.

»Photos? Which photos? Are you stalking me like some kind of secret agent? You would stoop to this kind of methods? Don't you have any decency at all? Instead of decency, you have Photoshop, right? You're such a hypocrite to ask me about my methods when you have the dirtiest motives of all!«

June looked around the room with revenge written all over her. To my regret, I could see in their faces that some of the participants sympathized with June—I suppose because they knew her, but not me. I was now in the unfortunate position of having to defend myself.

»Let's stay objective, please,« I said. »I just want to know what your relationship is with the Nigerian army—an organization that is unhappy about being under observation by the International Criminal Court. I know that you had contact with the army. You're denying that. So let's resolve it. Like I said, I have photos.«

»There is nothing to resolve!« June screamed. »Don't be so stubborn. Joshua already said that your accusations are all in your head!«

Still on the defensive, I said, »Are you not listening to me? He did not confirm it. He…«

»Yes, he did,« June shot back hatefully. »And now I would still like to know what López's manipulative interests are and what legitimation she has to be writing about Nigerian sentiments.«

The positions were deadlocked, the discussion was going in circles. In this situation, López had an idea that seemed ingenious in the moment, even if unable to prevent a total breakdown in the long run. She changed the subject.

López flattened the folds in her slacks with the palms of her hands, stretched her torso and inhaled deeply and calmly. »My interests? My legitimation? That's what you want to know? Okay, I'll explain it to you. Listen carefully. I am a person of change. Part of an eternal cycle in which form and content constantly regenerate themselves. My real name is Calliope, like the Greek Muse of heroic poetry. She kept memories alive with her poems, including terrible memories, and helped release people from their torment by giving them the ability to forget.«

The audience, including June, didn't quite know what to do with López's words. A hush fell over the room; not even a breath was heard. Some people didn't understand, others were eager to hear more. Amelie leaned toward me from behind and whispered in my ear, »It's beautiful how she said it. I wrote in Mrs. MacDowell's poetry album, ›Memories make life beautiful, forgetfulness makes it possible.‹«

The quote was quite apt, I thought, although I didn't want to get caught up in a conversation with Amelie because I was curious to hear what López was going to say next.

»And since I'm not only Greek, but also Diné, I might just as well say that there is a changing woman in me. Something that I learned from my grandfather, the storyteller.«

Walter recognized that the story López was telling was steering away from the toxic exchange that had just taken place. »Thank you, López, for such a thorough introduction. Very interesting.«

He tried to make the most of it and risked a modest joke. »Calliope could be the patron saint of transitional justice, if I've understood you correctly—but I honestly know only very little about Greek Muses, and nothing at all about the venerable women of the Diné. When I look around the room, I have the feeling that we would all appreciate a brief explanation.«

»I'll try, although it's not easy,« said López. At the time, what followed seemed very intricate to me. Now, I know that López basically presented the final chapter of her autobiography.

»The creation myth of the Diné is quite complicated. Before the humans of today, who live in the Fifth World, there were insect people. Because of their mistakes, they were expelled from the First World to the Second World, and then to the Third and Fourth World. In each world, they went through a kind of metamorphosis. On their way, they were joined by the divine winds of the four cardinal directions, other gods, and coyotes. In the Fourth World, the Shadow People laid two white and two yellow ears of corn under a buckskin. This is how the First Man and First Woman came into being. They multiplied after they had arrived in our world, the Fifth World. Following the same procedure as the First People, Talking God and Calling God created Changing Woman. She accompanied the people in all their deeds, as their helper and rescuer, or as their mother, you might say. The First People still had to learn to live in partnership. For a while, women and men lived separately from each other. The men became brutal. The women masturbated with deer's antlers, long stones or birds' feather. Some of them even became pregnant, but gave birth to headless monsters, namely the Horned Monster, the Monster Eagle and the Monster Who Kicks People Down the Cliff. Changing Woman saved the people by mating with an invisible god and giving birth to the Holy Twins. They fought the monsters and killed them.«

June and her bodyguards could hardly wait to cut in on López, but they held off because they could see how fascinated the audience was. Then June lost her temper.

»Excuse me,« she interrupted López with an aggressively shrill voice. »Is this fairytale hour? We want to talk about your job, not the mythology of the Diné.«

»I was talking about my job. It may be much less secretive than you think, dear June, and at the same time more spiritual than you can grasp in your current state. You heard how, in the creation myth of the Diné, the *Diné Bahane'*, people constantly change. They never stop learning from their mistakes and experiences, they discover themselves and are accompanied by a benevolent power. You also heard how Calliope helps people grow. She forces you to face up to reality and rewards you with a better life. It is my deepest wish to be a reincarnation of these two remarkable women. That, and nothing else, dear June, is my job. For this reason, I am committed to Bukar's desire to transform the people in his home by achieving justice. That's why I like him. And I want to make it clear that I harbor no ambition of my own. Do you understand?«

Part of the audience broke into spontaneous applause. June glared at them angrily and the applause faded.

»With all due respect,« she ranted, still looking furiously in López's direction, »your myth may be interesting as a... fairytale. But it's quite dubious and doesn't count at all as an answer to my concrete question.«

»You're very quick to label the views of other cultures as dubious,« replied López. »I presume you wouldn't like it if I were to call your NGO's spiritual foundation dubious?«

»No I wouldn't,« said June defensively, »because JUICE's foundation is humanistic in every regard. Your foundation, dear López, is made up of outdated concepts of morality.«

López gave June a critical look, like a teacher who had expected a better answer from her pupil. She simply replied, »Really?«

»Do you know how misogynistic your stories are?« asked June. I wasn't sure whether her seething was real or an act.

»Now I'm curious,« answered López, her composure stiffening.

»Yes, your mythology is highly misogynistic. Aren't you ashamed of yourself?«

López tried, perhaps for the last time, to sound self-controlled and relaxed. »Dear June, please choose your words carefully. You don't actually think that I should be ashamed of my own tradition?«

But June continued down her path of destruction. »Yes! You should be ashamed! You're telling stories about a society that rewards heterosexual partnerships and punishes the others with monsters.«

López was speechless for a moment. Before she could answer, June turned it up a notch. »You're telling us about women who are considered perverse for living out their sexuality as they like, with rocks or feathers. Women who find their purpose in life only in submitting to a man. That's insane!«

López started stumbling. »You've misunderstood me,« she said defensively. »The *Diné Bahane'* is anything but misogynistic. On the contrary, it conveys a largely matriarchal world view. And in terms of sex and gender, it's much more diverse than you can imagine.«

»What is that supposed to mean?« asked June.

»There are not only male and female gods, but all kinds of in-between forms.«

June was baffled for a moment.

»We also had hermaphrodites as gods. As far as I know, hermaphrodites are not even part of the LGBTQIA acronym, am I right?«

»True, but they don't really exist,«replied June.

»But in Diné Bahane', they do exist. Don't put yourself on the same level as the missionaries who did everything they could to stamp out our very open idea of sexuality. And stop trying to label us as prudes.«

»I'm not doing that.« June walked onto the stage and took Gregory's microphone. Walter made an effort to cap June's highhandedness. He stood up, walked over to her and gently tried to show her that she should take her seat in the audience. She dismissed him brusquely.

»Why should I go back?« she asked into the mic. »Is this a two-class society?«

Walter's reply was inaudible.

June didn't give up. »My questions for López and Bukar are just as much part of this event as the useless ICC!«

Walter picked up his own mic and said, »Please, June, that's Gregory's mic. If you want to ask questions from your seat, you can use the mic that's designated for that purpose.«

Two or three calls came from the audience, asking June to drop the antics because they were a waste of time. She went back to her row, but immediately grabbed one of the mics in the audience and kept fulminating.

»Where were we? That's right. I'm not here to discuss gender diversity in your culture, you can do whatever you want. What I'm saying is that you think you can present yourself as the voice of Africa in the press with this«—she frowned in disgust—»very unusual background.«

»Hey June, are you the voice of Africa?« said a voice from the back of the room in a Latin American accent. A few people laughed. June ignored the comment.

López looked at June in disbelief. I felt like I could read her—obvious—thoughts. Why was June repeating accusations over and over that she, López, had already answered? That was more than dumb, it was mean. López ran her hand across her forehead and hastily emptied one of the glasses of water on the table in front of her. I could see that she was feeling very uncomfortable.

López tried again to explain herself. »June, do you really not understand? I am not presenting myself as the voice of Africa. I cannot do that and did not want to do that. Neither do I want you to take my stories from Greek and Diné mythology as advice for your own life or anyone else's life. It's about the essence.«

López repeated the essence in other words than she had used before in the hope that she would finally be understood. Although she surely realized that June did not *want* to understand her at all.

»It is about the opportunity offered to a troubled post-conflict community. Face reality, accept it. Speak the truth loudly and clearly. Then, in the next step, the community can heal its wounds and overcome the past. But the most important step on the path is speaking out. That is not only the responsibility of the judicial system, but also of literature. This is where Bukar and I come together. Can you understand that now? If you do, then you can spare yourself any other assumptions and suspicions.«

López drank another glass of water in one go. Her throat seemed to be tightening up. Then June's ponytailed bodyguard spoke again. June quickly gave him the microphone. She seemed pleased that she didn't have to respond to López herself.

»Excuse me, but that all sounds very flimsy to me,« he rumbled. »López, you're presenting yourself here as a literature-loving savior of the world who teamed up with Bukar, the savior of the world from the department of repressive lawyers. Do you think we're naive? You're talking our ears off with far-fetched, made-up stories. I wonder how the *New York Daily* can uphold its standards while publishing a Nigeria series with such a shaky and unethical basis.«

That was Gregory's cue. With deliberate calm, he raised the microphone to his mouth. »You're not a journalist, are you?« he asked.

»No.«

»Have you ever visited a news desk?«

»No, but…«

»No problem. I haven't visited your office either.«

Chuckles rippled through the room. Gregory had made a winning entrance.

»We have editorial meetings where we talk about everything we publish. In the case of the Nigeria series, it was clear. Great quotes from Bukar, very topical, well edited by López. We've worked with her on other projects before and already valued her as a very competent and skilled colleague.«

»And it never occurred to you that Bukar's, that is, López's material could be one-sided?« cut in the guy with the ponytail.

»No. Why would it?« replied Gregory. »Bukar had written similar articles for Nigerian publications in the past and his authority and authenticity were never questioned. And the stories are consistent with what we otherwise hear from African justice circles.«

»African justice circles, you say. Hm. I'm sure you know that there are completely different circles in Africa.«

»Of course,« Gregory agreed. »The blogs published by some of the human rights NGOs are particularly interesting.«

»And you especially like to read the ones that share your preconceived notions,« countered the ponytail guy.

»We don't have any preconceptions.«

»Ha ha. Don't try to pull one over on me and everyone else here. Among America's major news organizations, the *New York Daily* is the most vehement supporter of the International Criminal Court. But, of course, you don't have any preconceptions. Again: ha ha.« The ponytail guy looked at Gregory as if he'd just caught a little boy telling a particularly clumsy lie.

»Please don't go looking for a bogeyman where there isn't one. If two independent sources, I mean the *New York Daily* and Nigerian NGOs, reach the same conclusion, that doesn't mean it's wrong, does it?« argued Gregory.

»You're right. But what if the sources aren't independent at all? If the deal between you and Bukar is just a set-up—and for all I know he works for one of your favorite NGOs on the side? Then there would be strong grounds for mistrust, wouldn't there? Then maybe the true voice of Africa, which works together with JUICE, is being suppressed? Because you don't give a damn that the International Criminal Court is being used to destroy Nigeria from the inside!«

Bukar interrupted the ponytail guy. »That sounds almost verbatim what the Nigerian military advisor told me three days ago. Did *he* put those wise words in your mouth?«

I was glad that Bukar had finally stepped into the discussion. He had been squirming in his chair for quite a while, ready to pounce and swing the pendulum in the other direction when the time was right. Now he was turning the page, I hoped. However, the ponytail guy had a rhetorically clever answer ready and delivered it arrogantly.

»Bukar, do me a favor. Listen to Gregory, your accomplice, from time to time. Didn't he just say that something isn't necessarily wrong if two independent sources both come up with it?«

Before Bukar could provide more evidence for June's cooperation with the military advisors, she took the lead again. The counter-offensive had failed.

»So, Gregory, why don't you say a few words about how you work,« she said into the microphone agitatedly. »Tell us which Nigerian NGOs you deal with, which domestically political destabilization you trigger, how the other side—the voice of reason—can be represented in your series. Your editorial conference hasn't thought about that at all, now has it?«

Gregory apparently wanted to remain as vague as possible. »I said the credentials were excellent, so the case was clear,« he reiterated.

»In insider jargon, that's called confirmation bias, right?« snapped June.

»We call it good judgment, based on years of experience. Nitpicking is a waste of time.«

The ponytail guy interjected, »Gregory, can I quote you in my next reader comment? Or maybe even in my own article?«

Gregory was visibly panicked. He never should have spoken so flippantly about the editorial conferences and the journalistic diligence of the staff. He hummed and hawed before answering. »You can write what you want of course, but just to be sure, you should call me first. I could help out with a bit of extra information.«

The ponytail guy smelled blood. »What kind of extra information?« he asked with exaggerated politeness.

Gregory kept improvising. »Well...I think that, in my department, we can have another look at whether, in this case, we've met the high standard of integrity that we're known for.«

»What do you mean exactly?«

»Well, I'll have to talk about that with my colleagues. But I think we could, for example, review whether our years of good collaboration with López justified our hasty assumption she had not crossed the fine line between linguistic improvements and amending content.«

»And you have doubts about that now?«

López's fury had been growing all along. It was enough. She looked at Gregory dumbfoundedly, but only said, hardly audibly without a microphone, »My goodness. Who are you? What are you doing? Are you nuts?«

Gregory tried to patch up his betrayal of López. »No, generally speaking, I have no doubt that our overall appreciation of López is well deserved.«

»Can I quote that, too? You don't have any doubts, *generally speaking*, but maybe, specifically, just enough to want to review everything again? And *overall* appreciation—does it means that where there's a rule, there are also exceptions?«

June took the reins again and snapped at López aggressively, as if her hunting instinct had told her to finish her off once and for all. »López, tell us the truth!«

Everything that followed was a slap in the face for López.

»How much of your work was checking typos and grammar, and how much did you write yourself?«

I saw fear in López's eyes. The fear of the accused in a public show trial. She made a huge effort to stay objective.

»My work is about more than spelling. It's about capturing a mood and putting it in my own words if need be. But quotes from Bukar's interview partners are non-negotiable, of course.«

»As a non-African you think you can capture African moods and put them in your own words?«

»It doesn't mean that I made anything up. Do you understand the difference between invention and literary refinement?«

»So you conveyed the mood by refining the text?«

»I made the moods more vivid, yes, you could say that.«

»You pursued certain intentions while you were doing that, of course.«

With each strike, López felt more and more cornered. Bukar had tried several times to come to her aid, but June was faster. Or more ruthless.

»So. What's your secret agenda?«

López's upper body was drooping. She wasn't sitting up as proudly as she had been a few minutes earlier, as if to protect herself from the blows. López didn't say a word. She no longer could.

»Haven't you noticed that nobody cares about your pseudo-profound myths?«

Another blow. Humbling and painful.

»Did you not hear that the gentleman from the *New York Daily* just stated with astonishing clarity that you cannot be trusted?«

López looked pleadingly at Walter and the audience, as if to say, *Spare me more torture! Help me in my distress!* Bukar tried again. This time he was quicker and louder than June.

»Dammit, June. If you think you have to defend your interests by lambasting an old lady, then at least have the courage to compete with *me*. With *me*—got it?—because this whole thing is about my articles. Leave López alone with your two-faced questions. Right now!«

Three or four people in the audience clapped faintheartedly. June turned toward Bukar with a look that said, *Don't worry, I'll get to you.* Then she went back to drilling López.

»Don't you see that your contradictions are also ruining Bukar?«

López held both hands in front of her face. Beads of sweat dotted her forehead, which was paler than I'd ever seen it before. Her upper body and her head were shaking as if she were sobbing. Despite her defeated demeanor, June asked López the meanest possible question she could think of.

»López, for the last time, are you finally ready to tell us the plain truth? Your truth and not somebody else's?«

López was still hiding her face in her hands. Walter told me later he had heard López murmuring a quiet prayer. He couldn't repeat it exactly, but it sounded something like *Hózhó is our path.*

Then it happened. One of López's elbows slipped off the armrest of her chair. Her entire upper body fell to one side and she cried out thinly. Bukar rushed to her and helped her sit upright again. López exposed her reddened eyes and tried to control her quick breathing by inhaling deeply. She spoke without a microphone, but those on stage and in the first few rows could hear her clearly. »If those are the new rules of the game for dealing with each other intellectually, then I will never write another word again as long as I…«

With the last words, she grasped her chest as a pained grimace contorted her sweat-dampened face and, a second later, fell face-down onto the floor.

Chaos ensued. I couldn't see everything because the people in front of me had stood up. Walter ran to the entrance and shouted, »Emergency! Quick!« I couldn't see Bukar, but assumed he was on his knees helping López.

Gregory stood there helplessly, horror-stricken, hopefully wondering how much responsibility he bore for López's interrogation ending like it did.

At the same time, I noticed movement in the rows behind me. I saw Bob limping as he bulldozed his way through the crowd to the stage. Amelie and Tony sat there as still as stones. I heard Amelie sigh, »Oh my God, the poor thing, at her age!«

Bob had reached the stage and stood before June. I couldn't understand what he said, but his expression was very unfriendly. He was waving his right arm around and signaling to her that she should buzz off—pronto.

It all went so fast. After a minute or so, two German security officers came in and went straight to López. One of them was carrying a small first aid case. They must have been trained for medical emergencies. I couldn't see what they were doing to López, but I heard a hush fall over the room. It was so quiet that I noticed the whirr of the ventilation system for the first time. Walter was pacing up and down the stage, talking on his phone.

Two or three minutes later, a siren approached the German House from down the street. The ambulance parked and the siren was turned off. A moment later, two paramedics arrived with a stretcher. They appeared to give López an injection. I wasn't able to see it, but some of the people standing close to her looked away. Then the paramedics must have put her on the stretcher. As they carried her out, I saw López lying there motionless with an oxygen mask covering her face. A minute later, the siren sounded again and the ambulance drove off.

I had no idea how López was doing. I heard two people from the front row, who had seen everything up close, say that they hoped she would get better soon. She must be alive, I derived. At least that.

All of the terrible things that could still happen passed through my mind. I felt guilty for staying frozen in my chair and not helping. But what could I have done?

And I thought about how awful it would be if these minutes were to become my last with López. What if our farewell were to be abrupt and wordless, like something that has been broken off, deserted? That couldn't be. In the two weeks we'd known each other, López had become a friend, an anchor for everything I was dealing with, both personally and academically. And despite her uncountable years of life, she was still so vital, as if she'd risen above aging. She seemed ageless.

As I pondered these dismal farewell fantasies in the conference room of the German House, I did not yet know that they would come true very soon.

It was good that I didn't know that. Otherwise, I also would have known that Amelie and Tony, who had just been sitting in the row behind me, had disappeared forever. I could have run outside and cried uncontrollably— but then I would have missed the unforgettable moment that was looming on stage.

Walter grabbed the microphone and somberly asked everyone not to leave right away but to please take their seats again. While most of the people were doing that, he summed up what had taken place. Everyone had just witnessed López suffer a medical emergency, he said, and she was en route to the hospital. On their way out of the building, the paramedics had told him that her pulse and breathing had stabilized. Walter wished López a speedy recovery and noted, as tactfully as he could, that he deeply regretted the escalation that had led to her collapse. As he said this, he deliberately avoided making eye contact with June and her bodyguards who were all back sitting on their seats. Instead, he was looking into the semi-darkness behind the spotlight that was directed onto the stage from the back of the room. That's where the grand piano was.

Melancholic blues music was pouring from the instrument, muffled by the closed lid. The sacral atmosphere emanating from the swaying rhythm and rich chords gripped us all. I immediately knew who was playing. The other people in the audience could hardly see Bob.

After three or four bluesy chord progressions, just twelve bars each, ornamented chords with no melody, he started to speak while he continued to play. He was leaning back from the keyboard, making angular movements with his upper body and looking upward into the unlit space above him. I don't know whether he was really looking into space or just closing his eyes and looking into the dark depths within himself.

Everyone could hear his voice clearly. It was raw, scratchy at times. Not loud, but its slow, nasal lilt made it easy to hear. Bob changed pieces and started talking.

»Shitty afternoon, wasn't it? López, you didn't deserve that. I want to say sorry…from all of us. Get well soon.«

He played a few more bars without speaking, and then he began to explain the music to the audience.

»Guys, listen. *Goin' Home*. López liked this number, I know. So rich in ideas and colors, just like herself. López, this is for you. Dvořák's *New World Symphony*, American symphonic music, a bit of Black, a bit of Indigenous, a lot of Bohemian homesickness. The second movement. Gorgeous! It was not a spiritual, but it sounded like one. Then came William Arms Fisher, a student of Dvořák's. His lyrics and choral part turned the piece into a gospel song. *Goin' Home*.[46] And then Art Tatum! Wow! He turned the piece into a real American jazz number. Art understood better than anyone that *Goin' Home* wasn't a funeral hymn, but a cheerful hiking song. Listen to how romantically the right hand yearns.«

Bob accompanied that romantic yearning with his scratchy voice which unfolded its unpolished beauty and gave us all goose bumps as he sighed Fisher's lyrics:

> There's no break, there's no end
> Just a living on
> Wide awake with a smile
> Going on and on

---

46 William Arms Fisher, a student of Dvořák's, wrote the text to the second movement of Dvořák's *New World* Symphony in 1922 and arranged the movement for a mixed

»That was it! Going on and on! The hiking song! The right hand again. Up and down the keyboard. Left hand: stride piano with the weirdest harmonies. Wild! Dvořák, Scott Joplin, Liszt, Tatum! They're all in there!«

Bob kept playing the piece, virtuosically and without commenting, and ended it brusquely just half a minute later.

»Hey guys, did you follow? How often has that piece been put in a box, then taken out and moved to the next? Always in search of otherness. Without barriers, without regard for political correctness—that's true art. Give and take. In art, there's no virgin conception. Give and take.«

Then Bob's voice suddenly became grimmer and sank half an octave. »Remember that before you judge others.«

His words automatically made me think of June and her bodyguards. He was obviously talking about them. I looked around. How was June reacting? I couldn't see her anywhere. She and her entourage must have snuck out of the room during Bob's speech which had magnetized everyone, including me.

---

choir. The piece quickly became popular, especially at funerals. Here is Fisher's full text:

Going home, going home
I'm a-going home
Quiet light, some still day
I'm just going home

It's not far, just close by
Through an open door
Work all done, care laid by
Going to fear no more

Mother's there 'xpecting me
Father's waiting, too
Lots of folk gathered there
All the friends I knew
    I am going home
Nothing's lost, all's gained
No more fear nor pain
No more stumbling on the way
No more longing for the day
Going to roam no more

Morning star lights the way
Restless dreams all done
Shadows gone, break of day
Real life just begun

There's no break, there's no end
Just a living on
Wide awake with a smile
Going on and on

Going home, going home
I'm a-going home
It's not far, just close by
Through an open door

I'm just going home

Going home, going home

Bob played another few bars of *Goin' Home*, then closed the lid over the keys. When he stood up, he hugged Gladys who had been standing at the upper end of the keyboard, and whispered something in her ear. Then some members of the audience helped him off the stage. One of them said, »I understand what you meant. You're so right.«

»Take care of yourselves, kids,« he grunted to them, adding a few words that no one would understand: »Otherwise you'll end up in Creedmoor.«

He shuffled over to Bukar and me. We gave him a hug and Bukar said, »You spoke the words people needed to hear. You're good, man, real good.«

Outside the German House, we suggested to Bob that we all go somewhere to get something to eat, but he declined the offer. »It's been a rough day. I'd better go home.«

I wasn't sure whether his pun was intended. A desperately needed homecoming for Bob; a new departure for Bukar and me.

We made an appointment for the next day.

* * *

The sun rose at the usual time. The sky was cloudy, as it had been for days. The street noises were familiar: sirens from fire trucks and ambulances; the clop-clop of garbage bin lids being closed; the murmur of motors spinning and tires finding traction, punctuated by shouts here and there.

And yet, everything was different. We sat apathetically at the breakfast table. A feeling like a blackout. Like the crash of a nearly completed manuscript into an incomprehensible Orkus.

Walter had told me the night before that López had been brought to the cardiology department at Mount Sinai Hospital at the corner of 17th Street and First Avenue. The hospital that had built its extension at the expense of Dvořák's former residence. If you save López, I'll forgive you, I thought.

When I called, they said they couldn't give me any information. I didn't even know López's last name. Clearly, I wasn't next of kin.

After breakfast, I tried again, pretending to be a family member anyway. There was a lot of back and forth until I was finally put through to a friendly nurse, who confirmed that López was in the hospital. She wasn't allowed to give me a diagnosis, she said, but it appeared to be a heart attack.

López's condition was critical, but not life-threatening. She was in pain. It would be better for her if I waited two or three days before visiting, said the nurse.

I thanked her and emphasized how much López meant to me and that I really needed to see her again. The nurse hesitated for a moment, then did something she allegedly never did. I say allegedly because I'm convinced that she does it all the time, simply because she has a good heart. She gave me her cell phone number and said I could call her in case of an emergency.

After I hung up, Bukar and I got dressed and went to the Ottendorfer. We wanted to talk to Bob. See how he was doing without López. A sign hung on the door: *Closed until Thursday*. Five more days. Our attempt to contact him hit a dead-end.

Frustrated, we went to the pizzeria on the corner of 10th Street and First Avenue where the Café Boulevard used to be. The place where Dvořák liked to drink his morning coffee and read the newspaper.

Our secret hope that the spirit of the past would suddenly turn up next to us, renew our motivation and lift our mood, was in vain. Sure, spirits don't really exist.

The restaurant welcomed us with clammy plastic furniture. The pizza pies on display in the case looked disgusting with their cold layer of sticky cheese and dried-out basil. We ate them anyway, and it wasn't long before Bukar and I agreed that our time in New York had come to an end.

We managed to rebook our flights for later that night without any extra fees. While I canceled our apartment rental and tried in vain to dig up Bob's phone number via the switchboard at the New York Public Library, Bukar ran back to the United Nations to say good-bye to Walter and Joshua.

Finally, we packed our bags and took a taxi to Newark. No farewell sentimentality, no final dreamy view of the skyline. We just wanted to get out of there.

* * *

With our return to Brussels, this report comes full circle. The result: no dissertation, no progress with the Nigeria trial at the International Criminal Court.

Bukar and I wondered whether our trip had been a failure.

The first thing that came to mind was the tragic turn it took at the end. The loss of at least three of our four daily companions whom we had come to love and cherish.

Amelie and Tony had disappeared without a trace after López's hospitalization. There was nothing we could do about it.

Even López had gone away. When I called the helpful nurse at Mount Sinai three days later from Brussels, she told me that the old lady had suddenly been transferred to another hospital the day before. To Ganado.

»What? Ganado?« I asked her. »Where is that?«

Somewhere in Arizona, the nurse said. Sage Memorial Hospital. Medically speaking, it wasn't a great choice, she said, because Mount Sinai had the best cardiology department in the country. But it was what the old lady wanted.

I googled the hospital and found that it was run by the Navajo Health Foundation. Its mission, according to its website, was to ›provide quality healthcare for the Diné people with respect, unity, beauty, harmony in honor of *K'é* (kinship) and the sacredness of life.‹

That sounded like López, I thought. She deserved a peaceful place—and *K'é*, at least the spiritual return to her grandfather and the rest of her family.

> Mother's there 'xpecting me
> Father's waiting, too
> Lots of folk gathered there
> All the friends I knew
> Goin' home.

Who knows what she was up to in Ganado. I was happy for her, although it seemed impossible to get in touch with her there.

I called the Ottendorfer the day it reopened. My hope was fulfilled. Bob answered the phone, edgy as always. When I asked how he was doing, his reply was brief. »I'm fine. Last week was pretty tough, you know. I'm gonna take it easy. Time to retire. Wanna play the piano and compose a bit.«

He paused, then said hastily, »Take care of yourself, Petra. And say hi to Bukar.« He hung up without waiting for me to reply.

A few days later, I called back. A young man with a friendly voice was on the line. »Bob left his position as doorman. I'm new here. I'm an intern.«

Gladys's successor. Yet another deadbeat classical musician? I was about to ask him what color his skin was, but bit my tongue. Being Black in the classical music world is a good reason to run into a brick wall, but not the only one. The world is full of washed-up musicians of all colors. Wasn't I a good example myself?

»So Gladys has left?« I asked simply. »Did she get a job as a musician?«

»No, I don't think so. Not yet. But she seems really hopeful. She said she wants to get ready for her next job.«

The new intern couldn't tell me how to reach Bob.

»You should drop by,« he said. Good idea, I told him, as soon as I'm in town again.

Bukar called Walter. Nothing new on the Nigeria trial. In December, the deputy chief prosecutor at the International Criminal Court was going to be elected, said Walter; maybe that would bring some forward motion. He hadn't seen June since that fateful afternoon. Thank goodness. He heard that she had celebrated the panel discussion as a victory. But she also lost a great deal of support, apparently. The final installment of Bukar's Nigeria series had been published, as if nothing had happened, and the *New York Examiner* campaign had simply fallen silent. A lot of unnecessary fuss, as is so often the case these days.

»I'm still on the ball, now more than ever,« Bukar said. Then he talked with Walter a bit about the NGO scene in Brussels, although he hadn't really gained a foothold since we'd been back. Both Walter and Bukar agreed that they should meet up again soon.

After a few days, the impressions of loss and farewell began to fade. We focused on what we'd gained from our New York friendships, especially the things they had in common. Over the course of their lives, each one of our New York friends had engaged with the cultural *other*—musically or literarily, in one way or another. Overall, they had affirmed the value of cultural encounters, wrestled with the proper form of encountering, gotten caught up in contradictions, corrected themselves.

Bukar put it in a nutshell. Perhaps we were so impressed by our friends, he said, because their strength rested in their mature, self-critical approach to their various states of mind, to their ambivalences and their at times conflicting priorities.

I thought of Amelie. Her behavior and her way of thinking were often caught in the corset of her era. By the time I met her in New York, she was an elderly woman and had managed to reflect on herself.

And I thought of Arthur Farwell, perhaps the most perplexing of all the musicians I'd come across in the past few weeks. His search for an identity outside of industrialized society; his missionary phase inspired by the world-conquering spirit of the pioneer period; his mellowing out later in life; all of this revealed both a deep connection to his time and a quest for individuality.

Bukar thought of another example to make his point. June, he said, had a long way to go before she would be able to practice self-criticism as a remedy to her problems. Her constant craving for attention and her theatrical show of consternation and unassailable moral superiority were behaviors aimed at avoiding discourse, and laying bare her insecurity and immaturity, Bukar theorized.

When I asked whether he thought June would ever be able to move forward on the long path toward self-criticism, Bukar said he didn't know, but that we should assume the best. After all, we'd learned that from Amelie, Tony and Bob.

I was literally about to write the last sentence of my report when the phone rang. Bukar answered it and spoke in a language I didn't understand.

»Guess who that was,« he said, his eyes shining like they always do when he's planning a new adventure. »It was Joshua. After the discussion at the German House, he was fed up. He quit his job and now he's coming to Brussels. He and I, we're really going to turn up the heat here and in The Hague. You bet we will!«

Bukar added hastily, »He can stay with us for the first few days, can't he?«

Of course he could.

I embraced Bukar out of sheer joy. I pulled him close to me, ran my fingers through his hair, and said, »A new departure, isn't it?«

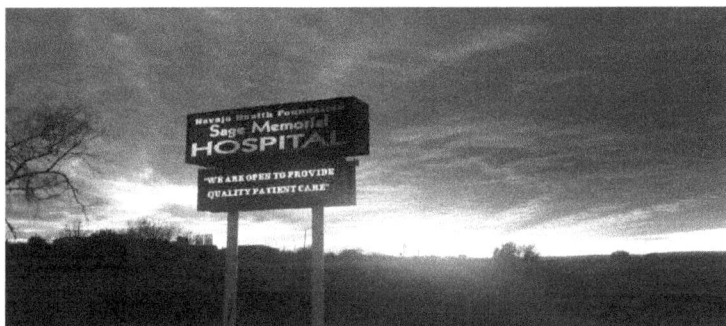

Short Biographies and Recommended Listening

Agassiz, Jean Louis Rodolphe (1807-1873) was a Swiss zoologist and glaciologist who moved to the US in 1846. He was the teacher of Frederic Ward Putnam, a significant supporter of Franz Boas. In his research on the history of the earth, Agassiz presumed that humanity had several divinely ordained roots (so-called polygenism). This theory was disproved primarily by Charles Darwin, but also by Franz Boas. In the US, polygenism was associated with racism.

Anderson, Marian Elina-Blanche (1897-1993) was an internationally celebrated American alto. In 1955, she became the first Black soloist to perform at the Metropolitan Opera in New York. Her 1939 performance at the Lincoln Memorial in Washington, DC, made her an icon of the civil rights movement. See footnote 22.

Apthorp, William Foster (1848-1913) was an influential music critic and music writer in Boston. He studied composition with John Knowles Pain and composed songs, but primarily wrote books about Hector Berlioz, Richard Wagner and opera in general. He wrote the program notes for the Boston Symphony Orchestra for many years.

Ballard, Louis Wayne (1931-2007) was an American composer. His father was a Cherokee, his mother a Quapaw. He earned a degree from the University of Oklahoma, then went on to study composition with Béla Rósza, Darius Milhaud and Mario Castelnuovo-Tedesco. During his college years, he resisted his teachers' efforts to assimilate him into Western culture, instead developing his own personal, contemporary style. Nevertheless, he called Dvořák's appreciation of Indigenous music an inspiration. Ballard's piece for chamber orchestra, *Incident at Wounded Knee*, which refers to the massacre of 300 members of the Lakota on December 29, 1890, received national and international acclaim.

Four *American Indian* Piano Preludes ♦ p. 19, fn. 9
Emanuele Arciuli

Bartók, Béla (1881-1945) was a Hungarian composer, pianist and ethnomusicologist; he was one of the most influential composers of the 20th century. After his early Romantic-nationalist period, the young Bartók started recording, transcribing and adapting folk music, first in Hungary, Romania, Serbia, and Ukraine, and later in Turkey and North Africa. He incorporated the folk melodies into his own compositions—to the great displeasure of Hungarian nationalists—and developed a distinctive musical language characterized by the extension of the diatonic scale and energetically leaping rhythms. Bartók also found the simplicity of folk melodies in sounds of nature which he likewise integrated into his works. An opponent of National Socialism, he emigrated from Hungary to the US in 1938, but found it difficult to settle. His immigration corresponds to his later mature period which followed on the heels of his expressionist phase. Bartók constantly faced financial woes and died of leukemia in New York in 1945.

Five Hungarian Folk Tunes for Violin and Piano ◆ p. 140
(adapted by Joseph Szigeti from Bartók's piano cycle *For Children*)
Joseph Szigeti/Béla Bartók (historical recording)

Beach, Amy Cheney (1867-1944) was an American composer and pianist. She grew up as a particularly intelligent and musically talented wunderkind in Boston, a city where the fine arts were flourishing more than anywhere else in the US. She was highly acclaimed in Boston and beyond as an excellent pianist and a composer on a par with her male colleagues. After the death of her well-meaning but restrictive husband, she secured her status by touring abroad (mainly in Germany and Italy) and advocating for strengthening the role of women in the music business. In 1893, she disputed with Antonín Dvořák about the extent to which composers can and should use foreign musical idioms. Over time, she revised her initial rejection of the practice and later included Indigenous melodies in her own works. As a representative of the Second New England School, she composed in a Late Romantic style with a distinct European influence. In her later works, she expanded her vocabulary by using whole-tone scales and emphasizing dissonance. Beach died of heart failure in 1944.

Gaelic Symphony in E-Minor, Op. 32 ◆ p. 16
Detroit Symphony Orchestra/Neeme Järvi

Variations on Balkan Themes, Op. 60 ◆ p. 183
Virginia Eskin

***Eskimos* (Four vignettes for piano), Op. 64** ◆ p. 183
Joanne Polk

Theme and Variations for Flute and String Quartet, Op. 80 ◆ p. 161
Ambache Chamber Ensemble

***From Blackbird Hills*, Op. 83** ◆ p. 148
Kirsten Johnson

String Quartet in One Movement, Op. 89 ◆ p. 63
Ambache Chamber Ensemble | Composed in1921, revised in 1929
The middle section incorporates three Inuit melodies. Prior to its publication in 1994 (!), the piece was very rarely performed.

Five Improvisations, Op. 148 ◆ p. 143
Joanne Polk

Boas, Franz (1858-1942) was a German-American anthropologist. His book *The Central Eskimo* (1888) and his research papers on the music and art of the Kwakwaka'wakw (Kwakiutl), Chinook, Inuit, and Sioux made him a leading figure of early North American anthropology. A cultural relativist, he was an early critic of racism and rejected the evolutionist concept of 'race' that was widespread in his time. Despite valid criticism of some of his research methods (he participated in the human exhibits at the 1893 Chicago World's Fair as an assistant in the anthropology department), he remains a prominent pioneer of enlightened anthropology.

Bülow, Hans von (1830-1894) was a celebrated German pianist and conductor with close ties to the prominent composers of his day, including Richard Wagner, Johannes Brahms and Antonín Dvořák. As a conductor, he transformed the Meiningen Court Orchestra and the Berlin Philharmonic into world-class ensembles. In 1875, he went on two extensive tours of the US and Canada.

Burleigh, Henry "Harry" Thacker (1866-1949) was an American baritone, composer and arranger of hundreds of spirituals (e.g. *Deep River*). He was Dvořák's assistant at the National Conservatory and one of the catalysts for Dvořák's interest in African-American music.

Busoni, Ferruccio (1866-1924) was an Italian pianist, composer and music theorist. In addition to his adopted home of Berlin, he had strong ties to the US after accepting a professorship in Boston from 1891-1894. During a US tour in 1910, his former student Natalie Curtis gave him her definitive book on ethnomusicology, *The Indian's Book - Authentic Native American Legends, Lore & Music*. This inspired Busoni to compose his 'Indian' pieces. After his Late Romantic period, his oeuvre paved the way for the development of new music and electronic sounds.

Indian Diary, Book I, BV 267   ♦ p. 65
Stephanie Bruning / Ferruccio Busoni (1866–1924): Indian Diary, Book I (Four piano studies), BV 267. | Busoni's Indian Fantasy for Piano and Orchestra, Op. 44, utilizes the same themes.

Cacioppo, Curt (*1951) is an American composer. Many of his works incorporate Indigenous American perspectives. His string quartet cycle *Womb of The Sacred Mountain* is based on the creation myth of the Diné, also known as Navajo (I. *A distant voice calling – Nítch'i dine'é* | II. *Coyoteway – Mạ' iijí hatáál* | III. *Kinaaldá: The Rite of Changing Woman* | IV. *Monsterslayer – Nayénězg ni*). The II. string quartet refers to a healing ceremony whose music Cacioppo researched and documented together with the Navajo spiritual leader John Co'ií Cook.

String Quartet Kinaaldá: The Rite of Changing Woman   ♦ p. 19, fn. 6
Borromeo String Quartet

Cadman, Charles Wakefield (1881-1946) was an American composer. After studying music, he followed the advice of Alice Fletcher (whose book, *Study of Omaha Indian Music*, he'd read) and traveled to Nebraska where he recorded and transcribed Omaha melodies and learned to play Indigenous instruments. He often performed his Indianist works together with Indigenous Americans.

Four Idealized Indian Themes, Op. 54
Stephanie Bruning

Cardin, Fred (1895-1960) was an American composer and member of the Quapaw Nation. He completed his composition studies at the Curtis Institute of Music in Philadelphia in 1927 and went on to compose numerous works in the Western tradition but based on Quapaw melodies. As founder and principal violinist of the Indian String Quartet and the Indian Art and Musical Company—groups composed entirely of Indigenous players who often performed in the traditional dress of their tribes—he toured the US and played a significant role in emphasizing Indigenous culture as part of the American identity.

Chadwick, George Whitefield (1854-1931) was an American composer. After studying music in Germany, he returned to Boston. Together with Edward MacDowell and Horatio Parker, he became an exponent of the New England School of Music which welcomed the use of Indigenous music.

Four Symphonic Sketches (especially No. 1 *Jubilee*)
Eastman Rochester Symphony Orchestra/Howard Hanson

Clarke, Kenny (1914-1985) was an American percussionist and vibraphonist. While playing in a trio with Freddie Green and Lonnie Simmons, he developed a new way of manipulating the drum set. The drummer used the right hand on the ride cymbal and the left foot on the hi-hat to keep the rhythm, while the accents and the melody were given with the left hand on snare and the right foot on bass drum. Clarke's technique, which he used in his collaborations with Count Basie, Dizzy Gillespie, Miles Davis, Bud Powell and many others, helped shape the sound of bebop. A founding member of the Modern Jazz Quartet, he lived in Paris from 1956 to his death.

Copland, Aaron (1900-1990) was an American composer. He was born into a Lithuanian-Jewish immigrant family in Brooklyn, New York. He went on to study with Nadia Boulanger in Paris who sent him home with the resolution to develop an American style of music. Early on, he was influenced by Igor Stravinsky and European modernism. With *Fanfare of the Common Man* (1930), his work became more accessible. Incorporating elements of jazz, Jewish chant, Anglo-American and Latin American folksongs, and film music, Copland's music can be considered an example of American diversity. An avid teacher, lecturer and facilitator, he was a significant figure for music in the US.

Dawson, William Levi (1899-1990) was an American composer best known for his *Negro Folk* Symphony and numerous spirituals. He grew up in a working-class family of nine, his parents being former slaves. He left home at the age of 12 to study music at the Tuskegee Institute. In 1930, he became its director and developed the institute's choir to a world-class ensemble. In 1946, it became the first Black choir to perform in the Constitution Hall in Washington, DC. Dawson frequently incorporated spirituals into his works, and occasionally West African folk melodies.

Negro Folk Symphony ◆ p. 118
American Symphony Orchestra/Leopold Stokowski

Dvořák, Antonín (1841-1904) was a Czech composer. Born into a butcher's family in rural Bohemia, he trained as an organist and worked for many years as a violist in a dance orchestra in Prague. With the help of Johannes Brahms, his *Slavic Dances* were published in 1878. They brought him instant fame and earned him international attention as a representative of Czech national music. Concert tours to Russia and England allowed him to leave behind the conflicts around national identity in the multi-ethnic Habsburg Empire. In 1892, he accepted a position as director of the National Conservatory in New York. Its president and patron, Jeannette Thurber, had recruited him with the request that he give advice on developing an American style of music independent of the European tradition. During his time in New York (1892-1895), he composed some of his most successful works, including his Symphony No. 9 *From the New World* which borrows melodies and rhythmic elements from the Black and Indigenous American traditions and makes use of his own folk style. Dvořák spent the summer of 1893 with his family in Spillville, a Bohemian immigrant village in Iowa, where he composed his *American* String Quartet No. 12. It was there that he also got to know Indigenous American music. In his later years, Dvořák devoted himself exclusively to the composition of programmatic works and opera. He is considered one of the most significant composers of the Romantic period and remains to this day the most frequently played Czech composer.

Symphony No. 9 *From the New World* in E Minor, Op. 95   ♦ p. 15
New York Symphony Orchestra/Leonard Bernstein

American String Quartet No. 12 in F Major, Op. 96   ♦ p. 121
Emerson String Quartet

American Suite for Piano in A Major, Op. 98
Benjamin Pasternack

Sonatina for Violin, Op. 100 (2nd movement: *Larghetto*)
Zhou Qian/Edmund Battersby

Eight Humoresques for Piano (e.g. No. 4 and 7), Op. 101
Benjamin Pasternack

Ellington, Edward Kennedy ('Duke') (1899-1974) was one of the most influential jazz pianists of his time. He achieved global fame with his own stride piano technique and the 'jungle style' soundscape of his Duke Ellington Big Band which frequently performed in the Harlem Cotton Club. Throughout his life, he sought to bridge racial divides and increasingly composed large-scale symphonic suites. The first highlight of this development was a 1943 concert in New York's Carnegie Hall with his three-movement work, Black, Brown and Beige, which refers to the complex history of the origins of African-Americans.

Black, Brown and Beige   ♦ p. 196
Buffalo Philharmonic Orchestra/JoAnn Falletta

A Tone Parallel to Harlem   ♦ p. 129
Detroit Symphony Orchestra/Neeme Järvi/Walter White and William Lucas (trumpets)

Farwell, Arthur (1872-1952) was an American composer, publisher and teacher. He studied composition in France, Germany (with Engelbert Humperdinck and Hans Pfitzner), and the US (with George Whitefield Chadwick). During his first teaching position at Cornell University (1899-1901), he came into contact with Alice Fletcher's book *Indian Story and Song from North America* and composed his *American Indian Melodies*. Subsequently, he vehemently turned against European, and in particular German, influences in American music and became one of the most significant Indianists. In 1901, he founded Wa-Wan Press with a focus on publishing 'Indian' music. The name Wa-Wan means 'to sing for someone' and was taken from a ceremony of the Omaha. In Indigenous American spirituality, Farwell found a role model for his own healing fantasies. In 1916 in New York, he founded his first community choir and went on to found others after moving to the West Coast. With the choirs, some of which grew to become huge ensembles, he promoted visions of a collective destiny, reminiscent of Richard Wagner. Farwell saw these efforts as a step toward realizing a future American style of music that would stem from 'new people' and replace European music. Farwell occasionally lost himself in supremist, esoteric perspectives. He was later a professor of music in California, Michigan and New York where he also conducted research on the topic of intuition.

From Mesa and Plain, Op. 20: No. 2 (*Pawnee Horses*) for Piano ♦ p. 153
Benjamin Pasternack

Navajo War Dance No. 2 for Piano, Op. 29 ♦ p. 119
Emanuele Arciuli

Orchestral Suite *The Gods of the Mountain*, Op. 52 ♦ p. 23
Royal Philharmonic Orchestra/Karl Krueger

String Quartet *The Hako* in A Major, Op. 65 ♦ p. 23
Dakota String Quartet

Four Indian Songs, Op. 102: No. 3 (*Pawnee Horses*) for Choir ♦ p. 150
University of Texas Chamber Singers/James Morrow

Fisher, William Arms (1861-1948) was an American composer and music historian. He was a student and friend of Antonín Dvořák's in New York. With his thorough research on the musical history of the US, he had a significant influence on the Czech composer. Fisher joined Dvořák in advocating for the admission of Black students to the National Conservatory of Music.

Goin' Home ♦ p. 229, fn. 46
Alex Boyé/Mormon Tabernacle Choir
Cantus (Minneapolis)
Or from Yo-Yo Ma's Silk Road Ensemble, an art collective which uses a variety of non-Western instruments. The recording offers plenty of fodder for a lively discussion on cultural appropriation. ♦ p. 234

Fletcher, Alice Cunningham (1838-1923) was an American anthropologist specializing in the music of Indigenous peoples in North America. She lived with the Omaha tribe in Nebraska from 1881-1883. Together with **Francis La Flesche**, she published her *Study of Omaha Indian Music* in 1893. La Flesche, the son of an Omaha mother and a French father, was her informant and later became her adoptive son. For Amy Beach, Charles

Cadman and Arthur Farwell, Fletcher's studies on 'Indian' music were decisive in sparking their interest in Indigenous American music. Fletcher had a particularly strong influence on Charles Cadman and others. Farwell was inspired by Fletcher's description of the Pawnee Hako ceremony in his String Quartet (*Hako*).

Foster, Stephen (1826-1864) was one of the best-known American songwriters of his time, but was soon forgotten. As a young man, he was influenced by Western art music as well as the traveling minstrel shows, in which African-Americans were ridiculed by white actors in blackface. Foster began writing songs for the minstrel shows, but without offensive expressions. His goal was rather to stir empathy with the slaves and thus impact audiences' taste. Although some of his songs (e.g. *Oh, Susanna* and *Old Black Joe*) became American classics, Foster died in poverty in 1864 after the Civil War ruined his livelihood.

Gershwin, George (1898-1937) was an American composer who had a significant influence on opera, jazz, musicals, rock, pop, and film music. The son of Russian-Jewish immigrants, he integrated a variety of musical idioms in classics like *Rhapsody in Blue* and *West Side Story*.

Gillespie, Dizzy (1917-1993) was a jazz trumpeter, band leader and composer. He was the prototype of the smart, hip jazz intellectual (hipster) of the 1940s and 1950s and was one of the main developers of bebop, along with Thelonious Monk and Charlie Parker. He was known for pointing his trumpet to the sky and puffing up his cheeks while playing.

Griffes, Charles Tomlinson (1884-1920) studied music in Berlin—first piano, then composition. After returning to the US, he taught music at a high school near New York. Fascinated by the latest works by French and Russian composers such as Debussy and Scriabin, he became a leading representative of American Impressionism. His oeuvre includes piano pieces, orchestral works, songs, and two Indianist pieces for string quartet possibly inspired by Arthur Farwell.

Two Sketches Based on Indian Themes, A.99 ◆ p. 114
Kohon Quartet

Hale, Philip (1854 -1934) was an American music critic for the *Boston Post* and an organist. He was known for writing program notes for the Boston Symphony Orchestra from 1902 until his death. Hale published two periodicals, *Musical Record* (1897-1901) and *Musical World* (1901-1902).

Hier, Ethel Glenn (1889-1971) was an American composer and pianist of Scottish origin. She was a good friend of Amy Beach. In 1908, she studied at the Cincinnati Conservatory of Music and started teaching at the Institute of Musical Art (later the Juilliard School) in 1917. Hier co-founded the American Association of Women Composers. Her works combine an impressionist style with influences from jazz and popular music.

Higginson, Henry Lee (1834-1919) was an American banker and philanthropist. He founded the Boston Symphony Orchestra in 1881, using the personal wealth he had accumulated as a banker. He was both the business director and artistic director of the orchestra throughout his life. In 1900, he sponsored the Symphony Hall, the orchestra's home to this day.

Hubach, Charlotte (1891-1966) was a librarian at the Ottendorfer Library from the 1920s until 1957. Previously, she had been a librarian in Brooklyn. She was the daughter of Otto Hubach, a reporter for the *New Yorker Staats-Zeitung* owned by Valentin Ottendorfer. In the late 1930s, at the beginning of World War II, Hubach became politically active by organizing free radio performances of the Metropolitan Opera as well as events for German emigrants (literary readings with exiled writers, exhibitions by exiled painters) which she paid for out of her own pocket.

Hughes, James Langston (1901-1967) was an American writer and political activist. In his work, Hughes dealt with the everyday life of Black Americans and advocated for a proud, self-confident Black national culture with its own aesthetic. In the 1930s, he became the voice of the Harlem Renaissance. He contributed texts to works by Harry Burleigh, William Grant Still and Kurt Weill, among others. His poem, *I, Too, Sing America* became an icon of the civil rights movement.

Ives, Charles (1874-1954) was an American composer who kept his day job as an insurance broker in order to maintain his artistic freedom. Influenced by nature-loving Transcendentalist writers such as Ralph Waldo Emerson and Henry David Thoreau, he composed highly idiosyncratic works in his search for an authentic America.

Krehbiel, Henry (1854-1923) was a German-born music critic for the *New York Tribune* from 1880 to 1923 and considered to be one of the most influential persons in his field. He helped popularize Dvořák's *New World* Symphony and supported Dvořák's views on the value of African-American music both as a publicist and through his own studies (*Afro-American Folksongs*, 1914).

Lion, Alfred (1908-1987) was the German-born founder of the jazz record label Blue Note which became known as the best of its kind. Lion knew how to secure the loyalty of his artists by taking good care of them and paying them fairly, even for their practicing time.

MacDowell, Edward Alexander (1860-1908) was an American composer and pianist. He studied music in France and Germany and returned to the US in 1888. There he worked as a composer and pianist with the Boston Symphony Orchestra and convinced his wife Marian to found the MacDowell Colony for artists in Peterborough, New Hampshire. In 1896, he became the first professor of art and music at Columbia University in New York. He made a name for himself with his piano pieces, songs and orchestral works, including his *Indian* Orchestral Suite. His piano concerto drew attention from outside the US.

***Indian* Suite for Orchestra No. 2 in E Minor, Op. 48**   ♦ p. 20
Westphalian Symphony Orchestra/Siegfried Landau

Monk, Thelonious (1917-1982) was an American jazz pianist, a founder of bebop, and Bud Powell's mentor. His unorthodox, abrupt style of playing, his eccentric appearance, and his reputation for being unreliable first kept him at a distance from bebop's growing wave of success. However, recordings from the 1950s and 1960s (with Miles Davis, John Coltrane and Dave Brubeck among others) solidified his status as a soloist and composer.

Michelot, Pierre (1928-2005) was a French jazz bassist. He frequently performed with Bud Powell, as well as Rex Stewart, Coleman Hawkins, Chet Baker, Thelonious Monk, Lester Young, Dexter Gordon and Dizzy Gillespie on their European tours.

Nikisch, Artur (1855-1922) was a Hungarian-born conductor. He was at the helm of the Boston Symphony Orchestra from 1889-1893, followed by the Leipzig Gewandhaus Orchestra and the Berlin Philharmonic.

Ørsted Pedersen, Niels-Henning (1946-2005) was a Danish jazz double bassist known for his unique four-finger technique. Count Basie invited Ørsted Pedersen to play in his orchestra when he was only 16 years old. In the 1960s, he toured with American jazz musicians like Sonny Rollins, Bill Evans, Dexter Gordon, Ben Webster and Bud Powell. In the 1970s, he began what would become a long collaboration with pianist Oscar Peterson.

Ottendorfer, Valentin Oswald (1826-1900) was an American journalist and patron. Born in Moravia (Svitavy), he fled to the US during the 1848 Revolution. In New York, he started as a journalist for the German-language *New Yorker Staats-Zeitung* and later became its director after marrying the widow of the newspaper's previous director. Ottendorfer and his wife funded numerous charity projects in New York and Svitavy, including the Ottendorfer Library, two hospitals, a poor-house, and an orphanage.

Parker, Charles (Charlie "Bird") (1920-1955) was an American jazz saxophonist and composer. With his virtuosity, clever use of harmony and rhythmic creativity, he played a significant role in shaping the stylistic development of jazz. Together with Dizzy Gillespie, Kenny Clark, Thelonious Monk, Coleman Hawkins, Oscar Pettiford, Max Roach, Bud Powell, and others, he laid the foundation for bebop—often performing in Minton's Playhouse. Parker's nickname Bird (short for Yardbird) inspired the name of the popular jazz club Birdland. Already quite ill, he gave his last concert in the club shortly before his death in 1955.

Pettiford, Oscar (1922-1960) was a double-bassist and cellist, arranger and composer. He was a significant figure of modern jazz and, along with Charlie Parker and Dizzy Gillespie, helped shaped the development of bebop.

Powell, Earl Rudolph ("Bud") (1924-1966) was an American jazz pianist and composer. Thelonious Monk brought Powell early on into the inner circle of musicians who developed bebop in the mid-1940s by jamming at Minton's Playhouse. According to Miles Davis, Bill Evans, Herbie Hancock, and others, Powell was the best bebop pianist around. In 1945, Powell was beat up during a police search in Philadelphia. Disoriented from the incident, he was committed to a psychiatric clinic, beginning a long series of temporary psychiatric treatments. Between clinic stays, Powell gave concerts and abused alcohol and medication. From 1959-1963, Powell lived in Paris, where Francis Paudras, a young fan, helped him get clean. Powell returned to New York and screwed up a number of concerts (e.g. in Birdland), relapsed, and was admitted to psychiatric clinics numerous times. Powell died of the effects of tuberculosis, malnutrition and alcoholism in 1966.

Tea for Two ♦ p. 69
Bud Powell Trio (Bud Powell/Ray Brown/Buddy Rich), 1950

Wee (Allen's Alley) ♦ p. 25
Charlie Parker Quintet (Charlie Parker/Dizzy Gillespie/Bud Powell/ Max Roach/Charlie Mingus), 1953

Willow Weep for Me ♦ p. 99
Bud Powell/George Duvivier/Art Taylor, 1955

Willow Weep for Me ♦ p. 100
Bud Powell/Oscar Pettiford/Kenny Clarke, Essen 1960

Round Midnight ♦ p. 73
Bud Powell/Pierre Michelot/Kenny Clarke, 1961

Price, Florence (1887-1953) was an American composer and the first African-American woman to achieve renown as a composer of classical music. Despite minor successes, such as her Symphony No. 1 (1932), she remained relatively unknown during her lifetime, eking out a living in Chicago as a piano teacher, organist and arranger for hire. Price didn't gain attention until 2000, and especially in 2009, when many of her scores were discovered during the renovation of her former summer residence.

Symphony No. 3 in C Minor
Philadelphia Orchestra/Yannick Nézet-Séguin

String Quartet No. 2 in A Minor (1935)
Catalyst Quartet

Still, William Grant (1895-1978) was an American composer and arranger. In 1955, he became the first Black conductor of a major US orchestra, in New Orleans. After teaching himself early on, he later studied with Edward MacDowell and avant-garde composer Edgard Varèse. Still's oeuvre includes five symphonies, cantatas, songs, and film music.

Symphony No. 2 in G Minor (*A New Race*, 1937) ♦ p. 194
Detroit Symphony Orchestra/Neeme Järvi

***And They Lynched Him on a Tree* (1940)**
Philippe Brunelle & Orchestra/Leigh Morris Chorale/ Hilda Harris (mezzo-soprano), William Warfield (baritone)

Tatum, Arthur ("Art") (1909-1956) was an American jazz pianist. His background was in swing and stride piano. With his breathtakingly fast runs and surprising rhythmic twists, he paved the way for bebop.

Goin' Home   ♦ p. 11
(Complete Capitol Recordings)

Taylor, John Deems (1885-1966) was an American music critic, radio presenter and largely self-taught composer. His oeuvre includes several operas and the orchestral suite *Through the Looking Glass*.

***Through the Looking Glass*, Op. 12**   ♦ p. 114
Seattle Symphony Orchestra/Gerard Schwartz

Shekau, Abubakar (between 1965 and 1975-presumably 2021) was the leader of the terrorist organization Boko Haram from approximately 2009 until his death. He succeeded Boko Haram founder Mohammed Yusuf whom he had met while in prison. Numerous reports of Shekau's death from the Nigerian government proved to be unfounded. In 2015, Boko Haram allied with the Islamic State, led by Abu Bakr al-Baghdadi. This caused Boko Haram to split: One part remained under the leadership of Shekau, while the other part, led by Abu Musab al-Barnawi, an alleged son of Mohammed Yusuf, called itself the Islamic State Western African Provinces (ISWAP). Shekau reportedly killed himself with a suicide vest to avoid capture during a battle with ISWAP in May 2021.

Verrett, Shirley (1931-2010) was an internationally renowned American mezzo-soprano. She and her family said that Marian Anderson was a role model for her in her singing career. See footnote 23.

Williams, Mary Lou (1910-1981) was an American jazz musician (pianist, composer and arranger) who helped pave the way for gender equality in jazz. She learned piano as a child and came to jazz by playing in vaudeville orchestras. In 1936, she arranged for Benny Goodman and later for Duke Ellington. In the mid-1940s, she began playing with the pioneers of bebop. For many decades, Williams was considered to be the greatest female jazz musician.

Wells, Ida (1862-1931) was an American journalist and activist for civil rights and women's rights. She was born as a slave six months before the Emancipation Proclamation was issued. Wells co-founded the NAACP and the National Association of Colored Women (NACW) and protested against the widespread lynching of African-Americans. Wells played an important role in the emergence of the civil rights movement in the US and was inducted into the National Women's Hall of Fame in 1988.

West, Kanye Omari (*1977) is an American rapper, singer and music producer. He rose to fame by producing for rapper Jay-Z and collaborating on his successful album *The Blueprint*. West is an influential figure in hip-hop and pop music of the 21st century. In the US alone, he has sold over 60 million records and downloads. Since 2018, West has been a vocal supporter of Donald Trump and has received negative attention for making public racist and anti-Semitic comments.

Places and Institutions

The original jazz club **Birdland** was located in New York on Broadway between 52nd Street and 53rd Street from 1949 to 1965. The name of the club was derived from jazz saxophonist Charlie Parker's nickname, Bird. Birdland enjoyed success from the very beginning, hosting nearly all of the great jazz musicians of the time. Live radio recordings were also made there. Shortly after Birdland was founded, Oscar Goodstein took over its management. Bud Powell felt exploited by him. In 1986, the club moved to Harlem. In 1996, Birdland was re-established near Times Square on West 44th Street.

Minton's Playhouse is a jazz club founded in 1938 by tenor saxophonist Henry Minton in the former dining room of Hotel Cecil in Harlem. Starting in the early 1940s, jazz greats like Thelonious Monk, Kenny Clarke, Dizzy Gillespie, Roy Eldridge, Coleman Hawkins, Lester Young, and Bud Powell played in the jam sessions at Minton's, considered the birthplace of bebop. When the jazz scene moved to Midtown Manhattan in the 1950s, Minton's popularity faded. In 1974, the club was damaged in a fire. It was rebuilt with a new look and reopened in 2006.

The **Ottendorfer Public Library** was built in 1884 in what was then known as Little Germany, now Manhattan's East Village. New York's oldest public library, it was funded by German-Moravian immigrant Valentin Ottendorfer, at that time the director of the *New Yorker Staats-Zeitung*, a German-language newspaper. He sponsored the library to fulfill the wish of his terminally ill wife Anna. German-born architect William Schickel designed the library in a Neo-Renaissance style and decorated the brick facade with terracotta busts. Located next to the Ottendorfer-sponsored hospital, the library originally housed an equal number of English and German books. Today, most of its inventory is in English, with a large collection of Polish and Ukrainian titles due to the influx of Eastern European immigrants to the neighborhood in the 1930s.

The **Creedmoor Psychiatric Center** was built in 1912 as the Farm Colony of the Brooklyn State Hospital in what was then a rural part of Queens. It was intended as a place for psychiatric patients to live self-sufficiently and pursue physical labor outdoors. The institution was understaffed and severely overcrowded, with as many as 7,000 people living there in the mid-1940s. As a result, many patients suffered from neglect and physical abuse. Since the 1960s, inpatient psychiatric treatment has drastically decreased. The center now houses a much smaller number of people.

The **International Nuremberg Principles Academy** is a Nuremberg-based institution dedicated to the promotion of human rights and the application of international criminal law. It provides educational opportunities for individuals involved in the conduct of trials for war crimes, crimes against humanity, and the crime of aggression. The Academy was founded by the German Ministry of Foreign Affairs, the Free State of Bavaria and the City of Nuremberg.

Boko Haram is an Islamic terrorist organization operating in northern Nigeria, Chad, Cameroon, and Niger. It fights to suppress Western values and aims to impose an Islamic legal system that is rejected by most Muslims due to its archaic rigorousness. However, Boko Haram has managed to capitalize on widespread discontent among Nigerians with social developments in their country (corruption, social inequality, the role of the army). Founded in the early 1990s by Mohammad Yussuf, the organization has split several times. After Yussuf's death around 2019, Abubakar Shekau became the leader of Boko Haram. He was succeeded after his death in 2021 by Bakura Modu. The acts of terror which are largely conducted against other Muslims, but also against Nigerian Christians, have claimed approx. 350,000 victims to date. Some 2 million people have been displaced.

The **MacDowell (Colony)** is a foundation that awards fellowships to outstanding artists in a variety of disciplines. Recipients are offered residency at a 36-unit campus on the outskirts of Peterborough, New Hampshire. The organization was founded in 1908 by pianist Marian Griswold Nevins (1857-1956) to fulfill the wish of her terminally ill husband, composer Edward MacDowell. In 2020, it dropped the word 'colony' from its name.

The **National Conservatory of Music** was founded in 1885, primarily by Jeannette Meyers Thurber (1850-1946), the daughter of a Danish violinist. Its aim was to offer music education programs up to the doctoral level and to develop a national American musical culture. At Thurber's invitation, Dvořák served as its director from 1892 to 1895. After several financial crises and location changes, the school closed for good in 1952, although things had been going downhill since 1900. Around 3,000 students attended the Conservatory.

Milton Keynes UK
Ingram Content Group UK Ltd.
UKHW021857130924
448328UK00006B/85